NEW DIRECTIONS IN GERMAN STUDIES
Vol. 5

Series Editor:

Imke Meyer

Editorial Board:

Katherine Arens, Roswitha Burwick, Richard Eldridge, Erika Fischer-Lichte, Catriona MacLeod, Jens Rieckmann, Stephan Schindler, Heidi Schlipphacke, Ulrich Schönherr, Silke-Maria Weineck, David Wellbery, Sabine Wilke, John Zilcosky.

New Directions in German Studies

Volumes in the series:

Improvisation as Art: Conceptual Challenges, Historical Perspectives
by Edgar Landgraf

The German Pícaro and Modernity: Between Underdog and Shape-Shifter
by Bernhard Malkmus

Citation and Precedent: Conjunctions and Disjunctions of German Law and Literature
by Thomas O. Beebee

Beyond Discontent: 'Sublimation' from Goethe to Lacan
by Eckart Goebel

Vienna's Dreams of Europe: Culture and Identity beyond the Nation-State
by Katherine Arens (forthcoming)

Image in Outline: Reading Lou Andreas-Salomé
by Gisela Brinker-Gabler (forthcoming)

Thomas Mann in English: A Study in Literary Translation
by David Horton (forthcoming)

Out of Place: German Realism, Displacement, and Modernity
by John B. Lyon

The Tragedy of Fatherhood: King Laius and the Politics of Paternity in the West
by Silke-Maria Weineck

The Laughter of the Thracian Woman: A Protohistory of Theory
by Hans Blumenberg, translated by Spencer Hawkins (forthcoming)

From Kafka to Sebald

Modernism and Narrative Form

Edited by
Sabine Wilke

BLOOMSBURY
NEW YORK • LONDON • NEW DELHI • SYDNEY

Bloomsbury Academic
An imprint of Bloomsbury Publishing Inc

1385 Broadway	50 Bedford Square
New York	London
NY 10018	WC1B 3DP
USA	UK

www.bloomsbury.com

Bloomsbury is a registered trade mark of Bloomsbury Publishing Plc

First published 2012
Paperback edition published 2014

© Sabine Wilke and Contributors, 2012, 2014

All rights reserved. No part of this publication may be reproduced or transmitted in any form or by any means, electronic or mechanical, including photocopying, recording, or any information storage or retrieval system, without prior permission in writing from the publishers.

No responsibility for loss caused to any individual or organization acting on or refraining from action as a result of the material in this publication can be accepted by Bloomsbury or the author.

Library of Congress Cataloging-in-Publication Data
From Kafka to Sebald : modernism and narrative form / edited by Sabine Wilke.
  p. cm.
Includes bibliographical references and index.
ISBN 978-1-4411-2267-4 (hardback) 1. Narration (Rhetoric) 2. German fiction--19th century--History and criticism. 3. German fiction--20th century--History and criticism. 4. Modernism (Literature) I. Wilke, Sabine, 1957-
PN3383.N35F76 2012
833'.90923--dc23
2012019025

ISBN: HB: 978-1-4411-2267-4
PB: 978-1-6289-2862-4
ePub: 978-1-4411-0936-1
ePDF: 978-1-4411-9823-5

Typeset by Fakenham Prepress Solutions, Fakenham, Norfolk NR21 8NN

For Rick and Cora

Contents

	Contributors	ix
1	Introduction: Kafka, Modernism, and Beyond Sabine Wilke	1
	I Kafka's Slippages	**9**
2	Ritardando in *Das Schloß* Stanley Corngold	11
3	Kafka's "A Hunger Artist" as Allegory of Bourgeois Subject Construction Imke Meyer	27
	II Kafka Effects	**47**
4	Hofmannsthal after 1918: The Present as Exile Jens Rieckmann	49
5	Yvan Goll's *Die Eurokokke*: A Reading Through Walter Benjamin's *Passagen-Werk* Rolf J. Goebel	65
	III Narrative Theory	**79**
6	Else Meets Dora: Narratology as a Tool for Illuminating Literary Trauma Gail Finney	81
7	"Das kleine Ich": Robert Menasse and Masculinity in Real Time Heidi Schlipphacke	97
8	Sebald's Encounters with French Narrative Judith Ryan	123

	IV Autobiography	143
9	Gender, Psychoanalysis, and Childhood Autobiography: Christa Wolf's *Kindheitsmuster* *Lorna Martens*	145
10	Provisional Existence *Walter H. Sokel*	167
	Index	177

Contributors

Stanley Corngold
Professor of German and Comparative Literature Emeritus, Princeton University

Upon his retirement, Professor Corngold received the Behrman Award for distinguished achievement in the humanities at Princeton. He has published widely on modern German writers and thinkers (e.g., Dilthey, Nietzsche, Musil, Kraus, Mann, Benjamin and Adorno, among others), but for the most part he has been studying and translating the work of Franz Kafka. He co-edited *Franz Kafka: The Office Writings* (Princeton University Press, 2009) with Professor Benno Wagner (of the University of Bochum) and has also translated Kafka's stories for Bantam and Norton. His Norton Critical Edition of *Kafka's Selected Stories* (2007) includes new translations of thirty of Kafka's stories, along with notes, essays and commentaries. His previous critical work on Kafka includes *Lambent Traces: Franz Kafka* (Princeton University Press, 2004).

Gail Finney
Professor of Comparative Literature and German at the University of California, Davis

Professor Finney's books include *The Counterfeit Idyll: The Garden Ideal and Social Reality in Nineteenth-Century Fiction* (Niemeyer, 1984); *Women in Modern Drama: Freud, Feminism and European Theater at the Turn of the Century* (Cornell University Press, 1989, 1991); *Look Who's Laughing: Gender and Comedy* ed. (Gordon and Breach, 1994); *Christa Wolf* (Twayne Simon and Schuster, 1999); *Visual Culture in Twentieth-Century Germany: Text as Spectacle* ed. (Indiana University Press, 2006); and *The Dark Side of the Screen: Family Trauma in Contemporary American Cinema* (in progress). Finney has also published numerous articles and book chapters over the years.

Rolf J. Goebel
Professor of German at the University of Alabama in Huntsville

In addition to numerous articles and conference papers, he has published three books: *Kritik und Revision: Kafkas Rezeption mythologischer, biblischer und historischer Traditionen* (Critique and Revision: Kafka's Reception of Mythological, Biblical and Historical Traditions, 1986), *Constructing China: Kafka's Orientalist Discourse* (1997), and *Benjamin heute: Großstadtdiskurs, Postkolonialität und Flanerie zwischen den Kulturen* (Benjamin Today: Urban Discourse, Postcoloniality and Flânerie between Cultures, 2001). He is also a co-author of *A Franz Kafka Encyclopedia* (2005) and has edited *A Companion to the Works of Walter Benjamin* (2009).

Lorna Martens
Professor of German, University of Virginia

Professor Martens is the author of *The Diary Novel* (Cambridge: Cambridge University Press, 1985); *Shadow Lines: Austrian Literature from Freud to Kafka* (University of Nebraska Press, 1996); *The Promised Land? Feminist Writing in the German Democratic Republic* (State University of New York Press, 2001); *The Promise of Memory: Childhood Recollection and its Objects in Literary Modernism* (in progress). She has published numerous articles and book chapters on related topics.

Imke Meyer
Helen Herrmann Professor of German, Bryn Mawr College

Professor Meyer is the author of *Männlichkeit und Melodram: Arthur Schnitzlers erzählende Schriften im Kontext der Wiener Moderne* (Königshausen & Neumann, 2009) and *Jenseits der Spiegel kein Land: Ich-Fiktionen in Texten von Franz Kafka und Ingeborg Bachmann* (Königshausen & Neumann, 2001). Her recent articles and book chapters include "Empire's Remains: The Ghosts of History in Michael Haneke's *Le Temps du Loup*." (*Modern Austrian Literature* 43.2, 2010); "Globalization, Consumer Culture and Mediated Affect in Barbara Albert's *Böse Zellen/Free Radicals*," (in Dassanowsky, Robert von and Oliver Speck, (eds), *New Austrian Film*, Berghahn, 2010); "The Insider as Outsider: Representations of the Bourgeoisie in Fin-de-Siècle Vienna." (*Pacific Coast Philology* 44, 2009); "Gender, Cultural Memory, and the Representation of Queerness in Ingeborg Bachmann's Narrative 'A Step Towards Gomorrah'." (*Studies in Twentieth- and Twenty-first-Century Literature* 31.1, 2007).

Jens Rieckmann
Professor Emeritus of German, UC Irvine

Professor Rieckmann is the author of *Der Zauberberg: Eine geistige Autobiographie Thomas Manns* (Stuttgart: Akademischer Verlag Heinz, 1977 and 1979); *Aufbruch in die Moderne: Die Anfänge des Jungen Wien. Österreichische Literatur und Kritik im Fin de Siècle* (Königstein, Ts.: Athenäum, 1985 and 1986); *Hugo von Hofmannsthal und Stefan George: Signifikanz einer "Episode" aus der Jahrhundertwende* (Tuebingen u. Basel: Francke, 1997); and the editor of *A Companion to the Works of Stefan George* (Camden House, 2005). He has published numerous articles and book chapters on fin-de-siècle Austrian and German literature and culture.

Judith Ryan
Robert K. and Dale J. Weary Professor of German and Comparative Literature, Harvard University

Professor Ryan is the author of *Umschlag und Verwandlung* (Winkler, 1972), a book on Rilke's poetry; *The Uncompleted Past* (Wayne State University Press, 1983), which treats postwar German novels; *The Vanishing Subject* (Chicago University Press, 1991), which traces the relation of literature to empiricist psychology; and *Rilke, Modernism and Poetic Tradition* (Cambridge University Press, 1999). She is co-editor of *Cultures of Forgery: Making Nations, Making Selves* (Routledge, 2003), and *Imagining Australia* (Harvard University Committee on Australian Studies, 2004). She is also General Editor of *A New History of German Literature* (Harvard University Press, 2004). She has written articles on Franz Kafka, Paul Celan, Christa Wolf, Günter Grass, Durs Grünbein and W. G. Sebald, among others. She is currently at work on two book projects: *The Novel After Theory* and the *Cambridge Introduction to German Poetry*.

Heidi Schlipphacke
Associate Professor of German, Old Dominion University

Professor Schlipphacke is the author of *Nostalgia After Nazism: History, Home and Affect in German and Austrian Literature and Film* (Bucknell UP, 2010). Recent articles and book chapters include "Melancholy Empress: Queering Empire in Ernst Marischka's *Sissi* Films"; "The Trouble With Shane: Lesbians and Polygamy" (in Heller, Dana ed. *Loving the L Word*, I. B. Tauris, 2010); "Fragmented Bodies: Masculinity in Contemporary German Cinema" (in Fouz-Hernández, Santiago ed. *Mysterious Skin: The Male Body in Contemporary Cinema*, I B Tauris, 2009); "Postmodernism and the Place of Nostalgia in Ingeborg Bachmann's *Franza* Fragment" (*The German Quarterly* 79.1 (2006): 71–89); and "Melodrama's Other: Entrapment and Escape in the Films of Tom Tykwer" (*Camera Obscura* 62 (2006): 108–43).

Walter H. Sokel
Virginia Commonwealth Professor of German and Comparative Literature Emeritus, University of Virginia

Walter Sokel is among the most important interpreters of the work of Kafka. He is part of the emigrant generation of Jewish scholars who built the field of German Studies after the war. His *The Writer in Extremis: Expressionism in Twentieth-Century German Literature* (Stanford UP, 1957) has become a classical study of German expressionism, followed by *Franz Kafka* (Columbia UP, 1966), a seminal study of the works of this author. Sokel's *Franz Kafka: Tragik und Ironie. Zur Struktur seiner Kunst* (Fischer, 1983) has influenced an entire generation of Kafka scholars.

Sabine Wilke
Professor of German and Chair, the University of Washington

Professor Wilke's research and teaching interests include modern German literature and culture, intellectual history and theory, and cultural studies. She has written books and articles on body constructions in modern German literature and culture (*Ambiguous Embodiment: Construction and Destruction of Bodies in Modern German Culture*, 2000), German unification (*Ist alles so geblieben, wie es früher war: Essays zur Literatur und Frauenpolitik im vereinten Deutschland*, 2000), aesthetics and gender constructions (*Dialektik und Geschlecht: Literaturanalyse zwischen Ästhetischer Theorie und feministischer Schreibpraxis*, 1996), German colonialism (*Masochismus und Kolonialismus: Literatur, Film und Pädagogik*, 2006) and the overlapping concerns of postcolonialism and ecocriticism.

1. Introduction: Kafka, Modernism, and Beyond

Sabine Wilke

The question of narrative form is crucial to the meaning of cultural artifacts. Unless we carefully analyze the position from which a tale is told and how that perspective evolves in complex ways, we have but a hazy grip on how the narrative unfolds, whose point of view we fully or partially share, which perspectives on the narrated events are presented as truths, and how trustworthy the narrator really is, if at all. Scholars who work on narrative theory and analysis concern themselves with this issue: Wayne Booth in his attempt to understand the rhetoric of irony, Robert Scholes who coined the phrase of the "fabulator" to designate modernist writers of fiction who shy away from direct representation of the surface of reality, Hayden White in his many studies on the narrative discourse of historical reality, to name just a few milestones in the history of narrative among many others.[1] *From Kafka to Sebald: Modernism and Narrative Form* explores how this larger discussion of narrative form relates to German literary modernism. It also brings German scholarship on narrative into this discussion in the wake of the important work by Franz Karl Stanzel and Käthe Hamburger in the seventies.[2] Dorrit Cohn's research on narrative tense and narrative modes for presenting consciousness in fiction built the necessary bridge between narrative theory and German literary modernism and it is by no means an accident that the focus of her analyses is the work of Franz Kafka.[3]

In terms of historical coverage, *From Kafka to Sebald* ties together original scholarship on one of the most important German-language writers from the beginning of the twentieth century, Franz Kafka, with scholarship on his contemporaries and on postwar German-language fiction leading up to W. G. Sebald, Christa Wolf, Robert Menasse and others in an attempt to reflect on the specific trajectory German-language fiction has taken over the last century. The aim is not to be comprehensive and map all the possible avenues writers have traveled in expressing narrative modes of consciousness, but to highlight some crucial and recurring themes and formal problems that have preoccupied German-language modernism and continue to preoccupy self-conscious fiction to this day. Patricia Waugh, in her work on metafiction, characterizes the concerns and characteristics of self-conscious fiction as "a celebration of the power of the creative imagination together with an uncertainty about the validity of its representations; an extreme self-consciousness about language, literary form and the act of writing fictions; a pervasive insecurity about the relationship of fiction to reality; a parodic, playful, excessive or deceptively naïve style of writing."[4] In the German context, self-conscious fiction often relates to the narration of trauma. Dominick LaCapra has reminded us that "there is an important sense in which the after effects—the hauntingly possessive ghosts—of traumatic events are not fully owned by anyone and, in various ways, affect everyone" and that, as a historian, he prefers to "distinguish between victims of traumatizing events and commentators (or those born later)."[5] Cathy Caruth's work on the double wound of trauma locates trauma not "in the simple violent or original event in an individual's past, but rather in the way that its very unassimilated nature—the way it was precisely *not known* in the first instance—returns to haunt the survivor later on."[6] The notion of writing trauma is crucial to an understanding of postwar German-language fiction in the wake of the Holocaust and will be addressed in several of the essays in this volume.

While there are many individual books and articles written specifically on Franz Kafka and his fiction, this collection of essays brings Kafka's work into conversation not only with his contemporaries, fellow Hapsburg intellectuals such as Sigmund Freud, Hugo von Hofmannsthal, Arthur Schnitzler and other writers and artists of the period such as Yvan Goll, but also with contemporary authors that position themselves vis-à-vis the legacy left by Kafka's writings and in particular his articulations of narrative consciousness. The emphasis in *From Kafka to Sebald* is on the advancement of narrative form in German-language modernist fiction, not understood as a universal structure, but as the location of an aesthetic and formal struggle with the main issues of the period, with alienation, urban existence, deception, disjointed life experiences, the collapse of the belief in the possibility of an objective articulation of meaning, the role of language, the fictionality of modes of documentation and the presentation of historical material, the fictionality of life and the performance of cultures, and other issues that emphasize the cultural construction of life experiences in modernism. The book approaches the question of narrative via a set of important questions including gender, performance, trauma theory, exile, autobiography and memory in an attempt to establish relevance to ongoing debates. Narrative form in German-language modernist fiction is analyzed from a variety of perspectives that have comparative, deconstructive and historical dimensions. The relevance of the topic of modernism and narrative form rests on the idea that most twentieth-century modernist avant-gardes defined themselves through the critique of narrative as the quintessential form of modern identity and as a category in both aesthetic practice and theory. Narrative theory has experienced a major revival in the course of the last decade, transforming the heritage of structuralist literary narratology into a truly interdisciplinary, transmedial study of narrative practice. The papers collected in this volume investigate how these narrative practices in German-language fiction shape our perception of reality through these lenses.

The essays in this book are dedicated to Richard T. Gray, who turned sixty in July 2012. *From Kafka to Sebald* is a tribute to the work of this scholar of German literature who has devoted much of his intellectual and critical life to the interpretation of the works of Franz Kafka and, more recently, W. G. Sebald and other contemporary authors of fiction. The essays collected in this volume engage in a conversation with the topics that form the center of Gray's intellectual life as a teacher, mentor and scholar. Gray wrote a dissertation on Kafka's aphorisms under the direction of Walter H. Sokel at the University of Virginia. The work was later published as volume 91 in the "Studien zur deutschen Literatur" with Niemeyer, under the title *Constructive Destruction: Kafka's Aphorism: Literary Tradition and Literary Transformation*. It constituted the first systematic attempt at articulating Kafka's contribution to this genre.[7] *Constructive Destruction* charts the significance of the aphoristic form to the overall development of Kafka's fiction, leading up to the insight that Kafka's turn to aphoristic expression resolves dissatisfaction with his previous narrative practices and helps him evolve his parabolic style. Lessing's play *Emilia Galotti*, Schiller's *Die Räuber*, Heine's *Ideen: Das Buch Le Grand*, Büchner's *Woyzeck*, Hofmannsthal's "Reitergeschichte" and Kafka's "Das Urteil" constitute the *Stations of the Divided Subject* in Richard Gray's second book, which deals with questions of literary form in the context of displacement and subjugation of the political subconscious. In *Stations of the Divided Subject* Gray shows how aesthetic innovation in German bourgeois literature was shaped by the simultaneous accommodation with and rebellion against bourgeois reason on the part of the literary intelligentsia. Returning to Kafka, Richard Gray, together with Ruth Gross,

Rolf Goebel and Clayton Koelb, composed the entries in *A Franz Kafka Encyclopedia*, an extremely useful and practical tool for students of Kafka's works at all levels.

After a critical study of the "science" of physiognomics[8] and a study of the relationship between aesthetics and economic thought,[9] Gray's scholarly interests returned to the subject of narrative in the example of W. G. Sebald and autobiographic fiction. In his work on W. G. Sebald, Gray explores questions of memory and narrative, relations of exiles to the idea of "homeland" and "adoptive nation", the relationship between image and text, trauma, memorial, and the possibilities of post-Holocaust literature, narratives of physical and imaginative travel, and questions of the relationship between architecture, image and narrative structure, always keeping Sebald's literary precursors in mind. In a contribution to a collection of essays on literature in the century of totalitarianism, Gray discusses the idea of exile as displacement using the example of one of Sebald's figures, Dr Henry Selwyn.[10] A narratological examination of *Die Ringe des Saturn*, Gray's essay begins with "the observation that this text exhibits a structure of laminated layers reminiscent of an omnipresent narrative consciousness in negotiating the transitions between themes, episodes, historical events and intertextual allusions that constitute the text's compositional makeup."[11] These points of transition become Sebald's segues that function as points of cohesion in an otherwise disjointed text. The impression of continuity that this strategy evokes, however, depends on the narrator's art of transition; he makes them look as if they are not merely staged when in fact they are the product of conscious intervention on the part of Sebald's narrator whose "narrative consciousness is characterized above all by its capacity to choreograph subtle transitions and cross-references among disparate elements", thus making him into the quintessential bricoleur.[12]

This volume addresses narratological questions in a variety of formats. The first section on "Kafka's Slippages" includes two essays that deal with the logic of ministerial action and narrating allegory. In his essay on "Ritardando in *Das Schloß*", Stanley Corngold analyzes the narrative logic of Kafka's novel and shows the complexity faced by any project that tries to map a unified narrative field theory. Corngold sees very little progression in the episodic structure of the work. Particles of Kafka's earlier work are redistributed throughout the novel among various characters and contribute to the failure of assuming a totalizing view of Kafka's narrative that always slips away from itself. In a similar vein, Imke Meyer takes a critical look at "Kafka's 'A Hunger Artist' as Allegory of Bourgeois Subject Construction". The outlines of her allegorical reading capture for a moment, in the face of allegory's insistence that the "breach between sign and referent" cannot be healed, the shifting outlines of one of the text's possible meanings. Meyer contends that Kafka shows us a subject that must consume itself in the very process of its constitution.

The second section deals with "Kafka Effects". In his essay on "Hofmannsthal after 1918: The Present as Exile", Jens Rieckmann discusses exile in the context of Hugo von Hofmannsthal's understanding of the loss of the k.u.k ("kaiserlich und königlich"—imperial and regal) monarchy and his alienated existence in the Austrian Republic. Rieckmann reads Hofmannsthal's artistic crisis as a mode of exile compared to the creative output of his youth. In "Yvan Goll's *Die Eurokokke*: A Reading Through Walter Benjamin's *Passagen-Werk*", Rolf Goebel shows that although neither work influenced the composition of the other, Benjamin's monumental compilation of citations and reflections on Paris as the capital of European modernity in the age of high capitalism can serve as an interpretive framework for a new reading of Goll's rather neglected novel. The comparison of Benjamin's and Goll's texts helps elucidate the complex range of intellectual responses to the cultural crisis of interwar Europe.

The third section addresses questions of "Narrative Theory". In "Else Meets Dora: Narratology as a Tool for Illuminating Literary Trauma", Gail Finney discusses the correspondences between two distinct modes of analysis: narrative theory and trauma theory, elucidating the ways in which they borrow from and complement one another. Finney examines instances of literary trauma through the lens of narrative theory to suggest ways in which narratology might be useful in elucidating traumatic experience as depicted in literature, using the example of Sigmund Freud's *Fragment of an Analysis of a Case of Hysteria* (1905) and Arthur Schnitzler's *Fräulein Else* (1924). Heidi Schlipphacke takes a critical look at "'Das kleine Ich': Robert Menasse and Masculinity in Real Time", reflecting on the links between narrating masculinity and national identity. For Menasse, Austria stands for the retreat from a dialectical mode of history, and the metaphor of transvestism that he likes to employ embodies the mechanisms of borrowing, appropriating and harmonizing that characterize the various "clothing changes" of Austrian political identity in the twentieth century. Menasse's musings on Austrian identity call into question the future of gender in a post-dialectical world and, in particular, the previously hallowed relationship between the male body and the national body. In "Sebald's Encounters with French Narrative", Judith Ryan explores Sebald's work via important materials discovered at the Sebald archive in Marbach. Her essay begins with the question of the author-narrator relation, and moves from there through a series of French authors that Sebald read (Flaubert, Proust, Butor) to show the trajectory of his understanding of narrative theory. She concludes by considering the ways in which Sebald's learning about narrative strategies play into the effect his texts have on the reader.

The final section investigates modes of "Autobiography". In "Gender, Psychoanalysis and Childhood Autobiography: Christa Wolf's *Kindheitsmuster*", Lorna Martens shows that Christa Wolf draws on details from her own childhood in the presentation of memory within the novel. What the narrator then "discovers" about memory largely corresponds to previously known psychoanalytic theory about memory. Walter H. Sokel shares an autobiographical reflection about his life in Vienna as a new student at the University shortly before the *Anschluss* (the annexation of Austria by the Nazis). "Provisional Existence" is based on a lecture Sokel gave at the University of Vienna in 2008, where it was received enthusiastically. This personal essay, which is included in this volume in an English translation by Japhet Johnstone, serves as a case in point for autobiographical narration and as a reminder to the reader of the lived nature of narrative.

I wish to thank all contributors for their enthusiastic response to the idea behind this project and their tireless work on the book's execution and completion. The series editor, Imke Meyer, who supported the idea of a volume on German-language modernist fiction, provided great critical feedback on the planning and direction of the book. The humanities acquisitions editor for Continuum Press, Haaris Naqvi, guided us through the publishing process with ease and professional advice. The two of them deserve great credit for envisioning a book series on German literature and culture at a time when the discipline—and the institution of academic publishing—is under severe scrutiny in the context of serious budgetary constraints faced by institutions of higher education. Last but not least, my editorial assistant, Gloria Lucia Man, was a wonderful collaborator, a talented and hard-working editor, and a conscientious reader of academic prose. Japhet Johnstone finished copyediting the manuscript when Gloria Man had to return to her studies full-time and concentrate on her exams. He applied his talent as an editor and the publishing experience gained at the University of Washington Press very generously to this project and I am immensely grateful for his help. To all of them I wish to express my heartfelt thanks.

Seattle and Winthrop, August 2011

Bibliography

Booth, Wayne. *A Rhetoric of Irony*. Chicago: University of Chicago Press, 1975.
Caruth, Cathy. *Unclaimed Experience: Trauma, Narrative, and History*. Baltimore: Johns Hopkins University Press, 1996.
Cohn, Dorrit. *Transparent Minds: Narrative Modes for Presenting Consciousness in Fiction*. Princeton, NJ: Princeton University Press, 1978.
Gray, Richard T. *Constructive Destruction: Kafka's Aphorisms; Literary Tradition and Literary Transformation*. Tübingen: Niemeyer, 1987.

—*Stations of the Divided Subject: Contestation and Ideological Legitimation in German Bourgeois Literature, 1770–1914.* Stanford, CA: Stanford University Press, 1995.
—*About Face: German Physiognomic Thought from Lavater to Auschwitz.* Detroit: Wayne State University Press, 2004.
—Ruth Gross, Rolf Goebel, and Clayton Koelb. *A Kafka Encyclopedia.* Westport, CT.: Greenwood Press, 2005.
—*Money Matters: Economics and the German Cultural Imagination, 1770–1850.* Seattle: University of Washington Press, 2008.
—"Exile as Dis-Placement in W. G. Sebald's *Dr. Henry Selwyn*". In *Literatur im Jahrhundert des Totalitarismus,* edited by Elke Gilson, Barbara Hahn, and Holly Liu, 209–26. Hildesheim: Olms, 2008.
—"Sebald's Segues: Performing Narrative Contingency in *The Rings of Saturn*". *The Germanics Review* 84 (2009): 26–58.
Hamburger, Käthe. *Die Logik der Dichtung.* Stuttgart: Klett, 1968.
LaCapra, Dominick. *Writing History, Writing Trauma.* Baltimore: Johns Hopkins University Press, 2001.
Scholes, Robert. *Fabulation and Metafiction.* Urbana, IL: University of Illinois Press, 1979.
Stanzel, Franz Karl. *Theorie des Erzählens.* Göttingen: Vandenhoeck & Ruprecht, 2001.
Waugh, Patricia. *Metafiction: The Theory and Practice of Self-Conscious Fiction.* London: Routledge, 1984.
White, Hayden. *The Content of the Form: Narrative Discourse and Historical Representation.* Baltimore: Johns Hopkins University Press, 1987.

Notes

1 See Booth, *A Rhetoric of Irony*; Scholes, *Fabulation and Metafiction*; White, *The Content of the Form.*
2 Stanzel, *Theorie des Erzählens*; Hamburger, *Die Logik der Dichtung.*
3 Cohn, *Transparent Minds.*
4 Waugh, *Metafiction,* 2.
5 LaCapra, *Writing History, Writing Trauma,* xi.
6 Caruth, *Unclaimed Experience,* 4.
7 Gray, *Constructive Destruction.*
8 *About Face* (2004) tells the story of how physiognomics became popular during the Enlightenment as an empirically grounded discipline. Originally claimed to promote understanding and love, physiognomics evolved into a system aimed at valorizing a specific set of physical, moral and emotional traits and stamping everything else as "deviant". This development not only reinforced racial, national and characterological prejudices, but lent such beliefs a presumably scientific grounding.
9 In *Money Matters* (2008), Richard Gray investigates the discourses of aesthetics and philosophy alongside economic thought, arguing that their domains are not mutually exclusive.
10 See Gray, "Exile as Dis-Placement in W. G. Sebald's *Dr. Henry Selwyn*".
11 Gray, "Sebald's Segues".
12 Gray, "Sebald's Segues", 54.

I Kafka's Slippages

2. Ritardando in *Das Schloß*

Stanley Corngold

This essay is dedicated to Richard Gray, with special appreciation and admiration of his critical writings on the work of Franz Kafka.

"One is alone, a total stranger and only an object of curiosity. And so long as you say "one" instead of "I", there's nothing in it and one can easily tell the story; but as soon as you admit to yourself that it is you yourself, you feel as though transfixed and are horrified."

Kafka

I had originally set out to map the narrative of "ministerial action" in *Das Schloß*, that is to say, the story of the behavior of the Castle officials. But before doing so, I had to come to terms with the narrative logic of *Das Schloß*, and here I encountered difficulty. It is reported that Albert Einstein, on being lent *Das Schloß* to read by Thomas Mann, returned it soon after, declaring that the human mind was not constituted to grasp such perversity. Of course, it would be craven—inadmissible—to shelter in Einstein's shadow, but I want to stress the difficulty of *Das Schloß* and the many obstacles it puts in the way of mapping a unified narrative field theory.[1]

Individual episodes of *Das Schloß* have only a loose relevance to one another; they are less chapters in a progression with a detectable *telos* than a succession of novellas with a recurring cast of characters, not all of whom are easy to keep apart: we have the two "landladies", K.'s admittedly indistinguishable apprentices, the two Friedas, the officials Sordini/Sortini. This loose structure allows Kafka to improvise continually: I refer to the scattering of Kafka-"memes" throughout the novel, which are assigned to various personages. "Meme" normally means "a unit of cultural information [...] transmitted verbally or by repeated action from one mind to another."[2] Kafka-memes, particles of Kafka's earlier writings, are remembered in *Das Schloß*—and indeed, re-membered—since they are distributed throughout the novel to *many* characters and not to Kafka's shadow, K., alone.[3]

For example, it is not K. who registers the bliss and urgency of keeping one's own company but Gisa, the blond schoolteacher—whom Adorno describes as the Jew-hating Aryan—"weil sie die Bequemlichkeit und deshalb das Alleinsein über alles liebte und wahrscheinlich am glücklichsten war, wenn sie sich zuhause in völliger Freiheit auf dem Kanapee ausstrecken konnte."[4] Here one might think of Josef K. on his "divan": "Gewöhnlich lag er dann auf dem Kanapee seines Bureaus—er konnte sein Bureau nicht mehr verlassen, ohne eine Stunde lang auf dem Kanapee sich zu erholen—und fügte in Gedanken Beobachtung an Beobachtung" (P 248).[5] And we recall Kafka's innumerable journal entries of such a tendency, e.g.: "In mir selbst gibt es ohne menschliche Beziehung keine sichtbaren Lügen. Der begrenzte Kreis ist rein."[6] Again, it is the taproom prostitute Olga (of all persons!) who produces the great aperçu touching Kafka's most intimate beliefs on this very topic of correct interpretation—she speaks of contingency, of the impossibility of a natural end to this ordeal: "Und die Mitte zwischen den Übertreibungen zu halten, also die Briefe richtig zu beurteilen, ist ja unmöglich, sie wechseln selbst fortwährend ihren Wert, die Überlegungen, zu denen sie Anlaß geben, sind endlos, und wo man dabei gerade Halt macht, ist nur durch den Zufall bestimmt, also auch die Meinung eine zufällige" (S 363).[7] Now compare to *Der Prozeß*: "Du mußt nicht zuviel auf Meinungen achten", says the prison chaplain to Josef K., "Die Schrift ist unveränderlich und die Meinungen sind oft nur ein Ausdruck der Verzweiflung darüber" (P 298).[8]

Such examples of what I am calling "Kafka-memes" are legion throughout *Das Schloß*; and part of the novel's hermeneutic allure is the discovery and appreciation of them; but the result of this practice fits badly with a totalizing view of Kafka's narrative. For what we have here is a continual tension between opposite temporal thrusts. On the one hand, we encounter allegorical fragments from the history of Kafka's writings, whence we are turned back and away from the expectable progressive narrative of K.'s attempt to "enter" the Castle. We could speak of the hyperbolic force of this allegorical dimension; on our intuiting a Kafka-meme, we experience an immediate flare-up of recognition, the elation of felt meaning. This swift movement into the past contrasts, on the other hand, with the slow, underlit, forward-moving dimension of this narrative, which barely advances through its gloomy interiors (see "Eine große Stube im Dämmerlicht" at

Lasemann's [S 22])[9] and its dusky light, viz. "Nur fing es freilich schon zu dunkeln an und er beschleunigte die Schritte. Das Schloß, dessen Umrisse sich schon aufzulösen begannen, lag still wie immer, niemals noch hatte K. dort das geringste Zeichen von Leben gesehen, vielleicht war es gar nicht möglich aus dieser Ferne etwas zu erkennen und doch verlangten es die Augen und wollten die Stille nicht dulden" (S 156).[10] Again,"Die Blicke des Beobachters konnten sich nicht [am Schloß] festhalten und glitten ab. Dieser Eindruck wurde heute noch verstärkt durch das frühe Dunkel, je länger er hinsah, desto weniger erkannte er, desto tiefer sank alles in Dämmerung" (S 156–7).[11] Again, "K. trat auf die wild umwehte Freitreppe hinaus und blickte in die Finsternis. Ein böses, böses Wetter. [...] Eine intrigante Natur, scheinbar sinnlos arbeitend wie der Wind, nach fernen fremden Aufträgen, in die man nie Einsicht bekam" (S 186).[12]

If allegory supplies us with a sort of cognitive equivalence without waste, the Castle-narrative, by contrast, sets us to work distinguishing metal from dross to forge a possible chain of meaning from scant incident, talk and detail. Or, we will wonder, is the truth of this narrative precisely in the seeming dross-covert *embellishments* of the "plot", in the manner of *In der Strafkolonie*, where the message is not conveyed to the victim-reader until he has read with his wounds both the "authentic script" *and* its "adornments", never mind that the writing of the adornments will not stop until it has eaten out his body, so that no sensorium survives to apprehend the vaunted insight.

If we think further of *In der Strafkolonie*, we will be brought promptly to another Kafka-meme in *Das Schloß*. As Bürgel (the little guarantor) explains to the sleeping hero, "the bitter herb" K., "Die Leibeskräfte reichen nur bis zu einer gewissen Grenze, wer kann dafür, daß gerade diese Grenze auch sonst bedeutungsvoll ist. Nein, dafür kann niemand" (S 425).[13]

A few more examples of the countless Kafka-memes intuitable in their dream-like variation in *Das Schloß* may well be required, along with a general theory, supplied by Kafka in his correspondence with Milena, to explain their presence. Here, first, are the examples: We have K. in Klamm's carriage, slurping schnapps.

> Das war rücksichtsvoll, aber K. wollte ihn ja bedienen; schwerfällig, ohne seine Lage zu verändern langte er nach der Seitentasche, aber nicht in der offenen Tür, die zu weit entfernt war, sondern hinter sich in die geschlossene, nun, es war gleichgültig, auch in dieser waren Flaschen. Er holte eine hervor, schraubte den Verschluß auf und roch dazu, unwillkürlich mußte er lächeln, der Geruch war so süß, so schmeichelnd, so wie wenn man von jemand, den man sehr lieb hat, Lob und gute Worte

hört und gar nicht genau weiß, um was es sich handelt und es gar nicht wissen will und nur glücklich ist in dem Bewußtsein, daß er es ist, der so spricht. "Sollte das Kognak sein?" fragte sich K. zweifelnd und kostete aus Neugier. Doch, es war Kognak, merkwürdiger Weise, und brannte und wärmte. Wie es sich beim Trinken verwandelte, aus etwas, das fast nur Träger süßen Duftes war in ein kutschermäßiges Getränk. "Ist es möglich?" fragte sich K., wie vorwurfsvoll gegen sich selbst und trank noch einmal.

Da—K. war gerade in einem langen Schluck befangen—wurde es hell, das elektrische Licht brannte, innen auf der Treppe, im Gang, im Flur, außen über dem Eingang. Man hörte Schritte die Treppe herabkommen, die Flasche entfiel K.'s Hand, der Kognak ergoß sich über einen Pelz. (S 164–5)[14]

Now here is Red Peter, the ape, who in the "Bericht für eine Akademie" has achieved "the average cultural level of a European",[15] not much inferior to K.'s, if we are to trust the opinions of the principals of *Das Schloß*, the landlady of The Bridge Inn, Gardena of the Gentlemen's Inn, or indeed Pepi. For the first he is a blindworm, for the second dull of sense, and for the third the "least thing" there is. We will recall Red Peter's "pelt": "Ich, ich darf meine Hosen ausziehen, vor wem es mir beliebt; man wird dort nichts finden als einen wohlgepflegten Pelz und die Narbe nach einem—wählen wir hier zu einem bestimmten Zwecke ein bestimmtes Wort, das aber nicht mißverstanden werden wolle—die Narbe nach einem frevelhaften Schuß."[16] We will recall Rotpeter's shifting sense of the bliss and then the repulsiveness of the strong drink; we recall his ecstasy at spilling the drink *down inside* his pelt; we recall the sense the drink gives him of being kissed (for K., in *Das Schloß* the mere smell of the cognac is like hearing praise and kind words from someone whom one loves):

Was für ein Sieg dann allerdings für ihn wie für mich, als ich eines Abends [...] eine vor meinem Käfig versehentlich stehen gelassene Schnapsflasche ergriff, [...] sie schulgerecht entkorkte, an den Mund setzte und ohne Zögern, ohne Mundverziehen, als Trinker von Fach, mit rund gewälzten Augen, schwappender Kehle, wirklich und wahrhaftig leer trank; nicht mehr als Verzweifelter, sondern als Künstler die Flasche hinwarf; zwar vergaß den Bauch zu streichen; dafür aber, weil ich nicht anders konnte, weil es mich drängte, weil mir die Sinne rauschten, kurz und gut "Hallo!" ausrief, in Menschenlaut ausbrach, mit diesem Ruf in die Menschengemeinschaft sprang und ihr Echo: "Hört nur, er spricht!" wie einen Kuß auf meinem ganz schweißtriefenden Körper fühlte.

Die Stimme versagte mir sofort wieder; stellte sich erst nach Monaten ein; der Widerwille gegen die Schnapsflasche kam sogar noch verstärkter. Aber meine Richtung allerdings war mir ein für allemal gegeben.[17]

One's readerly memory is jogged again on hearing of Amalia's blouse. On the day that she is verbally assaulted by Sortini, we read in Olga's narrative: "Besonders das Kleid Amalias war schön, die weiße Bluse vorn hoch aufgebauscht, eine Spitzenreihe über der anderen, die Mutter hatte alle ihre Spitzen dazu geborgt, ich war damals neidisch und weinte vor dem Fest die halbe Nacht durch. [...] und [Amalia] borgte mir deshalb, um mich zu beruhigen, ihr eigenes Halsband aus böhmischen Granaten" (S 296).[18] In an agonizing passage from the "Brief an den Vater", Kafka refers to

> Eine kleine Aussprache an einem der paar aufgeregten Tage nach Mitteilung meiner letzten Heiratsabsicht. Du sagtest zu mir etwa: "Sie hat wahrscheinlich irgendeine ausgesuchte Bluse angezogen, wie das die Prager Jüdinnen verstehn, und daraufhin hast Du Dich natürlich entschlossen, sie zu heiraten. Und zwar möglichst rasch, in einer Woche, morgen, heute. Ich begreife Dich nicht, Du bist doch ein erwachsener Mensch, bist in der Stadt, und weißt Dir keinen andern Rat als gleich eine Beliebige zu heiraten. Gibt es da keine anderen Möglichkeiten? Wenn Du Dich davor fürchtest, werde ich selbst mit Dir hingehn."[19]

And so we have encountered in Olga's account of Amalia's fall a dream-like morphing of this web of blouse, marriage, Bohemia, brutal sex, and—for some perceptive readers like the late Arnold Heidsieck— the "Jewish" Barnabas family. The thrust of this pairing of families is allegorical: it punctually halts the narrative, which more and more seems like a dusky night illuminated only by allegorical flashes.

An irresistibly keen moment is the tale of K's extraordinary impudence in testing the sensitivity of the "Herren", the gentlemen but also the lord and masters, by allowing himself to be seen in the corridor of the Gentlemen's Inn. This is a grim fault, "denn das Zartgefühl der Herren sei grenzenlos" (S 443). Meanwhile, the reader may well recall comparable lines from *Der Prozeß* when such "sensitivity" distinctively characterizes the accused. In 1913, before writing *Der Prozeß*, Kafka had described himself to Felice as a man "mit unsichtbaren Ketten an eine unsichtbare Literatur gekettet [...], der schreit, wenn man in die Nähe kommt, weil man, wie er behauptet, diese Kette betastet."[20] This complaint takes us to the scene in *Der Prozeß*, in which an accused gentleman in the law offices screams when Josef K. touches his arm "quite loosely": "Aber er [K.] wollte ihm nicht Schmerz bereiten, hatte ihn auch nur ganz leicht angegriffen, trotzdem aber schrie der Mann auf, als habe K. ihn nicht mit zwei Fingern, sondern mit einer glühenden Zange erfaßt. [...] 'Die meisten Angeklagten sind so empfindlich', sagte der Gerichtsdiener" (P 95–6).[21] We are left to ponder the inversion in *Das Schloß* of the hierarchy of the sensitive ones. In der *Strafkolonie* occupies an intermediate position in this respect, since here, unlike *Der Prozeß*, the victim of the killing agent, the knife-wielder, is no longer the hapless accused but the officer, the high official, himself.

Finally, the meme is striking for the way it actually abets one tangle of the putatively forward-moving plot. If K., as the hero of the narrative, is, in Samuel Beckett's phrase, the author's "vice-exister", then, in the world of *Das Schloß*, K. has a vice-exister in the child Hans Brunswick, "[der] wolle ein Mann werden wie K" (S 236).[22] Hans's family represents a sort of repository of Kafka-memes: Hans's sister is called Frieda (think "Frieda Brandenfeld" of "Das Urteil", a 'vice-exister' of Kafka's fiancée Felice Bauer, as well as K.'s fiancée Frieda, a part-mask of Kafka's correspondent Milena Jesenská).[23] Hans's mother is suffering from a pulmonary complaint that requires good air. We are dealing with what I have been calling punctual allegorical relations. At the same time, K's relation to the Brunswick family is one of the more productive plot elements, for it is Hans's father who was "wenigstens nach dem Bericht des Gemeindevorstehers, der Führer derjenigen gewesen, welche, sei es auch aus politischen Gründen, die Berufung eines Landvermessers verlangt hatten" (S 235).[24] This fact moves the plot forward, as it were, by illuminating, perhaps, something of the prehistory of K.'s arrival in the village as the land surveyor: it appears that the matter was at least debated before his arrival in the village, and so K. may not be entirely an imposter—perhaps.

> Now, I can imagine the objection that such "discoveries", which generally retard the narrative tempo, are merely random associations and hence without "Erkenntniswert" (conceptual substance). Kafka, however, has written eloquently about the persistence of just such hauntings, of just such "Gespenster" (ghosts). Among the abundant documentary evidence, the richest is an often-cited, though rarely explained, passage from the letter to Milena, dated July 1922. Here Kafka writes about their correspondence, deploring letter-writing with the poignant image of insatiable ghosts who drink up the kisses mailed to the beloved before they arrive at their destination. "Briefe schreiben", he writes, "heißt, sich vor den Gespenstern entblößen, worauf sie gierig warten. Geschriebene Küsse kommen nicht an ihren Ort, sondern werden von den Gespenstern auf dem Wege ausgetrunken."[25] Who are

these ghosts? This image is haunting whether one understands it or not, but we could make the effort by referring to the context of Kafka's letter. He prefaces the image with the claim, "Die leichte Möglichkeit muß eine schreckliche Zerrüttung der Seelen in die Welt gebracht haben. Es ist ja ein Verkehr mit Gespenstern und zwar nicht nur mit dem Gespenst des Adressaten, sondern auch mit dem eigenen Gespenst, das sich einem unter der Hand in dem Brief, den man schreibt, entwickelt oder gar in einer Folge von Briefen, wo ein Brief den andern erhärtet und sich auf ihn als Zeugen berufen kann."[26]

J. Hillis Miller clarifies the image:

> The ghosts in question here are the distorted specters or phantoms of the sender and receiver of the letter, *generated by the words of the letter*. The letter is an invocation of ghosts, but these are not to be identified with the sender and receiver of the letter as such. The letter itself deflects the letter and the written kisses it contains away from its intended message and its goal, its destination. The letter is deflected toward the ghosts of sender and recipient *that the letter itself raises*, by a powerful incantation or conjuration.[27]

Emphasis is given to the work of the letter as the generator of ghosts. Kafka's letter is an essay on the generative power of words and, at the same time, a vital hint for an understanding of how the power of such "conjuration" accumulates. It is a matter of the history of (Kafka's) writing that precedes any individual act of writing. Again, "Writing letters is actually a communication with ghosts and by no means just with the ghost of the addressee but also with one's own ghost, which secretly evolves inside the letter one is writing *or even in a whole series of letters, where one letter corroborates another and can refer to it as a witness.*"[28]

For this idea of the letter, let us think of Kafka's acts of writing pure and simple, and we will see that we have here a compact expression of a theory pertinent to a reading of *Das Schloß*. The theory asserts the estrangement of the empirical person from the transcendental phantom that writing produces—hence, the estrangement of the flesh and blood author from his text. In this light, all Kafka's texts are, however paradoxically, not about the flesh and blood author even when, as in "Brief an den Vater", such identity would seem to be the text's explicit goal. Or they are "about" the person only in the sense of Heidegger's "um" in his apothegm "zum Sein des Daseins, um das es ihm in seinem Sein selbst geht."[29] Rather, I stress J. Hillis Miller's point: "the letter [i.e. the text] itself deflects the letter [i.e. the text] and the written kisses it contains away from its intended message and its goal, its destination"

(S 901–2). We can think of *Das Schloß* as containing a message as to the perpetual deflection of meaning from a circuit of communication. This deflection is enacted in the drift of K.'s project to communicate with the Castle. But if knowledge of that deflection is conveyed to the reader of *Das Schloß*, would that not mean that the message of non-arrival has in fact arrived at its destination? The answer to this paradox is that knowledge cannot be fixed; it is incomplete; it produces a vertigo of indetermination, a perfect *ritardando*, not yet a message: and *that* is the message.

The spectral remains in *Das Schloß* that interrupt the narrative require, in principle, an endless interpretation: we will put a limit to this project by stressing that these remains are not *empirical* references, such as references to the persons who, following Hartmut Binder, serve as models for its cast of characters.[30] Here I am appealing to another of Kafka's poetological claims, one invoking "das Freie der eigentlichen Beschreibung [...], die einem den Fuß vom Erlebnis löst."[31] *Das Schloß* is not a medium in which fragments suited to Kafka's putative autographical project are finally embedded. We are detecting ghosts not from Kafka's biography but from the history of his writing.

Where, now, have we been brought in our discussion of Kafka's *Schloß* narrative? These allegorical interruptions contribute only incidentally, if at all, to an understanding of the main narrative. Some do gesture by parody and inversion toward the work as a whole, but we are mainly inclined to consider these memes as formal obstacles to understanding the thrust of this epic. They retard the main narrative of K.'s advance toward the Castle. So what, then, is the core question to which the narrative might be supposed to supply an answer but is reluctant to do?

The overwhelming question in reading or understanding *Das Schloß* would appear to be: What does K. want? The question arises not only for the reader; Pepi asks it thirty pages before the end of this work of 495 pages: "Ja, woran denkt denn K.? Was hat er für besondere Dinge im Kopf? Will er etwas Besonderes erreichen? Eine gute Anstellung, eine Auszeichnung? Will er etwas derartiges?" (p. 465).[32] We have heard K. answer the question, if Pepi has not: "Meine Angelegenheiten mit den Behörden in Ordnung zu bringen ist mein höchster, eigentlich mein einziger Wunsch" (S 268).[33] K. wants a satisfactory resolution of his "affairs". This resolution requires a meeting with the Castle officials, who must first grant his wish to confront them. In this light, we read the novel as an epic account of K.'s quest to have his desire for a meeting granted and therewith obtain the resolution of his case. He figures the resolution as a face-to-face interview with Klamm:

"Was wollen Sie also von Klamm?" sagte die Wirtin. [...]

"[...] was ich von ihm will, ist schwer zu sagen. Zunächst will ich ihn in der Nähe sehn, dann will ich seine Stimme hören, dann will ich von ihm wissen, wie er sich zu unserer Heirat verhält" (S 137–8).[34]

K.'s case consists, importantly, of his impending marriage with Frieda, and so K. wants to have Klamm's views on the matter. The content of this crucial interview appears to be a conceptual void followed by something like an accidental reprise of *Das Urteil* and the "Brief an den Vater", yet another Kafka-meme: the subordinate (the son, the supplicant) seeks his superior's (his father's, the authority figure's) benediction on his marriage plans. But as if to subject this reminiscence to ridicule, we hear the landlady's contempt for any such enterprise, uttered in the presence of Momus the scribe, descendant of the Greek God of the Ridiculous: "Haben Sie nicht selbst erklärt, daß Sie zufrieden sein würden, wenn Sie nur Gelegenheit hätten vor Klamm zu sprechen, auch wenn *er Sie nicht ansehn und Ihnen nicht zuhören würde?*" (S 182, emphasis added).[35] The fulfillment of K.'s desire to have Klamm's views on his marriage is in no way dependant on words he might hear from Klamm.

We are returned to our first question: What does K. want? The hero K. arrives on Castle grounds with no apparent project in mind. He is an uncentered vagabond. His arrival is a kind of second birth: we infer this from the fact that, though he has a wife and child, he quickly starts a new family.

Here is the anthropological conclusion to Kafka's account of K.: man is born with a glimmer of a higher thing; otherwise he is without a concrete desire or a notion of what he might want. But he must live; he must go forward in time; and so he will attend to the interpretations that others put on his actions. This translates as the sentence: I will act in the light of what I think you detect to be the purpose of my action. It is, in fact, K.'s quintessential refrain: "'Ja, gewiß', sagte K. und überließ ihr [Olga] die Deutung der Worte" (S 58).[36] And what meaning could Olga find in K.'s words other than the meaning that she thinks K. intended her to grasp? But he is ignorant of his intentions. And so she is bound to echo his void of purpose.

Consider some earlier occurrences of the echo. "Hier", says K. in a telephone conversation with the Castle: "'Hier der Gehilfe des Herrn Landvermessers.' 'Welcher Gehilfe? Welcher Herr? Welcher Landvermesser?' K. fiel das gestrige Telephongespräch ein, 'Fragen Sie Fritz', sagte er kurz. Es half, *zu seinem eigenen Erstaunen*" (S 37, emphasis added). A moment later: "'ich aber bin der alte [Gehilfe], der dem Herrn Landvermesser heute nachkam.' Nein', schrie es nun. 'Wer bin ich also?' fragte K. ruhig wie bisher. Und nach einer Pause sagte die gleiche Stimme [...]: 'Du bist der alte Gehilfe'" (S 37).[37] The answer merely echoes his wild surmise, at which point he can intuit the perfect emptiness of his ploy. He has not told the truth of his being, his desire (he does not know it), and here the lie is merely echoed. Others do not bother to disabuse him, because they do not know it any better than he. What follows this conversation is the truth that K. very nearly fails to hear: "K. [...] überhörte [...] fast die Frage: 'Was willst Du?' Am liebsten hätte er den Hörer schon weggelegt. Von diesem Gespräch erwartete er nichts mehr. Nur gezwungen fragte er noch schnell: 'Wann darf mein Herr ins Schloß kommen?' 'Niemals', war die Antwort. 'Gut',sagte K. und hing den Hörer an" (S 37–8).[38] But "it" is not good: if Klamm, of the Castle, is K.'s putative center, in words that K. will afterwards address to Frieda, his exclusion is disastrous: "Du aber [...] wurdest von Klamm losgerissen, ich kann nicht ermessen, was das bedeutet, aber eine Ahnung dessen habe ich doch allmählich schon bekommen, man taumelt, man kann sich nicht zurechtfinden" (S 397).[39] And yet K.'s desire to be in connection with Klamm, to "stand next to" him, "face to face", has always described a merely formal relation to the non-thing he intuits as something merely indistinctly more powerful ("mächtig") than himself (S 82).[40]

In this light we might well be allowed to alter our first surmise and judge the overriding issue of the narrative no longer as *what* K. wants (Calasso: "election"; Burnett: "a grounding center") so much as its hiddenness.[41] The crux is to attend to the evident: the fact that we do not know what K. wants because he does not know what he wants. *Das Schloß* is finally a work about someone who does not know what he wants, which is to say: Everyman. We want, it would seem, what we think we want, judging from the response of others to the first *random* hits of our contacts with them. K.'s contingent inspiration is that he has been summoned as a land surveyor—a contingent hit because he knows he is unqualified. (Readers of Kafka's office briefs will not be surprised at the hit: at the time of Kafka's executing a policy to collect workers' compensation insurance premiums from farmers on a flat tax based on acreage, he complained to the Vienna office of the futility of the project in the absence of competent land surveyors: there was an abundance of pretend-surveyors).[42] To K.'s surprise, his pretense is accepted by the Castle, and thereafter he will declare that he has indeed been accepted as land surveyor but, then again, only "seemingly" ("scheinbar" [S 313]).

We have come to see the narrative as entangling two questions: the meaning of K.'s quest and the meaning of the fact that the answer is hidden. Where are the words that will tell us the truth of his original desire? After a time we might grow less attentive to K.'s adventures and to the speeches of the others, which fill the novel more and more;

look less to event, emotion, physical object or character in the round, for we are waiting for the words that K. might but does not pronounce: "This is what I want." Robert Walser's aphorism is perfect: "In starkem Grad besitzt einer nur, was ihm fehlt, da er's suchen muß."[43] K. must forever seek the desire that impels his quest. This—admittedly tension-producing gap at the very outset and continuously thereafter—contributes to the *ritardando* in *Das Schloß*. We are *waiting* for the answer.

There is a third dimension of delay: *Das Schloß* is riddled with counterfactuals, a peculiarly hesitant mode of enunciation. It supplies not so much information as hypotheticals, "facts" of the case existing in a hypothetical world, parallel to the brutally reduced world at hand: snow, coffee, gymnasium equipment, the odd tin of sardines. We have these surmises right from the start impacted in the word "scheinen", a fan of conjectures folding out from the aboriginal seeming of the castle itself, "die scheinbare Leere" ("the seeming emptiness" [C 2]).

I propose a very partial, merely representative sampling of such conditionals: "so etwa als würde" (S 58); "es schien ihm" (S 69); "wenn es so ist" (S 84); "nicht weit davon" (S 92); "so war ihm manchmal als" (S 156); "schien, so als sei" (S 207); "vielleicht [...] wäre es sogar auch Ihnen lieb" (S 209); "das war nur scheinbar" (S 313); "so als wolle er" (S 320); "tut sie so als" (S 475); "so als wolle" (S 479); "als wären es nicht viel mehr als" (S 488); "als träume sie" (S 489); "war es als überliefe sie" (S 490).[44] The reader is challenged to understand the relation of these parallel worlds. Things have something to do with one another; they are not assuredly the same; they are not entirely different; so what relation between them would be thinkable?

One is *probably* the other. They are probably but not provably the same. To take this matter further, one would rightly be drawn into the world of Kafka's professional writings, in which he is expert in risk insurance based on laws of probability. But that is another order of reference, whose proper treatment would burst the bounds of this essay. This connection of ideas is developed at length in a book recently published by Benno Wagner and myself, titled *Franz Kafka: The Ghosts in the Machine*. The reader is invited to turn to that book as supplying a proper conclusion to this essay. My main task has been to suggest three orders of delay and distraction from the reader's expectation of a narrative *telos* found, with or more or less clarity, in the nineteenth century, *dit* Realist, novels of Kafka's declared masters: Goethe, Stifter, Dickens, Flaubert, Dostoevsky. I call these factors of delay—thus *ritardando*—Kafka-memes, Void of Original Desire and Hypotheticals.

Bibliography

The American Heritage Dictionary of the English Language. Boston: Houghton Mifflin, 2000.

Bay, Hansjörg. "Das eigene Fremde der Kultur: Travestien der ethnographischen Situation bei Kafka". *DVjs* 83 (2009): 287–309.

Binder, Hartmut. *Kafka in neuer Sicht: Mimik, Gestik und Personengefüge als Darstellungsformen des Autobiographischen.* Stuttgart: Metzler, 1976.

Burnett, Jacob. "Strange Loops and the Absent Center in *The Castle*". In *Kafka for the Twenty-First Century*, edited by Stanley Corngold and Ruth V. Gross. Rochester, NY: Camden House, 2011.

Calasso, Robert. *K.* New York: Vintage, 2006.

Corngold, Stanley. "Something to Do with the Truth: Kafka's Later Stories". In *Lambent Traces: Franz Kafka*, 111–25. Princeton: Princeton University Press, 2004.

—and Ruth V. Gross. *Kafka for the Twenty-First Century*. Rochester, NY: Camden House, 2011.

Heidegger, Martin. *Being and Time*. Translated by John Macquarrie and Edward Robinson. New York: Harper and Row, 1962.

—*Sein und Zeit*. Tübingen: Niemeyer, 1963.

Kafka, Franz. "A Report to an Academy". In *Kafka's Selected Stories: New Translations, Backgrounds and Contexts, Criticism*, edited by Stanley Corngold, 76–84. New York: W. W. Norton, 2007.

—*Briefe an Felice*. Edited by Erich Heller and Jürgen Born. Frankfurt am Main: Fischer, 1976.

—"Brief an den Vater". In *Nachgelassene Schriften und Fragmente 2*, edited by Jost Schillemeit, 143–217. Frankfurt am Main: Fischer, 1992.

—*Das Schloss: Apparatband*. Edited by Malcolm Pasley. Frankfurt am Main: Fischer, 1982.

—*Der Prozess*. Edited by Malcolm Pasley. Frankfurt am Main: Fischer, 1990.

—"Ein Bericht für eine Akademie". In *Drucke zu Lebzeiten*, edited by Wolf Kittler, Hans-Gerd Koch and Gerhard Neumann, 299–313. Frankfurt am Main: Fischer, 1994.

—*Letter to His Father: Brief an den Vater*. Translated by Ernst Kaiser and Eithne Wilkins. New York: Schocken Books, 1966.

—*Letters to Felice*. Translated by James Stern and Elizabeth Duckworth. New York: Schocken, 1973.

—*Letters to Milena*. Translated by Philip Boehm. New York: Schocken, 1990.

—*Tagebücher*. Edited by Hans-Gerd Koch, Michael Müller and Malcolm Pasley. Frankfurt am Main: Fischer, 1990.

—*The Diaries of Franz Kafka: 1910–1913*. Translated by Joseph Kresh. New York: Schocken, 1948.

—*The Trial*. Translated by Breon Mitchell. New York: Schocken, 1998.

—and Mark Harman. *The Castle: A New Translation based on the Restored Text*. New York: Schocken, 1998.

—and Milena Jesenská. *Briefe an Milena*. Edited by Jürgen Born and Michael Müller Frankfurt am Main: Fischer, 1983.

—Stanley Corngold, Jack Greenberg and Benno Wagner. *Franz Kafka: The Office Writings*. Princeton, NJ: Princeton University Press, 2009.

Kleinwort, Malte. "Rückkopplung als Störung der Autor-Funktion in späten

Texten von Friedrich Nietzsche und Franz Kafka". In *Für alle und Keinen. Lektüre, Schrift und Leben bei Nietzsche und Kafka*. Edited by Friedrich Balke, Joseph Vogl and Benno Wagner, 179–200. Berlin: Diaphanes, 2008.

—"Incidental and Preliminary: Features of the Late Kafka". Unpublished conference presentation: "Kafkas Spätstil" [Kafka's Late Writing]. Princeton University, March 26–27, 2010.

Miller, Hillis J. "Derrida's Destinerrance". *MLN* 121, no. 4 (2006): 893–910.

Wagner, Benno and Stanley Corngold. *Franz Kafka: The Ghosts in the Machine*. Evanston, IL: Northwestern University Press, 2011.

Walser, Robert. *Lektüre für Minuten: Gedanken aus seinen Büchern und Briefen*. Edited by Volker Michels. Frankfurt am Main: Suhrkamp, 1978.

Notes

1. There has been relatively little sustained study of the distinctive features of the "late Kafka". Some steps in this direction have been taken by Stanley Corngold in "Something to Do with the Truth", 111–25; Hansjörg Bay in "Das eigene Fremde der Kultur", 287–309; and Malte Kleinwort in "Rückkopplung als Störung der Autor-Funktion", 179–200.
2. *American Heritage Dictionary*. The word "meme" fuses "gene" and the Greek word μιμητισμός, meaning "something imitated".
3. Hidden references to and reflections about his former literary works are characteristic of the late Kafka. These loose references are very much prefigured in Kafka's decision to assemble the first *Schloß*-notebook out of sheets of previous notebooks. See Kafka, *Das Schloß: Apparatband*, 31–3. One striking example is the telephone talk in *Das Schloß*, in which an allusion to Josef K., the protagonist of *Der Prozeß*, is found. Here, the land surveyor surprisingly introduces himself as Josef, "the old assistant of the land surveyor" (37). See Kleinwort, "Incidental and Preliminary".
4. Kafka, *Das Schloß*, 259. "Because she particularly valued comfort and thus solitude and was probably happiest at home, completely free, stretched out on the settee" (Kafka, *The Castle*, 164). All subsequent references to Kafka's texts will be indicated with the following abbreviations plus a page number in the body of the article: S (*Das Schloß*), C (*The Castle*), P (*Der Prozeß*), T (*The Trial*).
5. "Then he would generally lie on the divan in his office—he could no longer leave his office without an hour's rest on the divan—and mentally assemble his observations" (T 261).
6. Kafka, *Tagebücher*, 581. "In me, without human relations, there are no visible lies. The limited circle is pure" (diary entry for August 30, 1913 [my translation]).
7. "And staying in the middle between the exaggerations, that is, weighing the letters correctly is impossible, their value keeps changing, the thoughts that they prompt are endless and the point at which one happens to stop is determined only by accident and so the opinion one arrives at is just as accidental. And if fear for your sake comes into this too, then everything becomes confused; you shouldn't judge these words of mine too harshly" (C 231).
8. "You mustn't pay too much attention to opinions. The text is immutable, and the opinions are often only an expression of the commentators' despair" (T 220, translation modified).
9. "A large dimly lit room" (C 11).

10 "Only it was getting darker, and he hastened his step. The Castle, whose contours were already beginning to dissolve, lay still as ever, K. had never seen the slightest sign of life up there, perhaps it wasn't even possible to distinguish anything from this distance, and yet his eyes demanded it and refused to tolerate the stillness" (C 98).

11 "The observer's gaze could not remain fixed there, and slid off. Today this impression was further reinforced by the early darkness, the longer he looked, the less he could make out, and the deeper everything sank into the twilight" (C 99).

12 "K. stepped out on the wild blustery steps and gazed into the darkness. Nasty, nasty weather. [...] An intriguer by nature, operating like the wind, seemingly to no end, upon remote alien instructions that one never got to see" (C 117).

13 "One's physical strength has a certain limit, who can help it that this limit is significant in other ways too. No, nobody can help it" (C 271).

14 "That was considerate, but of course K. wanted to do him a service; cumbersomely, without changing position, he reached over to the side pocket, not to the one on the open door, that was too far, but to the one on the closed door behind him; but it didn't matter, there were bottles here too. He took one out, unscrewed the cap, smelled it, and then had to smile involuntarily; the smell was so sweet, so pleasing, so much like praise and kind words from someone whom you're very fond of, though you don't quite know what it is all about and do not want to know either and are simply happy in the knowledge that it is he who is saying such things. 'And this is supposed to be cognac?' K. asked dubiously, trying it out of curiosity. But it was indeed cognac, oddly enough, warm and burning. How it changed as one drank, from something that was virtually no more than a bearer of sweet fragrance into a drink fit for a coachman. 'Can it be?' K. asked as though reproaching himself, and drank again. At that—just as K. was engaged in taking a long sip—it became bright, the electric light came on, not only inside, on the stairs, in the passage and in the corridor, but outside above the entrance. Footsteps could be heard descending the stairs, the bottle fell from K.'s hand, cognac spilled onto a fur" (C 103–4).

15 Kafka, *Kafka's Selected Stories*, 83. All subsequent references to this edition will be abbreviated as KSS followed by page numbers.

16 Kafka, *Drucke zu Lebzeiten*, 302. "I, I have the right to lower my trousers in front of anyone I like; there is nothing to see there other than a well-groomed pelt and the scar left by a—let us choose here a specific word for a specific purpose, a word, however, that should not be misunderstood—the scar left by a profligate shot" (KSS 78).

17 Kafka, *Drucke zu Lebzeiten*, 310–11. "What a victory, then, for him as for me, when one evening [...], I grabbed a bottle of brandy that had accidentally been left outside my cage, [...] uncorked it very correctly, put it to my lips, and without dawdling, without grimacing, like a professional tippler, with round, rolling eyes and sloshing it around my throat, really and truly drank down the entire contents; tossed away the bottle, no longer like someone in despair but like an artist; I did forget to rub my belly; but in return, because I could not help it, because I felt the urge, because all my senses were in an uproar, in short, shouted 'Hello!', broke out in human speech, with this cry leaped into the human community and felt its echo, 'Just listen to that, he's talking!' like a kiss on my whole sweat-soaked body.

[...] My voice failed again immediately; it returned only after several months; my disgust with the brandy bottle returned even stronger. But my course was irrevocably set" (KSS, 82–3).

18 "Amalia's dress was very beautiful, her white blouse was billowing at the top with row upon row of lace, Mother had lent her all her lace. I was jealous then, and before the festival I wept half the night [...] and then to calm me down, she [Amalia] lent me her own necklace of Bohemian garnets" (C 188).

19 Kafka, *Nachgelassene Schriften 2*, 205. "A brief discussion on one of those few tumultuous days that followed the announcement of my latest marriage plans. You said to me something like this: 'She probably put on a fancy blouse, something these Prague Jewesses are good at, and right away, of course, you decided to marry her. And that as fast as possible, in a week, tomorrow, today. I can't understand you: after all, you're a grown man, you live in the city, and you don't know what to do but marry the next best girl. Isn't there anything else you can do? If you're frightened, I'll go with you'" (Kafka, *Letter to His Father*, 107).

20 Kafka, *Briefe an Felice*, 450 (Letter of August 22, 1913). "Chained to invisible literature by invisible chains [...], [who] screams when approached because, so he claims, someone is touching those chains" (*Letters to Felice*, 308).

21 "He had no intention of hurting him, however, and squeezed quite gently, but even so the man screamed as if K. had applied a pair of red-hot pincers, and not merely two fingers. [...] 'Most of these accused men are so sensitive', said the court usher" (T 70–1).

22 "He wanted to be a man like K." (C 149).

23 It is important to stress that, despite the mention above of Felice Bauer and Milena Jesenská, I am defining Kafka-memes not by Kafka's biography but by textual hauntings.

24 "For he was after all, at least according to the council chairman's report, the leader of the faction that had, even if merely on political grounds, demanded the summoning of a surveyor" (C 148).

25 Kafka, *Briefe an Milena*, 302. "Writing letters, on the other hand, means exposing oneself to the ghosts, who are greedily waiting precisely for that. Written kisses never arrive at their destination; the ghosts drink them up along the way" (Kafka, *Letters to Milena*, 223).

26 Kafka, *Briefe an Milena*, 301. "The easy possibility of writing letters [...] must have brought rack and ruin to the souls of the world. Writing letters is actually a communication with ghosts and by no means just with the ghost of the addressee but also with one's own ghost, which secretly evolves inside the letter one is writing or even in a whole series of letters, where one letter corroborates another and can refer to it as a witness" (Kafka, *Letters to Milena*, 223 [translation modified]).

27 Miller, "Derrida's Destinerrance", 901–2, emphasis added.

28 Miller, "Derrida's Destinerrance", 902, emphasis added.

29 "[Das] Sein des Daseins, um das es ihm in seinem Sein selbst geht" (Heidegger, *Sein und Zeit*, 123). "The Being of Dasein [...] is an issue for Dasein in its very Being" (Heidegger, *Being and Time*, 160).

30 Hartmut Binder, *Kafka in neuer Sicht*.

31 Kafka, *Tagebücher*, 87. "The freedom of authentic description [...] that *releases one's foot from lived experience*" (Kafka, *Diaries*, 100, emphasis added).

32 "So what is K. thinking of? What extraordinary ideas go through his head? Is there something special that he wants to achieve? A good appointment, a prize? Does he want something of that sort?" (C 297).

33 "My greatest and indeed my only wish is to settle my affairs with the authorities" (C 170).

34 "'So what do you want from Klamm?' said the landlady [...].
   'I want to listen quietly to all you have to say.' [...]
   'Gladly', said K., 'but it's difficult to say what I want from him. First, I want to see him close-up, then I want to hear his voice, then I want him to tell me where he stands concerning our marriage'" (C 84–5).

35 "Didn't you yourself state that you'd be satisfied if you could only have an opportunity to speak in the presence of Klamm, even if he neither looked at you nor listened to you?" (C 115).

36 "'To be sure', said K., leaving it to her to interpret the words he had spoken" (C 34).

37 "'This is the assistant of the gentleman who came as surveyor.' 'What assistant? What gentleman? What surveyor?' K. recalled yesterday's telephone conversation. 'Ask Fritz', he said curtly. It worked, to his own astonishment." Then, "'I'm the old [...] [assistant] who came today to join the surveyor.' 'No', the voice was now shouting. 'Who am I, then?' K. asked as calmly as before. And after a pause, the same voice [...] said: 'You're the old assistant'" (C 20–1).

38 "K. was still listening to the sound of the voice and almost missed the next question: 'What do you want?' Most of all he would have liked to put down the receiver. He was no longer expecting anything from this conversation. Only under pressure did he quickly add: 'When can my master come to the Castle?' 'Never', came the answer. 'Fine', said K., replacing the receiver" (C 21).

39 "But as for you, [...] you were torn from Klamm, I cannot gauge what that means, but I have gradually gained an idea of what that means, one staggers, one cannot find one's way" (C 253).

40 "A person with power" (C 50).

41 Calasso, *K.*, 5; Burnett, "Strange Loops and the Absent Center".

42 Stanley Corngold, Jack Greenberg and Benno Wagner, (eds) *Franz Kafka: The Office Writings* (Princeton: Princeton University Press, 2009), 78.

43 Walser, *Lektüre für Minuten*, 9. "In the strongest sense, one possesses only what one lacks, since one must search for it".

44 "As if he had, say, (C34); "it seemed to him" (C 42); "if that's so" (C 51); "almost" (C 57); "it was at times as if he were" (C98); "seemed [...] as if" (C 131); "you might have preferred" (C 132); "only in appearance" (C198); "as though determined" (C 203); "acts as though" (C 304); "as though she wanted" (C 306); "as if they didn't last much longer than" (C 312); "as if she were dreaming" (C 312); "it was as if [...] went running" (C 313).

3. Kafka's "A Hunger Artist" as Allegory of Bourgeois Subject Construction

Imke Meyer

In his "Notes on Kafka", Theodor W. Adorno maintained that Kafka's prose is "striving not for symbol but for allegory",[1] and specifically with regard to Kafka's 1922 narrative "A Hunger Artist",[2] James Rolleston goes so far as to declare: "That 'A Hunger Artist' is allegorical has never been in doubt."[3] Alice Kuzniar reminds us of the "oblique, disconcerting" manner in which allegory signifies,[4] as the meaning to which it points is of necessity never that which it is saying: "It is this oblique signification that makes allegory unreadable: the inexpressible, mysterious truth or ideal to which it would point can only be signified through a materiality and artifice that ultimately only deflect and defer meaning.[...] [A]llegory pretends to open, direct statement, while actually it calls attention to the breach between sign and referent."[5] Indeed, if one were to substitute "Kafka's texts" for the term 'allegory' in Kuzniar's quote, the description would seem quite apt.

Like allegory's signification, an encounter with Kafka's texts often strikes us as "disconcerting". Readers of Kafka frequently experience what Stanley Corngold has termed "the commentators despair", the impossibility to find any definitive meaning in Kafka's writings.[6] It is, of course, precisely the often enigmatic quality of Kafka's texts that produces in the reader the kind of disquiet that prompts him or her to try time and again to arrest their meaning, but since "no single reading of Kafka", as Corngold puts it, "escapes blindness",[7] any interpretation of Kafka's texts implicitly begs the next one. As Mark Anderson has pointed out, the puzzling character of Kafka's texts is partially owed to the fact that "Kafka eliminated the specific cultural signs that had traditionally served to locate a literary text in a particular place and time. Almost all place names, dates, proper names and other references to the world outside the text were effaced. Moreover, the physical laws and social norms of this external world were also suspended."[8] In this sense, then, "Kafka had done everything to encourage [...] an allegorical reception of his writings."[9] My reading of "A Hunger Artist" quite consciously takes Kafka's bait: I will add yet another allegorical reading of the text to the catalogue of those that already exist, and I will do so in the knowledge that my allegorical reading will map on to Kafka's text but imperfectly, just like all previous allegorical readings. I will argue that Kafka's "Hunger Artist" can be read as an allegory of bourgeois subject construction. The outlines of my allegorical reading will match those of the text in some parts, but the outlines will oscillate and be incongruous with those of the text in other areas. Yet this allegorical interpretation hopes to do what all others before it also aimed to achieve: to capture for a moment, in the face of allegory's insistence that the "breach between sign and referent" cannot be healed, the shifting contours of one of the text's possible meanings.

The Hunger Artist's Protestant Work Ethic

Time and again, commentators of Kafka's "Hunger Artist" have interpreted the protagonist as a figure chiefly characterized by his refusal to make himself part of the bourgeois world and its institutions. To name but a few of these commentators, Richard Sheppard has claimed that it is the hunger artist's "task [...] to be a man among men, but he refuses this and turns his back upon men out of a deep-seated sense of pride."[10] Gerhard Neumann, in his highly illuminating reading of the text, discusses the hunger artist's refusal to eat as an attempt to remain outside the realm of the bourgeois family, an institution whose rules are in no small part constituted by rituals centered on food and food consumption.[11] Neumann reads the hunger artist's fasting as "the attempt to repeal the social achievements of culture" ("de[n] Versuch, die soziale Leistung der Kultur zu widerrufen").[12] Michael Müller, too, stresses that the hunger artist has "segregated himself from the community of others."[13] Rolleston finds that the hunger artist "symbolically rejects the claims of ordinary (bourgeois) living."[14]

It is Kafka's narrator, of course, who repeatedly tempts us into reading the hunger artist as a figure who stands apart from the bourgeois world. After all, from the outset of the text, the very designation of the protagonist as an artist identifies him as someone who potentially occupies the position of an outsider and—as such—a privileged observer. The cage in which the hunger artist displays himself to his audience quite literally bars him from regular intercourse with others. And it is not least the protagonist's dying admission that he could not but starve himself ("because I couldn't find the food I like")[15] that marks him as someone who is different from the average person.

In other words, I think that there is ample justification to read the hunger artist as an outsider. And yet: I also believe that there is just as much justification to read the hunger artist as an allegory of the performative contradictions of bourgeois subject construction.[16] How can such a reading be supported? In 1974, Peter Beicken characterized the hunger artist in the following way: "The hunger artist's art does not illuminate, it does not communicate new knowledge, it does not create an explicit insight that productively transmits anything new; it is focused on itself in a circular fashion and given over to a one-sided fanaticism of achievement."[17] While the hunger artist's art is primarily characterized by negativity, absences and gestures of refusal, it is also a testament to a *Leistungsfanatismus*, a fanatical drive to achieve—both in spite and as a result of its one-dimensionality.

Seen in this light, the hunger artist's ascetic life seems to testify to a kind of Protestant work ethic. Here, the adherence to this ethic is, of course, practiced in a paradoxical way: it is precisely by doing absolutely nothing that the hunger artist does absolutely everything to fulfill the demands of his art. In fact, his art may be an art only when viewed from a particular perspective. As Margot Norris has pointed out, "fasting becomes hunger art when the point of view shifts from sufferer to spectator (since spectators can only see pain, not feel it) and thereby assumes an aesthetic form whose essence is stasis, like painting or sculpture."[18] From the point of view of the hunger artist, then, his fasting may be less an artistic calling and more a profession. In fact, after the interest in hunger artists is said to begin to wane, the narrator points out that the hunger artist feels too old "for adopting another profession" (HA 273),[19] and Kafka himself excised from an early draft of the story the words "it simply became his profession."[20] From this perspective, "it"—the fasting—appears much more prosaic, a choice made "just because" ("eben"), almost out of convenience, or because no better option seemed available. This "Beruf" ("profession"), then— rather than an artist's "Berufung" ("calling")—is performed by the hunger artist in a manner the text itself calls "fanatical" ("fanatisch", KKADL 343): he is, in fact, a "Leistungsethiker", a workaholic.

Towards the end of the text, the narrator states that the hunger artist "was working honestly, but the world was cheating him out of his reward" (HA 276)[21]: though, ironically, he does not need any bread while he starves himself, as fasting is the hunger artist's "Brotberuf." The "Lohn", of course—the reward the hunger artist truly wants—is appreciation from his fellow-human beings. This, however, is precisely what repeatedly eludes him, as his audience believes him to be cheating, i.e., to be eating secretly and to exaggerate the number of days for which he has starved himself already. The hunger artist does not feel appreciated, a feeling to which most average members of the bourgeoisie and salaried employees can surely relate.

What did the hunger artist's average work day look like during the time when "it used to pay very well to stage such great performances under one's own management"[22] and prior to "these last decades" during which "the interest in professional fasting has markedly diminished" (HA 268)?[23] Entire cities are gripped by interest in the hunger artist's presence in their midst, and supposedly everybody wants to see the hunger artist at least once a day. Subscribers pay to view his cage for days on end, and even at night showings take place. The hunger artist periodically answers questions from the audience and lets them feel his boney arms. At times, the hunger artist seems withdrawn, and during these periods he does not even care about "the all-important striking of the clock that was the only piece of furniture in his cage" (HA 268).[24]

Guards selected by the audience are watching the hunger artist day and night to ensure that he does not cheat by secretly consuming food. The narrator points out, though, that this is "nothing but a formality" ("lediglich eine Formalität"), because "the initiates" ("die Eingeweihten") know that the hunger artist would never eat even the tiniest morsel during a period of fasting, as "the honor of his profession forbade it" (HA 268–69).[25] The hunger artist feels tortured, therefore, by guards who do their jobs in a lax manner, ostensibly to give the hunger artist an opportunity to sneak in some food: the assumption on the part of these guards that the hunger artist's shows are built on deception insults him deeply. He therefore prefers to be watched closely by his guards, but many members of his audience remain suspicious. As frustrating as these experiences are for the hunger artist, the audience's mistrust and suspicions "were a necessary accompaniment to the profession of fasting" (HA 269).[26] Therefore, while the hunger artist desires the presence and admiration of an audience, in the end only he himself can be "the sole completely satisfied spectator of his own fast" (HA 270).[27]

The hunger artist here seems like an employee who is punching the clock—it is no accident that the only piece of furniture in his cage is a clock, and later on in the text we learn that a sign on the hunger artist's cage announces to the audience the number of days a given fast has already lasted. The hunger artist's work is interrupted by "small regular intervals of recuperation" (HA 272);[28] like a salaried employee, he is granted regular vacations. Ironically, of course, the work periods are the times during which the hunger artist—since he does nothing but starve himself—is at rest, whereas he can engage in actual activities during his periods of recuperation ("Ruhepausen").

In addition, the hunger artist perceives the "Ruhepausen" as forced breaks from his hunger art, which he practices fanatically. Here, a vexed image of Kafka's own feelings about his devotion to writing on the one hand and his work as a lawyer for the Workers Compensation Insurance Company might have been inscribed in the text: as is well known, Kafka thought that his salaried work as a lawyer kept him from realizing fully his calling as a writer. This constellation might be reflected in the text, albeit in a distorted way: here, the hunger artist's passion and his paid work are collapsed into one. The hunger artist is "fanatically devoted" (HA 273)[29] to his paid work, rather than to some pursuit outside the realm of labor. In a manner of speaking, it is the fact that his passion has to labor under the demands of a market economy that keeps him from performing it in a fashion he deems ideal.

Another frustration the hunger artist regularly experiences is the fact that his impresario has limited the fasting periods to no more than forty days. The hunger artist feels that this limit prevents him from displaying to the world the true extent of his fasting talents, and he regularly resists being taken from his cage at the end of the predetermined fasting period, but the impresario finds that even in major cities, and even with the help of advertizing and dramatic stagecraft, the interest of the audience cannot be maintained for more than forty days:

> So on the fortieth day the flower-bedecked cage was opened, enthusiastic spectators filled the hall, a military band played, two doctors entered the cage to measure the results of the fast, which were announced through a megaphone, and finally two young ladies appeared, blissful at having been selected for the honor, to help the hunger artist down the few steps leading to a small table on which was spread a carefully chosen invalid repast. And at this very moment the artist always turned stubborn. True, he would entrust his bony arms to the outstretched helping hands of the ladies bending over him, but stand up he would not. Why stop fasting at this particular moment, after forty days of it? (HA 270–1)[30]

That the imagery in this passage is a partially religious one has repeatedly been pointed out:[31] both Moses and Jesus spent 40 days fasting in the desert, the scene of the hunger artist's removal from the cage is reminiscent of the pietà, and the impresario later lifts his arms "as if inviting Heaven to look down upon its creature here in the straw, this suffering martyr" (HA 271).[32] And as Jan Mieszkowski has pointed out, it is, of course, highly ironic that "only when it ceases does hunger art allow for a truly successful spectacle"[33], complete with all manner of pomp and circumstance.

What interests me here is that the hunger artist's "Beruf" is now, after all, re-staged as a "Berufung", a calling—albeit not an artistic one, but rather a religious one. As Max Weber's *The Protestant Ethic and the Spirit of Capitalism* has taught us, it was Luther's conception of the calling (and its Calvinist reinterpretation) as an expression of—rather than precondition for—salvation from God that allowed for its entry into the secular realm and support of a capitalist economic system. Asceticism morphs from a devout practice into a mark of devoted work, and it can then leave the religious realm and become a characteristic of hard labor and secular morality. As the "Berufung" turns into the secular "Beruf", it can be instrumentalized for economic ends. The view Weber expresses in his *General Economic History*, published posthumously in 1923, is particularly bleak: "The development of the concept of the calling quickly gave to the modern entrepreneur a fabulously clear conscience—and also industrious workers; he gave to his employees as the wages of their ascetic devotion to the calling and of co-operation in his ruthless exploitation of them through capitalism the prospect of eternal salvation."[34] In Kafka's text, the ravaging effects of the secularization of asceticism, of a worker's fanatical devotion to paid labor, are literally in full view for thirty-nine days at a time. On the fortieth day, however, a Christian veil is quite simply draped over the scene, so that it may be made palatable again to a paying—and as such equally exploited—public hungry for stories of salvation in a world otherwise too obviously ruled by the ruthless spirit of capitalism.

The narrator's description of the fasting period's ending as a shamelessly pseudo-religious spectacle put on for the paying masses is followed by a passage that once again details the hunger artist's frustrations in the face of a public that takes as a cause of his "melancholy" (HA 272)[35] his fasting, rather than the limitations placed on this fasting by the economic demands to which he is subject. It is noteworthy that here the text again points to the false consciousness capitalism produces in western societies: the public willing to pay to see the hunger artist—i.e., a public that readily rushes to spend its hard-earned money on a spectacle that (while performed by an honest worker) was specially designed for commercial purposes—this public willing and eager to see the hunger artist is ready to attribute his unhappiness to an existential cause, namely the fasting, rather than to the conditions of labor, namely the economic parameters which shape public fasting. While the public's false consciousness adequately attributes to the hunger artist a kind of Hegelian unhappy consciousness, it misidentifies the immediate causes of the hunger artist's "Traurigkeit", which have their roots in the capitalist system.

On occasion, the hunger artist is so frustrated by the audience's misunderstandings of his fasting that he becomes enraged and literally rattles his cage—to no avail, of course. The narrator tells us that the impresario has a "way of punishing" (HA 272)[36] the hunger artist's outbursts on such occasions; he disciplines his worker in the following manner:

> He would apologize publicly for the artist's behavior, which was only to be excused, he admitted, because of the irritability caused by fasting; a condition hardly to be understood by well-fed people; then by natural transition he went on to mention the artist's equally incomprehensible boast that he could fast for much longer than he was doing; he praised the high ambition, the goodwill, the great self-denial undoubtedly implicit in such a statement; and then quite simply countered it by bringing out photographs, which were also on sale to the public, showing the artist on the fortieth day of a fast lying in bed almost dead from exhaustion. This perversion of the truth, familiar to the artist though it was, always unnerved him afresh and proved too much for him. What was a consequence of the premature ending of his fast was here presented as the cause of it! To fight against this lack of understanding, against a whole world of non-understanding, was impossible. (HA 272–3)[37]

The impresario praises the hunger artist's striving, his goodwill, and his self-denial—all traits of secular morality, of a good bourgeois, as well as of a devoted employee. It is indeed quite true that the hunger artist embodies the qualities of a virtually perfect and, to use Weber's terminology, "industrious worker." And yet he periodically engages in futile gestures of rebellion against the conditions under which he labors. In a perverse move, the impresario seamlessly incorporates these gestures into his commercialized narrative about the hunger artist—and into its equally commercialized interpretive template. The hunger artist's humiliation does not end with the substitution of the commercialized narrative for his "true" story, though: in addition, photographs are substituted for his living body, and the circulation of these photographs in the capitalist economy of the public sphere and their subjugation under its spectatorial regimes complete the commodification of the hunger artist's labor.[38]

Soon the hunger artist's problems shift, though: the masses have now lost interest in public fasting shows. A "change" ("Umschwung") has occurred, and there "may have been profound causes for it, but who was going to bother about that; at any rate, the pampered hunger artist suddenly found himself deserted one fine day by the amusement-seekers, who went streaming past him to other more-favored attractions" (HA 273).[39] The hunger artist, whose "great self-denial" ("große Selbstverleugnung") the impresario had repeatedly praised, is now described as "pampered" ("verwöhnt")—simply in terms of the attention an audience was willing to pay him. Quite in keeping with the capitalist spirit, as soon as an economic shift affects the conditions of labor, any anticipated complaints by the workers are simply attributed to the fact that they are "pampered." The audience's change in taste has economic consequences for the hunger artist and his impresario, but this change in taste may itself have economic reasons. The narrator, in fact, mentions that "more profound causes" ("tiefere Gründe") might be responsible for the taste change, but then claims that their pursuit is probably of no importance to people. In other words, while the audience's leisure time is spent feeding the capitalist economy (tickets are purchased for various "attractions" ["Schaustellungen"], people are discouraged from analyzing the economic structures and currents that govern and steer their own behavior. Rather, individuals vanish by becoming part of a mob—a "Menge", as the German original puts it—that "streams" in different directions for seemingly arbitrary reasons out of its control.

After the hunger artist's popularity has waned so much that the staging of public fasts is no longer possible, he and the impresario part ways. The hunger artist lets himself be hired by a circus, barely looking at the contract he signs "in order to spare his own feelings" (HA 273–74).[40] The hunger artist suffers, as he is no longer the center of attention of large crowds who have come to see him specifically. Rather, he is placed in a cage near the stables of the circus animals, and his audience mainly consists of passers-by who have no great interest in him. Nobody is even attempting to witness his achievement, and the circus workers eventually forget to change the sign that announces to the audience the number of fasting days completed. Occasional visitors even believe a sign with an older, lower, inaccurate number to be a shameless exaggeration. As in the past, the hunger artist, who works honestly and does not cheat, is suspected by his small remaining audience of being a charlatan.

Since he no longer needs to adhere to the protocol of a major forty-day fasting show, though, the hunger artist is now liberated to hunger "as he had once dreamed of doing" (HA 276).[41] The circus briefly appears like a space in which something is possible for which there is no room elsewhere in a world dominated by the culture industry. In their *Dialectic of Enlightenment*, Horkheimer and Adorno describe this space as one that can temporarily give rise to what they term "traces of something better" ("die Spur des Besseren"):

> Traces of something better persist in those features of the culture industry by which it resembles the circus—in the

stubbornly purposeless expertise of riders, acrobats, and clowns [...]. But the hiding places of mindless artistry, which represents what is human against the social mechanism, are being relentlessly ferreted out by organizational reason, which forces everything to justify itself in terms of meaning and effect. It is causing meaninglessness to disappear at the lowest level of art just as radically as meaning is disappearing at the highest.[42]

Indeed, the hunger artist, liberated to starve without limit, does gradually vanish. As he continues to fast, his body literally shrinks, and he is soon nothing but "[a] small impediment [...], one that grew steadily less" (HA 276)[43] on the audience's path to the animal cages. The hunger artist has soon shrunk so much that he is nearly invisible underneath the "dirty straw" (HA 276)[44] that covers the bottom of his cage, but an "overseer" (HA 276) and his colleagues do find his hiding place. The overseer's "organizational reason"—to use Horkheimer and Adorno's term—wonders why a "perfectly good cage" is left "unused" (HA 276).[45] The translation of the "organizational reason" into action is interrupted but briefly by the hunger artist's confession that he was wrong to desire the public's admiration for his fasting, since he feels he has to starve himself and "can't help it", "because I couldn't find the food I liked" (HA 277).[46] Moments later, the hunger artist dies, and the custodian reacts to his death with the simple admonition to his co-workers: "'Well, clear this out now!'" (HA 277).[47] Along with the rotten straw, the hunger artist is quickly buried. His "disappearance" is indeed "radical"—after his burial, his body is no longer an "impediment", and an order ("Ordnung") that reflects an "organizational reason" has been restored.

The Hunger Artist and Bourgeois Subjectivity

The hunger artist's existence demarcates the contested space in which bourgeois subjectivity is constituted. From its inception, the birth place of bourgeois subjectivity, the nuclear family, was beset by contradictions and blind spots. Jürgen Habermas states:

> Although there may have been a desire to perceive the sphere of the family circle as independent, as cut off from all connection with society, and as the domain of pure humanity, it was, of course, dependent on the sphere of labor and of commodity exchange—even this consciousness of independence can be understood as flowing from the factual dependency of that reclusive domain upon the private one of the market.[48]

Furthermore, "occupational requirements also contradicted the idea of a personal cultivation as its own end".[49] The sphere of supposedly pure humanity, then, owes its very existence to a world of commerce, and *Bildung*, the foundation of the acquisition of a nobility of spirit and secular morality, will ultimately be instrumentalized in the context of a profession which, in turn, is necessary to provide the economic foundation for the familial sphere. These contradictions may help explain why the characterizations of the activities of Kafka's protagonist oscillate between the poles of autonomous art and paid profession, between purity and commerce, between "Berufung" and "Beruf". Of course, the repeated references to the hunger artist's trade as an art ("Kunst") only imperfectly obscure the fact that he is, in the end, a frustrated employee who feels under-appreciated by the world.

While the hunger artist is not shown to be part of a nuclear family, he and the impresario do engage in a joint venture. Instead of showing us a family, then, Kafka presents us with a partnership that stands in for precisely what is hidden at the heart of the "sphere of the family circle" ("Sphäre des Familienkreises"), namely a shared economic interest. Kafka's text never leads us into a conventional home. Instead, the narrator describes for us the hunger artist's barren cages. One of them contains a piece of furniture ("Möbelstück") that strikes the reader as a grotesque leftover of bourgeois homeliness, namely a grandfather clock. This piece of furniture has, of course, no decorative purpose here whatsoever, but functions purely as an instrument for the measurement of time. When we hear of a bed in which the hunger artist is resting, it is in the context of the photographs the impresario sells—the commercialization distances us from what we might otherwise have perceived as a private space. The hunger artist seems always to be in a public realm, and yet the bars of his cage visibly separate the space he occupies from the individuals that form the public. The hunger artist's subjectivity even seems to constitute itself in the space that is clearly marked as his own and yet permeated by the gaze of the public. With Habermas, one might speak here of a "Privateness Oriented to an Audience."[50]

What kind of space gives birth to this type of privacy? In his discussion of bourgeois homes in the eighteenth century, Habermas states:

> The line between private and public sphere extended right through the home. The privatized individuals stepped out of the intimacy of their living rooms into the public sphere of the salon, but the one was strictly complementary to the other. Only the name of salon recalled the origin of convivial discussion and rational-critical public debate in the sphere of noble society. By

now the salon, as the place where bourgeois family heads and their wives were sociable, had lost its connection with that sphere. The privatized individuals who gathered here to form a public were not reducible to "society"; they only entered into it, so to speak, out of a private life that had assumed institutional form in the enclosed space of the patriarchal conjugal family.[51]

For Habermas, the private sphere and the public sphere are not only linked, but ultimately interdependent. The private sphere that the bourgeoisie carved out of the more open structures of a pre-Enlightenment society soon gives birth to a public sphere consisting of private individuals who, in essence, become each other's audiences. Thus when the intimate sphere of the nuclear family gives rise to subjectivity, this subjectivity is, as Habermas reminds us, "always already oriented to an audience", i.e. always already linked to the notion of a public.[52]

Habermas goes on to describe how these newly formed audiences of private individuals engaged in reasoned arguments eventually turned into a discursive sphere in which power could be subjected to critique. When we meet Kafka's hunger artist in early twentieth-century Europe, things have shifted, of course. The eighteenth century's "privateness oriented to an audience" has been inverted: it is no longer the bourgeois private sphere itself that gives birth to a notion of the public, but rather, an inauthentic notion of privacy is circulated in public by the culture industry.[53] A "Culture-Debating" ("kulturräsonierendes") public is thus turned into a "Culture-Consuming Public."[54] The audience that gathers to watch the hunger artist may, of course, not even be consuming culture anymore. Rather, it may be looking at a grotesquely enlarged reflection of the shrunken and panoptical space that its own formerly private sphere has become, and it may be gazing at a distorted image of its own frustrated self exploited on the labor market. The eighteenth century's productive proximity of the private and the public sphere has been replaced by the economic appropriation of the private sphere and the harnessing of subjectivity for commercial ends.

Horkheimer and Adorno, of course, explain this state of affairs with reference to the paradoxes and contradictions to which the dialectic of the Enlightenment gives birth:

> The human being's mastery of itself, on which the self is founded, practically always involves the annihilation of the subject in whose service that mastery is maintained, because the substance which is mastered, suppressed and disintegrated by self-preservation is nothing other than the living entity, of which the achievements of self-preservation can only be defined as functions—in

other words, self-preservation destroys the very thing which is to be preserved. The antireason of totalitarian capitalism, whose technique of satisfying needs, in their objectified form determined by domination, makes the satisfaction of needs impossible and tends toward the extermination of humanity—this antireason appears prototypically in the hero who escapes the sacrifice by sacrificing himself. The history of civilization is the history of the introversion of sacrifice—in other words, the history of renunciation.[55]

The very process of the constitution of the subject, in other words, must ultimately lead to its demise. As the subject gives shape to itself, it inadvertently represses, distorts and sacrifices so much of its substance that it begins to endanger its very existence. This, of course, is exactly the process in which the hunger artist is caught: his self is constituted in the course of fasting, yet the fasting quite literally consumes the substance of which his body is made up.[56] The satisfaction of the need indicated by hunger is impossible—the hunger artist cannot find the food that he likes. Hunger, then, is turned into an end in itself—it is meant to be the conscious self-sacrifice made to escape sacrifice, the "introversion of sacrifice." But this renunciation, the fasting prolonged *ad infinitum* that was meant to unite spirit and substance in the focus on a single purpose, the fasting that was supposed to heal the split that runs through the bourgeois subject, in the end only cements the mind-body separation: as the hunger artist dies, his body gives in, yet even "in his dimming eyes remained the firm though no longer proud persuasion that he was still continuing to fast" (HA 277).[57]

Conclusion

As Richard T. Gray has shown us in his seminal reading of "The Judgment", Kafka's text "depicts the dilemma of the bourgeois subject in terms of an aporetic choice between total assimilation of the rationalizing, reifying structures of bourgeois socioeconomic and discursive practice, or uncompromising withdrawal from bourgeois social and commercial circulation into the impotent isolationism of nonpraxis."[58] In 1922, as Kafka works on "A Hunger Artist" ten years after the completion of "The Judgment", he no longer seems to leave such alternatives open to his protagonist. However aporetic Georg Bendemann's choice might have been, even the sphere in which to select one bad option over the other seems to have vanished for the hunger artist. The hunger artist is always already subjected to a public-private spatial interplay that has become a mere commercial simulation and in which he is forced to do both: assimilate to the existing socioeconomic structures and, simultaneously, withdraw into an interiority that is in the process of dying along with the very possibility of the existence of bourgeois subjectivity. With the removal of choice, Kafka pushes the aporia of the split bourgeois subject to its apex: the very attempt of the constitution of the self cannot but lead to the annihilation of the bourgeois subject.

In "A Hunger Artist", Kafka's narrator introduces us to a diligent worker, a virtual embodiment of the Protestant work ethic, who is eaten up by the contradictions that mark the conditions under which he labors. Kafka shows us a subject that must consume itself in the very process of its constitution. After Kafka finished correcting the galleys for the *Hunger Artist* volume on his death bed, he is said to have cried.[59] With the hunger artist, he has left us the story of a torn and doomed individual—a story that is as disquieting as it is moving.

Bibliography

Adorno, Theodor W. "Aufzeichnungen zu Kafka". In *Prismen: Kulturkritik und Gesellschaft*, 250–83. Frankfurt am Main: Suhrkamp, 1977.

—"Notes on Kafka". In *Prisms*, translated by Shierry Weber Nicholsen and Samuel Weber, 243–71. Cambridge, MA: MIT, 1983.

Anderson, Mark. "Introduction". In *Reading Kafka: Prague, Politics, and the Fin de Siècle*, edited by Mark Anderson, 3–22. New York: Schocken Books, 1989.

Anderson, Patrick. *So Much Wasted: Hunger, Performance, and the Morbidity of Resistance*. Durham, NC: Duke University Press, 2010.

Beicken, Peter U. *Franz Kafka: Eine kritische Einführung in die Forschung*. Frankfurt am Main: Athenäum Fischer, 1974.

Corngold, Stanley. *The Commentators' Despair: The Interpretation of Kafka's 'Metamorphosis'*. Port Washington, NY: Kennikat Press, 1973.

Gray, Richard T. *Stations of the Divided Subject: Contestation and Ideological Legitimation in German Bourgeois Literature, 1770–1914*. Stanford, CA: Stanford University Press, 1995.

Guarda, Sylvain. "Kafkas *Hungerkünstler*: Eine Messiade in humorig verwilderter Form". *The German Quarterly* 81, no. 3 (2008): 339–51.

Habermas, Jürgen. *Der philosophische Diskurs der Moderne. Zwölf Vorlesungen*. Frankfurt am Main: Suhrkamp, 1988.

—*Strukturwandel der Öffentlichkeit. Untersuchungen zu einer Kategorie der bürgerlichen Gesellschaft*. Frankfurt am Main: Suhrkamp, 1990.

—*The Philosophical Discourse of Modernity. Twelve Lectures*. Translated by Frederick G. Lawrence. Cambridge, MA: MIT Press, 1990.

—*The Structural Transformation of the Public Sphere. An Inquiry into a Category of Bourgeois Society*. Translated by Thomas Burger, with the assistance of Frederick Lawrence. Cambridge, MA: MIT Press, 1991.

Horkheimer, Max and Theodor W. Adorno. *Dialektik der Aufklärung. Philosophische Fragmente*. Frankfurt am Main: Fischer, 1971.

—*Dialectic of Enlightenment. Philosophical Fragments*. Edited by Gunzelin Schmid Noerr. Translated by Edmund Jephcott. Stanford, CA: Stanford University Press, 2002.

Kafka, Franz. *Briefe 1902–1924*. Edited by Max Brod. Frankfurt am Main: Fischer, 1958.
—*Kritische Ausgabe der Schriften, Tagebücher und Briefe*. Edited by Jürgen Born, Gerhard Neumann, Malcolm Pasley and Jost Schillemeit. Frankfurt am Main: Fischer, 1982 ff.
—*The Complete Stories*. Edited by Nahum H. Glatzer. New York: Schocken Books, 1971.
Kuzniar, Alice A. *The Queer German Cinema*. Stanford, CA: Stanford University Press, 2000.
Lange-Kirchheim, Astrid. "Das fotografierte Hungern: Neues Material zu Franz Kafkas Erzählung 'Ein Hungerkünstler'". *Hofmannsthal-Jahrbuch* 17 (2009): 7–56.
Maier, Thomas. "Das anorexische Ich oder der Künstler als sein eigener Zuschauer: Überlegungen zu Kafkas Erzählung 'Ein Hungerkünstler'". In *Wege in und aus der Moderne: Von Jean Paul zu Günter Grass*, edited by Werner Jung et al., 199–217. Bielefeld: Aisthesis, 2006.
Mieszkowski, Jan. "Kafka Live!". *MLN* 116, no. 5 (2001): 979–1000.
Mitchell, Breon. "Franz Kafka and the Hunger Artists". In *Kafka and Contemporary Critical Performance*, edited by Alan Udoff, 236–55. Bloomington, IN: Indiana University Press, 1987.
Müller, Michael. "'Ein Hungerkünstler'". In *Franz Kafka. Romane und Erzählungen*, edited by Michael Müller, 284–311. Stuttgart: Reclam, 1994.
Neumann, Gerhard. "Hungerkünstler und Menschenfresser: Zum Verhältnis von Kunst und kulturellem Ritual im Werk von Franz Kafka". *Archiv für Kulturgeschichte* 66, no. 2 (1984): 347–88.
—"Kafka als Ethnologe". In *Odradeks Lachen: Fremdheit bei Kafka*, edited by Hansjörg Bay and Christof Hamann, 325–45. Freiburg: Rombach, 2006.
Norris, Margot. "Sadism and Masochism in 'In the Penal Colony' and 'A Hunger Artist'". In *Reading Kafka. Prague, Politics, and the Fin De Siècle*, edited by Mark Anderson, 170–86. New York: Schocken Books, 1989.
Rolleston, James. "Purification unto Death: 'A Hunger Artist' as Allegory of Modernism". In *Approaches to Teaching Kafka's Short Fiction*, edited by Richard T. Gray, 135–42. New York: The Modern Language Association of America, 1995.
Sheppard, Richard W. "Kafka's 'Ein Hungerkünstler': A Reconsideration". *The German Quarterly* 46, no. 2 (1973): 219–33.
Weber, Max. *General Economic History*. Translated by Frank H. Knight. New York: Collier, 1961.

Notes

1 Adorno, "Notes on Kafka", 246. Adorno maintained that "Kafkas Prosa [...] eher der Allegorie nacheifert als dem Symbol" (Adorno, "Aufzeichnungen zu Kafka", 251).

2 Unless otherwise noted, all Kafka quotes in the original German will be taken from Franz Kafka, *Kritische Ausgabe der Schriften: Tagebücher und Briefe*. The edition itself will be cited as KKA; individual volumes will be cited with the following abbreviations: T (*Tagebücher*); DL (*Drucke zu Lebzeiten*); and App. for any "Apparatband". Translations of Kafka's narratives will be cited from Nahum Glatzer's edition of Kafka's *Complete Stories*. Translations from the German not otherwise marked are my own.

 In a diary entry of May 25 1922, Kafka notes that he worked on "A Hunger Artist" on May 23 (see KKAT 922; KKADL App. 437). The story was first published in October 1922 in *Die neue Rundschau* (KKADL App. 436). Kafka eventually integrated the text into an eponymous story collection that appeared in 1924, after Kafka's death on June 3. Shortly before his death, Kafka corrected the volume's first galleys. For a detailed history of the volume's publication, see KKADL App. 388–99.

3 Rolleston, "Purification unto Death", 136. "But allegorical of what?", Rolleston goes on to ask (136), and he argues "that the text allegorizes the specific aspirations of modernist art" (140). Rolleston's reading allows him to shed a lot of light on Kafka's critical engagement with a modernism he himself espoused.
4 Kuzniar, *Queer German Cinema*, 14.
5 Kuzniar, *Queer German Cinema*, 8–9.
6 Corngold, *Commentators' Despair*.
7 Corngold, *Commentators' Despair*, v.
8 Anderson, *Reading Kafka*, 5.
9 Ibid.
10 Sheppard, "Kafka's 'Ein Hungerkünstler'", 231.
11 Neumann, "Hungerkünstler und Menschenfresser". Neumann offers another compelling reading in his "Kafka als Ethnologe".
12 Neumann, "Hungerkünstler und Menschenfresser", 364.
13 Müller, "'Ein Hungerkünstler'", 309. "Sich aus der Gemeinschaft der anderen ausgegrenzt".
14 Rolleston, "Purification unto Death", 140.
15 Kafka, "A Hunger Artist", 277. All subsequent references to the English translation are cited in the text as HA followed by the page numbers. "Weil ich nicht die Speise finden konnte, die mir schmeckt" (KKADL 349).
16 Neumann, " Hungerkünstler und Menschenfresser", 371. Neumann, too, states: "Kafkas Text repräsentiert die Inszenierung der 'Paradoxie der Identität' schlechthin." However, he argues that the hunger artist is seeking a space situated prior to and outside of culture, whereas I maintain that the hunger artist seeks to follow the rules for the construction of subjectivity in western culture in an especially rigid manner.
17 Beicken, *Franz Kafka*, 322. "Die Kunst des Hungerkünstlers illuminiert nicht, sie kommuniziert nicht neue Erkenntnis, schafft keine explizite Einsicht, die produktiv Neues vermittelte, sie ist zirkulär auf sich selbst gerichtet und einem einseitigen Leistungsfanatismus ausgeliefert."
18 Norris, "Sadism and Masochism", 176.
19 "Um einen anderen Beruf zu ergreifen" (KKADL 343).
20 "Es war eben sein Beruf geworden" (KKADL App. 442).
21 "Er arbeitete ehrlich, aber die Welt betrog ihn um seinen Lohn" (KKADL 347).
22 "Es sich […] gut lohnte, große derartige Vorführungen in eigener Regie zu veranstalten" (KKADL 333–34).
23 "Das Interesse an Hungerkünstlern sehr zurückgegangen [ist]" (KKADL 333).
24 "Den für ihn so wichtigen Schlag der Uhr, die das einzige Möbelstück des Käfigs war" (KKADL 334).
25 "Die Ehre seiner Kunst verbot dies" (KKADL 335). It is interesting to note, in the translation by Willa and Edwin Muir quoted here, the slippage from the original German's "Kunst" (art) to "profession". This slippage speaks to the point I am arguing, namely that the hunger artist is as much a salaried employee as he is an artist.

26 "Gehörte [allerdings] zu den vom Hungern überhaupt nicht zu trennenden Verdächtigungen" (KKADL 336).
27 "Der von seinem Hungern vollkommen befriedigte Zuschauer sein" (KKADL 337).
28 "Regelmäßigen kleinen Ruhepausen" (KKADL 341).
29 "Fanatisch ergeben" (KKADL 343).
30 "Dann also am vierzigsten Tage wurde die Tür des mit Blumen umkränzten Käfigs geöffnet, eine begeisterte Zuschauerschaft erfüllte das Amphitheater, eine Militärkapelle spielte, zwei Ärzte betraten den Käfig, um die nötigen Messungen am Hungerkünstler vorzunehmen, durch ein Megaphon wurden die Resultate dem Saale verkündet, und schließlich kamen zwei junge Damen, glücklich darüber, daß gerade sie ausgelost worden waren, und wollten den Hungerkünstler aus dem Käfig ein paar Stufen hinabführen, wo auf einem kleinen Tischchen eine sorgfältig ausgewählte Krankenmahlzeit serviert war. Und in diesem Augenblick wehrte sich der Hungerkünstler immer. Zwar legte er noch freiwillig seine Knochenarme in die hilfsbereit ausgestreckten Hände der zu ihm hinabgebeugten Damen, aber aufstehen wollte er nicht. Warum gerade jetzt nach vierzig Tagen aufhören?" (KKADL 338).
31 See, for instance, Neumann, " Hungerkünstler und Menschenfresser", esp. 356–8; Norris, "Sadism and Masochism", 184–5; Jan Mieszkowski, "Kafka Live!", 987; Sylvain Guarda, "Kafkas *Hungerkünstler*: Eine Messiade", esp. 346; or Astrid Lange-Kirchheim, "Das fotografierte Hungern", esp. 14–15. Neumann also points out that the history of public starving itself is linked to beliefs in religious miracles and attempts to restage the devil's temptation of Jesus in the desert (356). Following Deleuze, Norris's illuminating interpretation reads the Christian elements in the text "as providing a mystical justification for the masochist" (184), and Norris also reads them as Kafka's own highly ironic take on his diet and his own "nurturing, oral mother" (185). Mieszkowski reminds the reader that the imagery in question is not merely religious, but rather "an elaborate blend of biblical, maternal and sexual imagery" (987). Guarda reads the entire text as a dialogue with the passion of Christ. Lange-Kirchheim introduces a fascinating possible intertext for Kafka's "Hunger Artist", namely an 1896 series of articles and photographs from *Das interessante Blatt* on Giovanni Succi, the famous Italian hunger artist whom Mitchell had already identified in 1987 as a possible inspiration for Kafka's story (Breon Mitchell, "Franz Kafka and the Hunger Artists", 236–55). Lange-Kirchheim points out that the religious allusions were part of Succi's performance too, (and the way it is described in *Das interessante Blatt*). For a discussion of fasting and anorexia around the turn of the last century, and with reference to Kafka's text, see also Patrick Anderson, *So Much Wasted*, 57–84.
32 "So, als lade er den Himmel ein, sich sein Werk hier auf dem Stroh einmal anzusehn, diesen bedauernswerten Märtyrer" (KKADL 339).
33 Mieszkowski, "Kafka Live!", 987.
34 Weber, *General Economic History*, 269–70.
35 "Traurigkeit" (KKADL 341).
36 "Strafmittel" (KKADL 341).
37 "Er entschuldigte den Hungerkünstler vor versammeltem Publikum, gab zu, daß nur die durch das Hungern hervorgerufene, für satte Menschen nicht ohne weiteres begreifliche Reizbarkeit das Benehmen des Hungerkünstlers

verzeihlich machen könne; kam dann im Zusammenhang damit auch auf die ebenso zu erklärende Behauptung des Hungerkünstlers zu sprechen, er könnte noch viel länger hungern, als er hungere; lobte das hohe Streben, den guten Willen, die große Selbstverleugnung, die gewiß auch in dieser Behauptung enthalten seien; suchte dann aber die Behauptung einfach genug durch Vorzeigen von Photographien, die gleichzeitig verkauft wurden, zu widerlegen, denn auf den Bildern sah man den Hungerkünstler an einem vierzigsten Hungertag, im Bett, fast verlöscht vor Entkräftung. Diese dem Hungerkünstler zwar wohlbekannte, immer aber von neuem ihn entnervende Verdrehung der Wahrheit war ihm zu viel. Was die Folge der vorzeitigen Beendigung des Hungerns war, stellte man hier als die Ursache dar! Gegen diesen Unverstand, gegen diese Welt des Unverstandes zu kämpfen, war unmöglich" (KKADL 341–2).

38 In this context, see also Lange-Kirchheim, "Das fotografierte Hungern", esp. 27–9, who stresses that on the one hand, the photographs are part of a system of supervision and punishment directed at the hunger artist, but that on the other hand, the photographs, with their documentary function, help fulfill the hunger artist's wish that proof might be produced that he does not cheat during his fasts.

39 "Es mochte tiefere Gründe haben, aber wem lag daran, sie aufzufinden; jedenfalls sah sich eines Tages der verwöhnte Hungerkünstler von der vergnügungssüchtigen Menge verlassen, die lieber zu anderen Schaustellungen strömte" (KKADL 342).

40 "Um seine Empfindlichkeit zu schonen" (KKADL 343). For a reading of the circus engagement as the signing of a masochistic contract, see Norris, "Sadism and Masochism", 176.

41 "Wie er es früher einmal erträumt hatte" (KKADL 347).

42 Horkheimer and Adorno, *Dialectic of Enlightenment*, 114. "Die Spur des Besseren bewahrt Kulturindustrie in den Zügen, die sie dem Zirkus annähern, in der eigensinnig-sinnverlassenen Könnerschaft von Reitern, Akrobaten und Clowns [...]. Aber die Schlupfwinkel der seelenlosen Artistik, die gegen den gesellschaftlichen Mechanismus das Menschliche vertritt, werden unerbittlich von einer planenden Vernunft aufgestöbert, die alles nach Bedeutung und Wirkung sich auszuweisen zwingt. Sie läßt das Sinnlose drunten so radikal verschwinden wie oben den Sinn der Kunstwerke" (Horkheimer und Adorno, *Dialektik der Aufklärung*, 128).

43 "Ein immer kleiner werdendes Hindernis" (KKADL 346).
44 "Verfaulte[s] Stroh" (KKADL 348).
45 "Gut brauchbare[r] Käfig", "unbenützt" (KKADL 348).
46 "Kann nicht anders"; "weil ich nicht die Speise finden konnte, die mir schmeckt" (KKADL 348–9).
47 "'Nun macht aber Ordnung!'" (KKADL 349).
48 Jürgen Habermas, *The Structural Transformation of the Public Sphere*, 46. "Obschon die Sphäre des Familienkreises sich selbst als unabhängig, als von allen gesellschaftlichen Bezügen losgelöst, als Bereich der reinen Menschlichkeit wahrhaben möchte, steht sie mit der Sphäre der Arbeit und des Warenverkehrs in einem Verhältnis der Abhängigkeit—noch das Bewußtsein der Unabhängigkeit läßt sich aus der tatsächlichen Abhängigkeit jenes intimen Bereichs von dem privaten des Marktes begreifen" (Habermas, *Strukturwandel*, 110).

49 Habermas, *Structural Transformation*, 47–8. "[D]ie Bedürfnisse des Berufes [widersprachen] einer Idee von Bildung, die sich selbst einziger Zweck sein darf" (Habermas, *Strukturwandel*, 112).
50 Habermas, *Structural Transformation*, 43. "Publikumsbezogene Privatheit" (Habermas, *Strukturwandel*, 107).
51 Habermas, *Structural Transformation*, 45–6. "Die Linie zwischen Privatsphäre und Öffentlichkeit geht mitten durchs Haus. Die Privatleute treten aus der Intimität ihres Wohnzimmers in die Öffentlichkeit des Salons hinaus; aber eine ist streng auf die andere bezogen. Nur noch der Name des Salons erinnert an den Ursprung des geselligen Disputierens und des öffentlichen Räsonnements aus der Sphäre der adligen Gesellschaft. Von dieser hat sich der Salon als Ort des Verkehrs der bürgerlichen Familienväter und ihrer Frauen inzwischen gelöst. Die Privatleute, die sich hier zum Publikum formieren, gehen nicht "in der Gesellschaft" auf; sie treten jeweils erst aus einem privaten Leben sozusagen hervor, das im Binnenraum der patriarchalischen Kleinfamilie institutionelle Gestalt gewonnen hat" (Habermas, *Strukturwandel*, 109).
52 Habermas, *Structural Transformation*, 49. "Stets schon auf Publikum bezogen" (Habermas, *Strukturwandel*, 114). As an example, Habermas cites the culture of letter writing in eighteenth-century Europe: letters, a seemingly intimate expression of subjectivity, were usually written with a broader audience in mind, and were readily copied and shared.
53 Habermas, *Structural Transformation*, 161.
54 Habermas, *Structural Transformation*, 159. "[k]ulturkonsumierende[s] Publikum" (Habermas, *Strukturwandel*, 248). Habermas repeatedly emphasizes his belief, of course, that "bourgeois culture was not mere ideology" (Habermas, *Structural Transformation*, 160): "Die bürgerliche Kultur war nicht bloße Ideologie" (Habermas, *Strukturwandel*, 248). His conviction that modernity is ultimately an unfinished project inscribes itself into the structure of his argument: Habermas wants to avoid the very totalization of a "suspicion of ideology" ("Ideologieverdacht") he identifies in Horkheimer and Adorno's *Dialectic of Enlightenment*. See Jürgen Habermas, *The Philosophical Discourse of Modernity*, 106–30; here: 119. (Habermas, *Der philosophische Diskurs der Moderne*, 130–57; here: 144.)
55 Horkheimer and Adorno, *Dialectic of Enlightenment*, 43. "Die Herrschaft des Menschen über sich selbst, die sein Selbst begründet, ist virtuell allemal die Vernichtung des Subjekts, in dessen Dienst sie geschieht, denn die beherrschte, unterdrückte und durch Selbsterhaltung aufgelöste Substanz ist gar nichts anderes als das Lebendige, als dessen Funktion die Leistungen der Selbsterhaltung einzig sich bestimmen, eigentlich gerade das, was erhalten werden soll. Die Widervernunft des totalitären Kapitalismus, dessen Technik, Bedürfnisse zu befriedigen, in ihrer vergegenständlichten, von Herrschaft determinierten Gestalt die Befriedigung der Bedürfnisse unmöglich macht und zur Ausrottung der Menschen treibt—diese Widervernunft ist prototypisch im Heros ausgebildet, der dem Opfer sich entzieht, indem er sich opfert. Die Geschichte der Zivilisation ist die Geschichte der Introversion des Opfers. Mit anderen Worten: die Geschichte der Entsagung" (Horkheimer and Adorno, *Dialektik der Aufklärung*, 51).
56 On anorexia and subjectivity, see Maier, "Das anorexische Ich", 199–217. Maier states that "the fulfillment of anorexic subjectivity is identical with its

annihilation" ("Die Erfüllung anorexischer Subjektivität ist identisch mit ihrer Vernichtung", 209).
57 "Noch in seinen gebrochenen Augen war die feste, wenn auch nicht mehr stolze Überzeugung, daß er weiterhungre" (KKADL 349).
58 Gray, *Stations of the Divided Subject*, 272.
59 See Kafka, *Briefe*, 520–1.

II Kafka Effects

4. Hofmannsthal after 1918: The Present as Exile

Jens Rieckmann

In the years after 1918 and the collapse of the Habsburg Empire, Hofmannsthal suffered a profound, abiding sense of loss. Perhaps it was not wholly different in kind from the feeling of most people as they live on and the world changes around them. Values, customs, even the material life familiar in youth are receding into the distance or have long vanished, and we have trouble finding our way in the world around us and sympathizing with it. But usually the world one lives in changes "with no pace perceived", as Shakespeare put it, that is, gradually, almost imperceptibly, even though the distance from the remembered past may eventually seem enormous.

Hofmannsthal experienced this transition as an acute crisis, mainly for three reasons. For one thing, it did not seem to be a transition. For Hofmannsthal, as for so many of his generation, 1918 loomed in consciousness as a demarcation from the present, a date separating the lost world of yesterday, as Stefan Zweig put it; the fact that there was a definite date marked emphasized for consciousness how much of a change there had been. The loss had happened then. Secondly, with the fall of the Habsburg monarchy and the breakup of the empire, the political and social world of the Austrian elite collapsed. In 1926 Hofmannsthal wrote to Carl J. Burckhardt: "meine Heimat habe ich behalten, aber Vaterland hab ich keins mehr, als Europa."[1] A third cause of emotional crisis was more personal. The pre-war world with its political and social fabric was associated in Hofmannsthal's mind with his achievement as a writer. If after 1918 he felt himself an exile in his own land, so to some degree did many others. What was personal to him and incalculably distressing and bewildering was that he could not write as he had. He felt himself in exile from his own creativity. After reading Josef Redlich's *Kaiser Franz Joseph*, a work he considered "eine wahre Geschichte Österreichs im XIXten Jahrhundert", he explains why he cannot comment on the intellectual foundations of that era:

> Eben weil ich mit dem Zusammenbruch Österreichs das Erdreich verloren habe, in welches ich verwurzelt bin, [...] weil mein eigenes dichterisches Dasein in diesem Zusammensturz fragwürdig geworden ist (und fragwürdig werden mußte), [...] eben darum weil dies alles mir so furchtbar nahe, so unausdenklich bedeutsam ist—kann ich über diese Dinge nur schweigen.[2]

In a fine, recent novel by Walter Kappacher, *Der Fliegenpalast*, the protagonist, referred to simply as "H.",[3] is a fictional version of Hofmannsthal, and the setting and internal crises of H. were also experienced by his real-life counterpart. In this respect, the novel is comparable to Colm Tóibín's *The Master*, a fictional biography of the mature Henry James. Kappacher's novel dwells on approximately eight anxiety-ridden days, which Hofmannsthal spent in Bad Fusch in August 1924. But although the narrated time is short and the external events are few, the protagonist's reminiscences, which form the bulk of the text, reveal his entire life from his childhood through to his fiftieth year. Thus it is not preposterous to refer to the 165-page text as a fictional biography of Hofmannsthal.

To compare the fictional with the biographical representation of a person, and the respective possibilities and limitations of the two genres, constitutes, of course, a much discussed topic in narratology, and I do not intend to go into it here. But Kappacher explores some of the same themes in Hofmannsthal's emotional crisis that I do, and I shall cite him, among other sources, for supporting or contrasting views. If this seems controversial, the justification is simply that Kappacher knows his subject as well as any biographer could and that his interpretation is highly plausible. We should remember that, even though Hofmannsthal was averse to biographical writing (in a letter to Rilke he referred to it as the "läppischen Biographismus")[4] he also knew that each individual can be interpreted in multiple ways and that each of these interpretations can claim to be true.[5] Of course, no fictional biography can depict the whole truth, but precisely because fiction is not tethered to the information available in oral and written sources, it is freer to present a unified yet probing characterization of its subject.[6]

That the setting of Kappacher's text is Bad Fusch is appropriate for bringing into focus Hofmannsthal's perception of the changes the war has brought on post-war Austria and his emotional reaction to them. Hofmannsthal had spent part of the summer in Bad Fusch from his childhood until his marriage in 1901. It was a place he was thoroughly familiar with, emotionally attached to, and where he had written some of his most memorable poems, like the "Terzinen über Vergänglichkeit." In a 1900 letter he wrote to Hans Schlesinger from Bad Fusch:

> Seit 15 Sommern mit einer einzigen Unterbrechung gehen wir hierher. Zuerst habe ich die einfachen großen Formen gar nicht verstanden; jetzt aber scheint mir das ganze Tal, die unveränderten kleinen Fußwege, die einfachen Konturen der Berge überschwebt von tausendfachen, ganz innerlichen, wortlosen Erinnerungen, überall begegne ich mir selber und fühle, wie stark auch diese Landschaft an meinem Inneren gebildet hat.[7]

In Bad Fusch, and the nearby Strobl and Bad Aussee, he felt emotionally more at home than in Vienna.[8]

In the very few extant letters from the period narrated in *Der Fliegenpalast* there is no mention of Hofmannsthal's perception of post-war Bad Fusch, and here Kappacher makes full use of the advantages available to the writer of a fictional biography. The observations H. makes might well have been Hofmannsthal's, for they are not concerned primarily with the physical changes Bad Fusch has undergone, but rather with its social changes. These would have struck Hofmannsthal, who, after all, had been born into the upper middle classes and who, as his fame as a poet grew in Vienna, was also welcomed into the houses and salons of the upper classes.

H. is staying in a "besserer Gasthof", which, in keeping with the societal upheavals after 1918, boldly calls itself "Grandhotel" in an obvious attempt to lure the nouveau riches to its premises. The guests staying at the "Gasthof" differ markedly from those in pre-war days. In those days they were "Landgeistliche, Gymnasiallehrer, pensionierte Offiziere, unsäglich beruhigende, einlullende Provinzmenschen."[9] The present guests are hard to classify. H. notes disapprovingly that they do not dress formally for dinner and deplores their inconsiderateness: "Laut war es geworden in den Hotels, [...] kaum jemand dämpfte seine Stimme, lautes Lachen in der Nacht, Türenschlagen, Gekichere auf dem Gang."[10] During the day they do not take walks or hikes, as everyone had done before the war, but rather they sit on the terraces of the hotels and expect to be waited on (F 19). Generally speaking, they are more demanding than the members of the upper middle class had been during their vacations in "den Sommerfrischen der Monarchie"(F 7).[11] Occasionally, H.'s observations of decline take on a comical character. It seems to him, for example, that the waiters are not as skilled as they were in the Habsburg monarchy (F 36), and he laments that the quality of the pencils is not the same as before the war (F 18). His strong sense of alienation expresses itself in his hardly being able to bring himself to look at the guests' faces; they represent "eine völlig andere Gesellschaft als vor dem Krieg" (F 93).[12] When he is in his room looking out of the window, he is "selbstvergessen, in der Fusch von früher" (F 5),[13] but the moment he leaves his room and goes down to the lobby, he enters the alien world of the "Fliegenpalast", a more proper designation for the "Grandhotel", at least from H.'s point of view, flies being associated with something that is annoying, disturbing and unwelcome.

This alien world is a product of the "unselige Krieg" (F 7),[14] which ruined everything. Hofmannsthal initially shared the enthusiasm with which the outbreak of war had been welcomed by most of his fellow Young Viennese writers—the exception being Arthur Schnitzler—and most of his contemporaries, but by the time the war entered its third year, he characterized it as "die eigentliche Agonie des tausendjährigen heiligen römischen Reiches deutscher Nation."[15] Since the 1890s Hofmannsthal had been aware of the long sickness that preceded the war. In a 1898 conversation with Harry Graf Kessler, he painted the following pessimistic picture of the condition that the Austro-Hungarian Empire found itself in:

> An der Spitze das Herrscherhaus, das mit keiner Fiber mehr mit irgend einem Volk oder irgend einer Rasse ausser der eigenen Ahnenreihe zusammenhängt [...]. Darunter eine Aristokratie, die, ähnlich, wie das Herrscherhaus von der Menschheit abgesprengt ist, und die sich oben erhält durch rücksichtsloses Schüren des Nationalitätenhasses [...] und darunter grosse verwirtschaftete, feindliche Massen, auf denen Jene wie auf den Wellen eines Meeres schaukeln; Tschechen und Juden, Magyaren und Südslaven, Deutsche und Polen; unfähig sich über ihre gemeinsamen Interessen zu verständigen.[16]

The awareness of the systemic political and social problems within the Habsburg Empire, exacerbated by the nationalist tensions, together with the fear of a potential uprising of the masses, which haunted Hofmannsthal since the first May Day demonstration in Vienna in 1890, culminated in harrowing visions of the destroyed city.[17] The most haunting and perturbing of these was noted down in 1894:

> Wie merkwürdig auch das wieder ist, daß wir [Künstler] vielleicht in Wien die letzten denkenden, die letzten ganzen, beseelten Menschen überhaupt sind, daß dann vielleicht eine große Barbarei kommt, eine slavisch-jüdische, sinnliche Welt. Das

zerstörte Wien zu denken: alle Mauern verfallen, der innere Leib der Stadt bloßgelegt, die Wunden mit unendlichem Schlingkraut übersponnen, überall lichtgrüne Baumwipfel, Stille, plätscherndes Wasser, alles Leben tot.[18]

Apart from its poetic expressive language, this passage is remarkable in two respects: the equation of barbarism with a Slavic-Jewish, sensuous world and the privileging of the artist. In the second half of the nineteenth century a significant number of Jews and Slavs settled in the Viennese *Vorstädte* (outlying districts); they were perceived as the ethnic and racial Other and as a threat to the predominantly German population of the inner city.[19] The equation of Slavs and Jews with sensuality is part of the anti-migrant and anti-Semitic discourse of the turn of the twentieth century, and although Hofmannsthal was partly Jewish himself, he (and many of his contemporaries) shared the prevailing prejudices of his time.[20] The artist as the last thinking and animated human being in a declining world is a recurring *topos* in Hofmannsthal's thought. In 1894, for example, talking about himself and Leopold von Andrian, he wrote: "Wir glauben die Seele dieses Wien zu spüren, die vielleicht in uns zum letzten Mal aufbebt; wir waren triumphierend traurig."[21]

With the collapse of the Habsburg Empire these visionary fears had, at least in Hofmannsthal's mind, partially become reality. The end of the war indelibly marked a break in the continuum of time. As H. says in Kappacher's text: "Man weiß, das Leben wird von nun an in zwei Abschnitte geteilt sein: die Zeit davor und die Zeit danach" (F 84).[22] The structure of Kappacher's text reflects this dichotomy. The present ("die Zeit danach") is crowded out by H.'s memories of and reflections on the past ("die Zeit davor"); correspondingly, large parts of the text consist of analepses. Structurally, the novel mirrors the Nikolaus Lenau poem H. quotes:

Sahst du ein Glück vorübergehn
Das nie sich wieder findet
Ist's gut in einen Strom zu sehn
Wo Alles wogt und schwindet. (F 31)[23]

Here the "Glück" corresponds to the Bad Fusch of H.'s childhood and the "Strom" to H.'s stream of consciousness. But the closure that the speaker of the poem promises in the last stanza, "Hinträumend wird Vergessenheit/ Des Herzens Wunde schließen", is not obtainable for H. or for his historical counterpart.[24] The last stanza is not quoted in Kappacher's text.

For Hofmannsthal, the war and its aftermath also marked the end of his financial independence, something he had striven for ever since he was a young man and had finally achieved by 1913. Looking back, he wrote to Willy Haas: "1922 hatte ich weder mehr das geringste Vermögen—noch, für den Moment, ein Arbeitseinkommen, dazu drei halbgroße Kinder."[25] A further shock for Hofmannsthal was his realization that Austria and Germany were responsible for the outbreak of the war, caused by "grausige Zerfahrenheit, Dummheit, Nichtdurchdenken" in Vienna and Berlin.[26] He formed this opinion after having read in 1923 the memoirs of Tirpitz, Hötzendorf, and Maurice Paléologue, the French ambassador to Russia in 1914.

It was in these circumstances that Hofmannsthal read Spengler's *Der Untergang des Abendlandes* (*The Decline of the West*). He read the first volume in 1919 with mixed feelings. To Carl J. Burckhardt he wrote that the book had occupied and tired him, that he had been drawn to it and then again he had lost interest in it.[27] Yet of these mixed feelings, fascination was obviously the predominant one, for in 1922 he ordered Spengler's second volume, which he read and excerpted in the following year. His fictional counterpart recalls a conversation in which he told Burckhardt that he had not shared Spengler's theses when he had first read the *Untergang des Abendlandes* in the midst of the war,[28] but now it seemed to him that Spengler could have been right to argue that "unsere Epoche sei eine Spätzeit, eine seelenlose, kunstlose Zeit, in der das Geld herrsche und alles vom Geld entschieden werde" (F 117).[29]

As I mentioned above, for Hofmannsthal the loss of *Vaterland* was exacerbated by his increasing crises of creativity. In a conversation with the fictional Dr Krakauer, H. sums up this loss of national identity and creativity: "Auf irgendeine Weise bin auch ich verschüttet worden, in den letzten Kriegsjahren. Innerlich [...] sind Dinge in mir verschüttet, und ich finde keinen Zugang mehr" (F 94).[30] Hofmannsthal's and his fictional counterpart's choice of Bad Fusch as the place to work on the comedy *Timon der Redner* was determined, as it turns out, by the deceptive hope that in this magical place" ("magische[n] Ort" [F 15]) he would find the inspiration to write continuously for several days, as he had often done in his younger years. Attempts to do so failed in Lenzerheide, where he visited Burckhardt prior to his stay in Bad Fusch. The latter tried to help him by writing down a disposition based on his and Hofmannsthal's conversations about the comedy, but all Hofmannsthal accomplished in more than two weeks was to jot down some notes for *Timon der Redner*. Thus travelling to Bad Fusch represents a kind of desperate flight. But the magic place fails him too. In Bad Fusch he does not write a single line, all he takes away with him are a few promising notes and a few revised lines.

This search for a place where he could write is paradigmatic. Hofmannsthal knew that he had only three to four "good months per year" ("gute Monate im Jahr"), usually in the summer and early fall, in which he could be productive.³¹ The success or failure of these "gute Monate" was totally dependent on his surroundings and on the weather. In a letter to Georg von Franckenstein he went so far as to say "an der Art, wie ich in der Früh' den Duft des jungen Grüns und der Kastanienblüten mehr oder weniger spüre, kann ich voraus wissen, ob ich an dem Tag werde gut oder schlecht arbeiten können."³² Working on *Das kleine Welttheater*, he wrote in a similar vein to Arthur Schnitzler that the dark and rainy weather would slow down his progress on this one act play.³³ In *Der Fliegenpalast* H. refers to this state of affairs as the "Abhängigkeit von der Beschaffenheit der Luft, die furchtbare Wetterfühligkeit" (F 52).³⁴

Looking back on the 1890s, H. recalls the "traumwandlerische Sicherheit der frühen Jahre, als fast alles gelang" (F 39).³⁵ According to Josef Redlich's diary, Hofmannsthal himself called such productive days and weeks "Trancezustände",³⁶ and many of his letters from those years document such bouts of creativity. But even in these early years, the enormously productive phases regularly gave way to sterile periods. In a letter to Edgar Karg von Bebenburg he wrote: "ich hab überhaupt von 2 zu 2 Monaten ungefähr so einen Wechsel von Flut und Ebbe. Die Flut ist sehr hübsch; da fallen mir fortwährend hübsche oder gescheite Sachen ein; [...]. Die Ebbe dafür ist so unangenehm, öd und leer, taub und tot."³⁷ But in those years he was not greatly troubled by these changes of the creative tides: "Mich ängstigt diese Ebbe nicht", he wrote to Marie von Gomperz as early as 1892, "ich kenne es jetzt schon und man muss eben abwarten, dann kommt schon wieder die Renaissance."³⁸

Yet after 1899, there is an increasing number of planned and begun works that remain fragments or are never realized: "Vieles habe ich versucht, das mißlungen ist, unendlich vieles angefangen und wieder aufgegeben", he wrote to Andrian a few months before his death.³⁹ And in Kappacher's text, H., fearing that he would not be able to complete *Timon der Redner*, ruefully notes that the number of his completed works was surpassed by the number of folders containing works he had given up (F 50). The comparably fewer texts in his oeuvre of the 1890s that were not completed were so for reasons that the following 1926 letter to Georg Terramare illuminates. Commenting on *Der Kaiser und die Hexe*, Hofmannsthal wrote that he thought of this one act play not as a completed work, but rather as a plan or a draft: "Ich glaube zu verstehen, woher dies kommt. Daher, daß ich als recht junger Mensch in dieser Arbeit einen sehr großen, wahrhaft tiefen Stoff ergriffen habe, aber in halb traumwandelnder Weise, ohne ihm ganz gewachsen zu sein."⁴⁰ The same may be true of such fragments of the 1890s as the Renaissance tragedy *Ascanio und Gioconda*.

That the number of fragments, of unfinished or planned but not realized works, increased after 1899 is due primarily to the complexity and scope of Hofmannsthal's later works which remained unfinished, or plans which were hardly or not at all carried out.[41] Very early in his career he became aware of a tendency that developed more and more in the later, crisis-ridden years. Working on "Der Geiger vom Traunsee" in 1889, he noted in his diary "Versuch der Abfassung eines märchenartigen Feuilletons scheitert [...] an meiner leidigen Angewohnheit des Ausmalens und Erschöpfenwollens."[42] How debilitating this tendency could become is vividly depicted in Kappacher's text, particularly in those passages where H.'s thoughts turn to the novel *Andreas*, on which Hofmannsthal worked off and on for two decades. Whenever H. opened the manuscript,

> erschlug ihn das umfangreiche Konvolut von Notizen und Varianten, von Exzerpten, Literaturhinweisen; diese Notizen erzeugten ja unentwegt weitere Notizen, der Papierhaufen erschien ihm immer mehr als ein endloses Gebirge, wie das Höllengebirge oder das Tote Gebirge bei Aussee, das er seit seiner Jugend hatte besteigen wollen, jedoch nie bestiegen hatte. (F 138–9)[43]

This way of working stands in marked contrast to the creative process that Hofmannsthal had described to Schnitzler in 1892:

> Was ich aus späteren Acten [*Ascanio und Gioconda*] vorausarbeiten kann sind nicht geschlossene Scenen, sondern reine Farbenskizzen: Worte und Dialogstellen, die oft dann gar nicht wirklich aufgenommen werden, mir aber als Parfümflaschen, als Stimmungs-Accumulatoren und Condensatoren dienen, damit die Suggestion im Laufe der Detailarbeit nicht verloren geht.[44]

At the center of the process depicted in the latter quotation is inspiration. Notes and bits of dialogue serve the writer as stimulants to maintain the initial momentum that sets the creative process in motion. At the center of the process related in Kappacher's text is the search for inspiration, which the writer hopes to find in the accumulated materials. Ultimately, however, the oppressive mass leads to paralysis, which, in its turn, induces prolonged depressive periods that grow in length and frequency after 1899, the year which Hofmannsthal marked as the end of the most productive phase in his literary career: "Produktives bis zum *Abenteurer* [und die Sängerin]."[45] Kessler, who knew Hofmannsthal well and collaborated with him on *Der Rosenkavalier*, speculated, for good reasons, that the latter's mood swings, nervousness and excitability originated in "einem intimen Drama, einem Ringen nach Produktivität, einer Angst vor irgendwelcher plötzlich hereinbrechender endgültigen Impotenz."[46]

Although Hofmannsthal laid claim to the "formidable Einheit" of his works,[47] he himself was fully aware of the distinct phases of his production. In a letter to Max Pirker he spoke of an "erste vorwiegend lyrisch-sujektive Epoche: das Jugendoeuvre bis zirka 1899."[48] And in *Ad me ipsum*, in a section entitled "Zur Darstellung meines Lebens", he distinguished between the "Jünglingszeit", ending in 1899, and the present, approximately the years from 1912 to 1917, which he summed up as "Krise des Mannealters."[49] After the war the crisis was exacerbated by the loss of *Vaterland* and was to last intermittently for the remainder of his life. This crisis constitutes, as we have seen, the central theme of *Der Fliegenpalast*.

H. recalls that at some point in his married life he had thought: "Ich bin ins Leben eingetreten, [...] und meine lyrische Begabung ist bei der anderen Tür hinaus" (F 137). As far as I know, Hofmannsthal never made such a direct causal connection between getting married and the loss, for the most part, of his ability to write poetry. Yet Kappacher's assumption of such a connection does not lack a foundation in Hofmannsthal's biography. Hofmannsthal himself stated that the years of his engagement and subsequent marriage (1900/01) were marked by an "Erstarrung meiner produktiven Kräfte",[50] but he considered this to be a symptom of the troubled transition from his productive youth to what he obviously hoped would be an equally productive maturity. At the same time he remained convinced that there was a dichotomy between his life as a writer and his bourgeois existence. In 1912 he wrote to Ottonie Gräfin Degenfeld: "Manchmal scheint es so paradox, daß man zugleich Dichter sein soll und ein Mensch, ein Zeitgenosse, verheiratet, Vater, der Herr von Nr. 5 Badgasse [in Rodaun], durchaus unbegreiflich erscheint es."[51]

His marriage with Gertrud (Gerty) Schlesinger was essentially a *Vernunftehe*, partly born of the conviction that marriage is a form of life and of the belief that it liberates from the "Unmenschliche, das im Künstler-sein steckt."[52] He also entered into it partly because of a fear of loneliness, and it may have served partly as an attempt to come to terms with his homoerotic inclinations.[53] Hofmannsthal did not share the romantic concept of love, did not believe in the idea that there were only two individuals in the world meant exclusively for each other; rather he argued "wir sind hauptsächlich Männer und Frauen, sind Kinder von Eltern und werden Eltern von Kindern."[54] His marriage, like most, had its advantages and disadvantages. Gerty understood or tolerated his need to be alone in order to work, which meant that, particularly in the summer months, he was often away from home for extended periods. In a 1921 letter to Irene Hellmann he commented approvingly on "Gertys wohltuende Gabe, mit sich und den Kindern allein fertig zu werden und mich nicht zu sehr zu vermissen."⁵⁵ This may have been wishful thinking on his part; in one of her letters to Hofmannsthal, written during one of his absences, his wife asked rather wistfully if the "'Zusammenleben' [ihm] wieder Freude machen wird."⁵⁶ His understanding of the role of a married woman was the conventional one of his time. Gerty, he wrote rather complacently, "teilt sich zwischen dem Kochherd, der Nähmaschine und der Schreibmaschine [...] und so sind auch ihr die Tage ausgefüllt und lieb."⁵⁷ Apart from typing Hofmannsthal's manuscripts, she was largely excluded from his life as a writer. In a letter to Burckhardt he confessed that it never occurred to him to consider if the conversations he had with his friends interested her.⁵⁸

The marriage for Hofmannsthal, then, was a convenient one, but it also entailed a growing financial responsibility. Half jokingly, he wrote to Degenfeld that until he got married he had not even known that there was money in the world,⁵⁹ but he now had to think of his career in terms of that of a professional writer. This may partly explain why he increasingly turned to the theater after the turn of the twentieth century. At least this is how Kappacher's H. sees things. In a conversation with Dr Krakauer he says that after the publication of the fictional Lord Chandos letter, he would have preferred to continue in this genre, but "plötzlich habe er eine Familie gehabt, Kinder, er habe Geld verdienen müssen. Also habe er sich dem Theater zugewandt" (F 120–1).⁶⁰

There is, indeed, a correlation between Hofmannsthal's turn to the theater and his marriage, but it is not quite as clear-cut as his fictional counterpart has it. Hofmannsthal, after all, started writing for the theater as early as 1892. The theater, and in particular the *Burgtheater*, already fascinated Hofmannsthal during his school years. In his notes for an account of his life he emphasized the "natürliche Verbindung mit dem Theater" as essentially characteristic of the Austrian.⁶¹ Money was certainly another motivating factor. He felt morally obliged to gain financial independence from his father, and the theater seemed to be the best venue to gain such independence. In 1899 he pointed out to Andrian that the modest sums he earned in the theater "schon recht ins Gewicht fallen, sowohl tatsächlich als insbesondere moralisch, als eine Garantie der Zukunft gegenüber."⁶² The problem he encountered in the 1890s in his attempts to get his plays staged was that they were generally considered to lack theatricality. Schnitzler, for example, commented that although *Der Abenteurer und die Sängerin* had some "gute theatr.[alische] Momente", it was not "ein rechtes Stück."⁶³ When Hofmannsthal attended the rehearsals of this play, which was produced together with *Die Hochzeit der Sobeide* by the *Deutsches Theater* in Berlin, he became conscious of the "abwechselnden Zusammenstimmen und abwechselnden sehr fühlbaren Auseinandertreten dieser Gedichte und des Theaters."[64] Emphasized is the incompatibility of these plays and the theater, and by referring to the dramas as poems, Hofmannsthal puts his finger on the cause of the dissonance. From a dramaturgic point of view, the plays he wrote in the 1890s were more poetic than dramatic. He was well aware of this, but as he had written to Gustav Schwarzkopf in 1892, while he was working on *Ascanio und Gioconda*, he needed "Vers und Kostüm [...] das ist entweder einfach ein jugendliches Bedürfnis oder hat innere Gründe."[65]

Despite the negative reception *Die Hochzeit der Sobeide* had found in Berlin, Hofmannsthal was not discouraged. He hoped, as he said to Kessler, that he would still earn "viel Geld mit dem Theater."[66] He achieved his dramatic breakthrough with *Das gerettete Venedig* (1904) and indeed went on to make a small fortune, particularly through his collaboration with Richard Strauss. As H. leaves Bad Fusch, neither *Timon der Redner* nor *Der Turm* are completed. Hofmannsthal eventually ended *Der Turm*, but, as Michael Hamburger has pointed out, "auf zwei so verschiedene, sich widersprechende Weisen, daß sie für den Autor gewissermaßen unfertig und offen blieb."[67]

Bibliography

Aurnhammer, Achim. "Hofmannsthals Andreas: Das Fragment als Erzählform zwischen Tradition und Moderne". *Hofmannsthal Jahrbuch zur europäischen Moderne* 3 (1995): 275–96.

Hamburger, Michael. "Das Fragment: Ein Kunstwerk?". *Hofmannsthal Jahrbuch zur europäischen Moderne* 3 (1995): 305–18.

Hirsch, Rudolf. *Beiträge zum Verständnis Hugo von Hofmannsthals*. Frankfurt am Main: Fischer, 1993.

Hofmannsthal, Hugo von. *Briefe 1890–1901*. Berlin: Fischer, 1935.

—*Briefe 1900–1909*. Vienna: Fischer, 1937.

—"Briefe an Irene und Paul Hellmann". *Jahrbuch der Deutschen Schillergesellschaft*, edited by Werner Volke, 11 (1967): 170–224.

—*Briefwechsel mit Marie von Gomperz 1892–1916*. Edited by Ulrike Tanzer. Freiburg: Rombach, 2001.

—*Briefwechsel mit Ottonie Gräfin Degenfeld und Julie Freifrau von Wendelstadt*. Edited by Marie-Therese Miller-Degenfeld and Eugene Weber. Frankfurt am Main: Fischer, 1974.

—*Gesammelte Werke. Reden und Aufsätze 3. 1925–1929. Buch der Freunde. Aufzeichnungen 1889–1929*. Edited by Bernd Schoeller and Ingeborg Beyer-Ahlert, with the assistance of Rudolf Hirsch. Frankfurt am Main: Fischer, 1980.

—*Sämtliche Werke 3. Dramen 1*. Edited by Götz Eberhard Hübner. Frankfurt am Main: Fischer, 1982.

—*Sämtliche Werke 6. Dramen 4*. Edited by Michael Müller. Frankfurt am Main: Fischer, 1984.

—*Sämtliche Werke 29. Erzählungen 2*. Edited by Ellen Ritter. Frankfurt am Main: Fischer, 1978.

—and Carl J. Burckhardt. *Briefwechsel*. Edited by Carl Burckhardt, and Claudia Mertz-Rychner. Frankfurt am Main: Fischer, 1991.

—and Willy Haas. *Ein Briefwechsel*. Edited by Rolf Italiaander. Berlin: Propyläen, 1968.
—and Josef Redlich. *Briefwechsel*. Edited by Helga Fußgänger. Frankfurt am Main: Fischer 1971.
—and Rainer Maria Rilke. *Briefwechsel: 1899–1925*. Edited by Rudolf Hirsch and Ingeborg Schnack. Frankfurt am Main: Suhrkamp, 1978.
—and Arthur Schnitzler. *Briefwechsel*. Edited by Therese Nickl and Heinrich Schnitzler. Frankfurt am Main: Fischer, 1983.
—and Leopold von Andrian. *Briefwechsel*. Edited by Walter H. Perl. Frankfurt am Main: Fischer, 1968.
—and Karg von Bebenburg. *Briefwechsel*. Edited by Mary E. Gilbert. Frankfurt am Main: Fischer, 1966.
—and Eberhard von Bodenhausen. *Briefe der Freundschaft*. Edited by Dora von Bodenhausen. Düsseldorf: E. Diederichs, 1953.
Kappacher, Walter. *Der Fliegenpalast*. St Pölten-Salzburg: Residenz Verlag, 2009.
Kessler, Harry Graf. *Das Tagebuch 1880–1937*. Vol. 3 (*1897–1905*). Edited by Carina Schäfer, Gabriele Biedermann and Roland S. Kamzelak. Stuttgart: J. G. Cotta'sche Buchhandlung Nachfolger GmbH, 2004.
—*Das Tagebuch 1880–1937*. Vol. 4 (*1906–1914*). Edited by Jörg Schuster, Roland S. Kamzelak and Ulrich Ott. Stuttgart: J. G. Cotta'sche Buchhandlung Nachfolger GmbH, 2005.
Lenau, Nikolaus. *Werke und Briefe*. Vol. 2. Edited by Helmut Brandt et al. Vienna: Klett-Cotta, 1995.
Lüders, Detlev, ed. *Hugo von Hofmannsthal: "Gedichte und kleine Dramen"; Zeugnisse seiner Jugendzeit und seines frühen Werkes. Ausstellung*. Frankfurt am Main: Freies Deutsches Hochstift-Frankfurter Goethe Museum, 1979.
Meyer, Imke. *Männlichkeit und Melodram: Arthur Schnitzlers erzählende Schriften*. Würzburg: Königshausen & Neumann, 2010.
Rieckmann, Jens. "Zwischen Bewußtsein und Verdrängung: Hofmannsthals jüdisches Erbe". *DVjs* 67 (1993): 466–83.
—"Schools of Inauthenticity: The Role of the *Akademisches Gymnasium* and the *Burgtheater* in Hofmannsthal's Formative Years". In *Turn-of-the Century Vienna: Essays in Honor of Donald G. Daviau*, edited by Jeffrey B. Berlin, Jorun B. Johns and Richard H. Lawson, 67–77. Vienna: Edition Atelier, 1993.
—*Hugo von Hofmannstal und Stefan George: Signifikanz einer 'Episode' aus der Jahrhundertwende*. Tübingen and Basel: Francke, 1997.
Schmid, Martin E., in colaboration with Regula Hauser and Severin Perrig, eds. *Hugo von Hofmannsthal: Brief-Chronik. Regest-Ausgabe*. 3 vols. Heidelberg: Winter, 2003.
Schnitzler, Arthur. *Tagebuch 1893–1902*. Edited by Werner Welzig. Vienna: Verlag der Österreichischen Akademie der Wissenschaften, 1989.
Weinzierl, Ulrich. *Hofmannsthal: Skizzen zu seinem Bild*. Vienna: Zsolnay, 2005.

Notes

1 Hofmannsthal and Burckhardt, *Briefwechsel*, 224–5. The following translation and all subsequent translations are my own: "I have kept my *Heimat*, but except for Europe, I no longer have a fatherland."
2 Hofmannsthal and Redlich, *Briefwechsel*, 116–17. "Because with the collapse of Austria I had lost the earth in which I was rooted, because my own being as a writer had become questionable (and had to become questionable), because

all of this is so terribly near to me, so inconceivably meaningful to me—I can only be silent about these things."
3   "H." is addressed as "Herr von Hofmannsthal" only by other fictional characters in the relatively few mimetic parts of the text. Kappacher's choice of the initial "H." is intended to underline the fictionality of his protagonist.
4   Hofmannsthal and Rilke, *Briefwechsel*, 149.
5   Hofmannsthal, *Reden und Aufsätze*, 3:45.
6   Written sources for the period narrated in Kappacher's text are particularly scarce: only four of Hofmannsthal's letters and two notes for "Timon der Redner" are extant, but, of course, Kappacher draws on other biographical material for H.'s reminiscences and reflections.
7   Hofmannsthal, *Briefe 1890–1901*, 311. "For fifteen summers with only one exception we have come here. At first I did not understand the simple, grand forms at all; but now the entire valley, the small trails that have not changed at all, the simple outlines of the mountains, connected to thousands of wholly inner, wordless memories; everywhere I meet myself and feel how strongly this landscape too has formed my character."
8   See the letter to Leopold von Andrian, dated July 22, 1898. Hofmannsthal and Andrian, *Briefwechsel*, 108.
9   Letter to Josephine von Wertheimstein, dated July 6, 1893. Hofmannsthal, *Briefe 1890–1901*, 80. "Country parsons, high school teachers, retired officers, immensely soothing, sleep inducing provincial people."
10 Kappacher, *Fliegenpalast*, 36. Subsequent references to Kappacher's *Fliegenpalast* are cited in the text as F followed by the page numbers. "The hotels were noisy now, [...] hardly anyone kept his voice down, loud laughter in the night, doors slamming, tittering in the hallway."
11 "The resorts of the monarchy."
12 "A society totally different from the one before the war."
13 "Unconscious of himself, in the past."
14 "Unfortunate war."
15 Letter to Eberhard von Bodenhausen, dated July 13, 1916. Hofmannsthal and Bodenhausen, *Briefe der Freundschaft*, 235–6. "The actual throes of death of the thousand-year-old holy Roman empire of the German nation."
16 Kessler, *Tagebuch*, 3:144. Diary entry of May 14, 1898. "At the top the House of Habsburg that is not connected in any way with any people or any race except with its own ancestors [...]. Below the aristocracy that, like the House of Habsburg, is separated from mankind, and that retains its position by recklessly inciting nationalist hatred [...] and below them impoverished, hostile masses, on which these bob as upon waves; Czechs and Jews, Magyars and Southern Slavs, Germans and Poles; incapable of coming to an understanding of their common interests."
17 Hofmannsthal and Gomperz, *Briefwechsel*, 53. Discussing Hauptmann's *Die Weber* in a letter to Marie von Gomperz (dated 1 May 1892), he wrote: "Ich habe zu viel Taine gelesen, um für die großen Massen ein anderes Gefühl zu haben als das der Furcht; es ist das einzige, wovor sich auch ein gentleman fürchten darf, denn es ist etwas unpersönliches, blindes und allen wertvollen, menschlichen Dingen gefährliches in ihnen" ("I have read too much Taine than to have any other feeling for the masses than fear; it is the only thing of which even a gentleman may be afraid, because there is something impersonal, dim in them that endangers all valuable, human things").

18 Hofmannsthal, *Gesammelte Werke*, 3: 383. "How strange it is that we [artists] are perhaps the last thinking, the last whole, animated men in *Vienna*, that after us a great barbarism will perhaps come, a Slavic-Jewish sensuous world. To imagine the destroyed Vienna: all walls in ruins, the inner body of the city laid bare, the wounds covered with tangles of creepers, everywhere light green treetops, silence, splashing water, all life dead."

19 For a recent discussion of the changing relationship between the middle class and the Jewish and Slavic immigrants see Meyer, *Männlichkeit und Melodram*, 14–30. The association of Slavs and Jews with sensuality is evident in the portrayal of many literary figures at the turn of the twentieth century, e.g., Vuic in Hofmannsthal's "Reitergeschichte" or Tonka in Musil's novella of the same name to name just a few.

20 For a detailed discussion of Hofmannsthal's ambivalent attitude towards his Jewish heritage, see Rieckmann, "Zwischen Bewußtsein und Verdrängung", 466–83, and Weinzierl, *Hofmannsthal*, 17–48.

21 Hofmannsthal, *Gesammelte Werke*, 3: 382. "We believe to be feeling the soul of this Vienna that, perhaps for the last time, wells up in us; we were triumphantly sad."

22 "One knows that from now on life will consist of two parts: the time beforehand and the time afterwards."

23 Lenau, *Werke und Briefe*, 2: 422. "If you saw happiness passing by / that will never be found again / Then it's good to look into a river, / where everything fluctuates and disappears."

24 "Dreaming on forgetting / will heal the heart's wound."

25 Hofmannsthal and Haas, *Briefwechsel*, 81. "In 1922 I had neither the smallest fortune—nor, for the time being, an income from my work, moreover I had three adolescent children."

26 Schmid, *Hugo von Hofmannsthal*, 2462. Letter of 8 December 1923. "An awful carelessness, stupidity, no thinking things over carefully."

27 See Schmid, *Hugo von Hofmannsthal*, 2063.

28 Here H.'s memory fails him. The first volume of Spengler's *Der Untergang des Abendlandes* was published in 1918.

29 "Our era is at an advanced stage, a soulless time, lacking in art, in which money rules and everything is decided by money."

30 "In some manner or form I too was lost in the last years of the war. Internally [...] things were lost in me, and I cannot access them anymore."

31 Hofmannsthal, *Briefe 1890–1901*, 111.

32 Schmid, *Hugo von Hofmannsthal*, 628. Undated letter, probably written in July 1900. "By the way, how I sense the fragrance of the young green and of the chestnut blossoms early in the morning, I can know in advance whether on that day I shall work well or badly."

33 Hofmannsthal and Schnitzler, *Briefwechsel*, 92.

34 "Dependence on the state of the air, the terrible sensitivity to the weather."

35 "The sleepwalking security of the early years when almost everything succeeded."

36 Hofmannsthal, *Sämtliche Werke*, 3: 323.

37 Hofmannsthal and Bebenburg, *Briefwechsel*, 45–6. "Indeed I experience every two months or so a changing of the tides. The high tide is very pretty; during it pretty or intelligent things occur to me all the time; [...]. The low tide on the other hand is so unpleasant, bleak and empty, numb and dead."

38 Hofmannsthal, *Briefwechsel mit Marie von Gomperz*, 41. Letter of 18 April 1892. "The low tide does not alarm me, I know it now already, and one just has to wait, then the renaissance will surely emerge." The editor of the letters has "aber" instead of "eben". My own reading of the letter and the context favor "eben".
39 Hofmannsthal and Andrian, *Briefwechsel*, 433. "I have attempted many things that failed, immensely many things I have begun and given up again."
40 Hofmannsthal, *Sämtliche Werke*, 3: 707–8. "I think I understand why this is so. It is because as quite a young man I had got hold of a very great and truly profound subject matter, but in a partly sleepwalking manner, without being quite equal to it."
41 See Hamburger, "Das Fragment", passim. For further discussions of the fragmentary character of Hofmannsthal's works see also Mayer and Aurnhammer.
42 Hofmannsthal, *Sämtliche Werke*, 29: 264. "The attempt to compose a fairytale-like feuilleton foundered upon my tiresome habit of wanting to imagine every detail thoroughly."
43 "The bundle of notes and variants, of excerpts and bibliographical reminders knocked him down; these notes brought forth more and more notes, the bundle of papers seemed to him more and more to be infinite mountains like the *Höllengebirge* or the *Totes Gebirge* near *Aussee*, which he had wanted to climb since his youth, but which he had never climbed."
44 Hofmannsthal and Schnitzler, *Briefwechsel*, 26. "What I can work out in advance of the following acts [of *Ascanio und Gioconda*] are not complete scenes, but rather colored sketches: words and parts of dialogue, which do not become part of the finished play, but serve me as perfume bottles, as atmospheric batteries and condensers, so that the suggestion does not vanish in the course of detailed work."
45 Hofmannsthal, *Gesammelte Werke*, 3: 616. "Productive up to *Der Abenteurer und die Sängerin*."
46 Kessler, *Tagebuch 1880–1937*, 4: 467. Diary entry of 10 May 1908. "In a very personal drama, in a wrestling for productivity, in a fear of some suddenly erupting definitive impotence."
47 Hofmannsthal, *Gesammelte Werke*, 3: 620.
48 Hofmannsthal, *Sämtliche Werke*, 6: 271. "First period predominantly lyrical-subjective: the early works up to roughly 1899."
49 Hofmannsthal, *Gesammelte Werke*, 3: 616. "On the representation of my life", "youthful years", "crisis in the years of manhood."
50 Letter of 14 February 1902 to R. A. Schröder. Hofmannsthal, *Briefe 1900–1909*, 67.
51 Hofmannsthal, *Briefwechsel mit Ottonie Gräfin Degenfeld*, 230. "Sometimes it seems to be so paradoxical that one should be both a poet and a human being, a man of the time, married, a father, the master of No. 5 Badgasse, it seems absolutely incomprehensible."
52 Hofmannsthal, *Gesammelte Werke*, 3: 426.
53 For a detailed discussion of Hofmannsthal's reflections on homoerotic friendship between men and heterosexual marriage, see Rieckmann, *Hugo von Hofmannsthal*, 158–79.
54 Hofmannsthal, *Briefe 1900–1909*, 76. Letter to Dora Michaelis, dated 14 June 1902. "Above all we are men and women, are children of parents and will be parents of children."

55 Hofmannsthal, *Briefe an Irene und Paul Hellmann*, 194. "Gerty's comforting gift to cope by herself with the children and not to miss me too much."
56 Quoted in Hirsch, *Beiträge*, 242.
57 Letter to Irene Hellmann of 4 November 1923. Quoted in Hofmannsthal, *Gedichte und kleine Dramen*, 8. "Gerty shares her time among the stove, the sewing machine and the typewriter [...] and in this way her days are also fulfilled and lovely."
58 Hofmannsthal and Burckhardt, *Briefwechsel*, 231.
59 Hofmannsthal, *Briefwechsel mit Ottonie Gräfin Degenfeld*, 398.
60 "Suddenly he had had a family, children, he had had to earn money. And so he turned to the theater."
61 Hofmannsthal, *Gesammelte Werke*, 3: 626. For a more detailed discussion of the role the theater played in Hofmannsthal's education, see Rieckmann, "Schools of Inauthenticity", 67–77.
62 Hofmannsthal and Andrian, *Briefwechsel*, 136. "Carry quite great weight, both factually and morally, as a guarantee for the future."
63 Schnitzler, *Tagebuch*, 295–6. "Some good theatrical moments", "[it was] not really a play."
64 Hofmannsthal, *Briefe 1890–1902*, 284. Letter of 4 April 1899 to Felix Oppenheimer. "The alternating harmony and alternating noticeable discrepancy between these poems [plays] and the theater."
65 Hofmannsthal, *Briefe 1880–1937*, 54. "Verse and costume [...] that is simply either a youthful need or has internal reasons."
66 Kessler, *Das Tagebuch 1880–1937*, 3: 230. Diary entry of 22 March 1899.
67 Hamburger, "Das Fragment", 310. "In two such different and contradictory ways that for the author it remained in a manner of speaking incomplete and open-ended."

5. Yvan Goll's *Die Eurokokke*: A Reading Through Walter Benjamin's *Passagen-Werk*

Rolf J. Goebel

1927 witnessed two seemingly coincidental literary events: In this year, Yvan Goll published his Parisian novel *Die Eurokokke*[1] and Walter Benjamin began the compilation of what came to be known as the *Passagen-Werk* (*The Arcades Project*), his monumental assemblage of citations and reflections for his reading of Paris as the capital of the nineteenth century.[2] Their authors' biographies seem remarkably similar. Both were Jewish intellectuals whose lives were marked by exile, border-crossings, and cosmopolitanism. Born in Berlin in 1892, Benjamin emigrated to Paris in 1933 before committing suicide, in 1940, on the French-Spanish border while trying to escape the National Socialists. Goll was born Isaac Lang in Saint-Dié (Vosges) in 1891, lived in Swiss exile from 1914–18, moved to Paris in 1919, stayed intermittently in Berlin from 1931–35, and lived in New York from 1939–47 before returning to Paris; after a stay in Strasbourg from 1948–49, he died in Paris in 1950.[3]

Whereas Benjamin's *magnum opus* has become one of the most important cultural analyses of European modernity, Goll's novel has remained a rather obscure work, appreciated mainly by literary connoisseurs. Indeed, as the editors of a collection of essays revaluating Yvan and Claire Goll's oeuvres argue, the literary fortunes of the couple were for a long time characterized by a good deal of scholarly neglect. The reasons for this problem, at least on Yvan's part, are manifold: in addition to the vicissitudes of his life, Goll evades easy literary-historical classification, having been affiliated with expressionism and surrealism. Further philological questions arise from his many pseudonyms, his habit of rewriting his texts, from unsubstantiated dates, and so forth.[4] Despite Goll's relative obscurity on the one hand, and the seminal status of the *Passagen-Werk* in current cultural studies on the other, the two texts share a number of surprisingly similar themes and stylistic features, which deserve closer critical attention.

My following remarks are guided by the assumption that the very structure of the *Passagen-Werk*—its anti-systematic understanding of philosophy; its fragmentary, and, indeed, ruinous body; and its often cryptic allusiveness—always already refers to something other than itself, accounting for the text's radical openness and its ability to be transposed into different time frames and cultural contexts that go beyond Benjamin's original intentions. Thus the *Passagen-Werk* can serve as a conceptual framework for analyzing other texts, opening up hermeneutic avenues that are not necessarily available through an immanent reading of these texts alone.[5] Goll's brief and dense novel, in turn, is centered around a number of literary tropes that may seem obscure within the text's own parameters but reveal their deeper, and more concrete, cultural implications when decoded, as it were, in the light of Benjamin's more analytical categories and figures of thought. Moreover, each text's genre displays some formal elements of the other: the *Passagen-Werk*, although predominantly an essayistic text of cultural philosophy, contains many descriptive passages that border on quasi-fictional narrative, while Goll's novel makes up for its poverty in plot and action by the reflective character of its protagonist's interior monologue. Thus each text seems eminently translatable into the other. Together they constitute an intertextual relation that produces one of the most penetrating analyses of Paris as the metropolitan space of European modernity: Benjamin's *Passagen-Werk*, although focusing on the origins of Parisian culture during the nineteenth century, anticipates many features of the city during the late 1920s as depicted in *Die Eurokokke*; conversely, Goll's novel spells out many of the hypermodern implications already found throughout the various convolutions of Benjamin's textual collection.

The settings of Goll's and Benjamin's works are remarkably similar. For Benjamin, nineteenth-century Paris is a phantasmagoric dream-city, where the imitation of past cultural styles and the import of exotic images from colonial lands intermingle with the most modern technological advances, such as cast-iron constructions, electric light fixtures, broad boulevards and commercial novelties. Panoramas imitate nature; world exhibitions transfigure the exchange value of commodities; the bourgeois apartment, filled with decorative artifacts from the past and foreign cultures, becomes the owner's loge seat from which to view the entire world like a theatre performance; the urban crowd functions as the veil through which the city appears as a spectacle to the *flâneur*;

and Baron Haussmann's boulevards are designed like theater stages celebrating Napoleonic imperialism and the rise of financial capital.[6]

Similarly, from the beginning, Goll's 1920s Paris figures as a phantasmagoric mixture of dream and reality. The protagonist wakes up as if from a dream whose conclusion he experiences like an expulsion from Paradise. Suddenly feeling that he is drowning in reality, Paris appears to him nonetheless like an enchanted city: in the public parks, the tulips are made of wax; to save money, the seasons have been abolished and merely show up as decorations in the tailor's shop windows; and the steamboats on the Seine are only paintings on the quay walls because the city council claims that they are necessary for promoting the image of the city (E 5–6). Goll offers a metaphorically medical explanation for this pervasively phantasmagoric space: a cultural bacillus—the eponymous eurococcus—is rapidly destroying the organic fabric of Western culture and the health of its inhabitants, turning material actuality and intellectual truth into hollow shells and insubstantial facades. The eurococcus is the entire narrative's imaginative master trope, that within the fictional horizon of Goll's novel cannot be deciphered in socioeconomic terms. The reason for this resistance to interpretive analysis is that the novel is told exclusively as a first-person narrative from the point-of-view of the nameless protagonist. Obsessively fixated on the eurococcus, he remains trapped in his radically subjective imagination, which, like that of the protagonist of Rainer Maria Rilke's *The Notebooks of Malte Laurids Brigge* (1910), perhaps the greatest novel of modern Paris in the German language, is characterized by a strange dialectic of inside and outside, leading to the dissolution of the metaphysical self-certainty of the autonomous subject: "Je mehr ich mich [...] in mich selber verkroch, desto näher rückte die Außenwelt an mich heran, in mich hinein [...]. Aus allen Zimmern ringsum flossen die geheimen Gefühle der Insassen, die Sehnsuchten, die Hoffnungen, die Ängste, alle Leiden. Keine Existenz kann sich in Paris hermetisch gegen die Außenwelt abschließen" (E 11–12).[7]

Benjamin, too, deconstructs the notion of the autonomous subject, positing the *flâneur* not as a real person but as the medium for, and the product of, various discourses of the city, such as cultural anthropology, sociology, utopian revolutionary ideas, etc. But as a critic transcending the limited perspective of the *flâneur*, Benjamin employs the instruments of a Marxist-inspired social critique that unveils the dreamlike state of the French capital as a simulacrum effect instigated by capitalism's manipulation of market forces and its pervasive commodity fetishism, its entertainment industry and colonialist fantasies. Capitalism comes over Europe like a collective hallucination, a seemingly natural sleep filled with dreams, leading to a reactivation of the mythic forces of primordial times (K1a,8; P 494, AP 391).[8] In this sense, Benjamin's Marxist-inspired philosophy of cultural materialism seeks to uncover social, economic, and historical reasons for the phantasmagoria of the French capital that are beyond the subjective horizon of Goll's fictional narrator.

Like Benjamin's modernist *flâneur*, Goll's protagonist roams the boulevards of Paris, suffering from the loneliness that is typically felt most severely when moving within the anonymous and teeming crowds of accelerated modernity (E 18). As the perambulatory media of the city's textual representation, these figures read historical traces off the dispersed reality details that make up the topographical space of urban modernity. Their perceptions crystallize in the shape of a literary montage text, assembling what has been discarded and half-forgotten by the incessant powers of progress (N1a,8; P 574, AP 460). Benjamin's *flâneur* is able to forge his impressions into constellations in which past images attain their sudden legibility in a particular present, an epiphany captured in Benjamin's famous concept of the dialectic at a standstill (N3,1; P 577–8, AP 462–3). By contrast, Goll's protagonist remains lost and trapped in the whirlpool of phenomenal appearances without attaining lasting insights into the workings of historical meaning. The novel chronicles this predicament through the portrayal of a single day in the life of its narrator.

After rising early one morning in his hotel room, the protagonist meets his neighbor, the joyfully cynical nihilist Henry d'Anglade, who will become his mentor of sorts. D'Anglade loans the narrator his favorite book, a poisonous treatise on all the decay, lies and stupidities that make up the diseased body of modern culture (E 16–17). In the streets the protagonist observes the passers-by, who do not see and feel anything because they have no time (E 19–20). They believe in the illusory promises of advertisement but are without a God; their voices muted by the noise of the asphalt, car horns, phonographic records and turbines (E 20–23), they echo Benjamin's claim that technological progress promises a false sense of continuous innovation without truly liberating humankind from its self-imposed misery. Hence Goll's narrator feels free only because he is not accountable to any other human being, laughing at the world and lying to it because he believes that there is no truth beyond the deceptive proclamations issued by the newspapers and insurance companies (E 26–7). The absence of metaphysical truth and the dictatorship of technology correspond to the revolting ugliness of the city (something Goll's Paris again shares with Rilke's): "Ein Kran wühlt wie ein Zahnstocher im eiternden Munde des Himmels herum" (E 33).[9] Benjamin describes modern Paris as being built on a subterranean mythological underground, where the shopping arcades lead from daylight and consciousness into the dreamlike past, and the Metro tunnels evoke the Hades and the Minotaur's Labyrinth (C1a,2; P 135–6, AP 84). Similarly, Goll's Paris is a decaying, superannuated space, resembling ancient Egyptian and Roman cultural cities, because the capital's cultural history is rendered obsolete by new building projects announcing the illusions of culture in slogans like "WIR WISSEN NICHT" (E 35).[10] At a time when everything has been discovered and everything seems technologically possible, this pronouncement proclaims the last redemption from godless time while promising only a vague new beginning after the existing culture (E 36). Through the good offices of a seedy job-broker, the protagonist earns twenty francs by selling people their salvation in the form of paperback bibles advertised sensationally as the adventure novel of a young Jew; having finished his job, he retreats again into the cavernous interiority of his lonely life (E 50–3).

In Benjamin's *Passagen-Werk*, the representation of metropolitan space remains firmly ensconced within European modernity despite its numerous references to exotic imports from colonial territories. By comparison, Goll's novel links the decay of ruinous Europe more specifically to its historical Other, America, a country whose commercial and technological innovations invade and strangulate Paris irresistibly (E 34). In the grand boulevards, little booths can be seen, which amidst American-style modern stores artificially conjure up the wretched world of the Middle Ages by offering horoscopes, African charms, and other such cheaply romantic tokens of a pitilessly clairvoyant world of ancient belief (E 48). In this phantasmagoric, groundless and ruinous cityscape, the despairing protagonist feels an overwhelming desire for redemption, longing for the spirituality of various traditions, which, however, he can only envision with utter disgust: "Nach allem habe ich Sehnsucht: nach dem Wasserreis des Buddhisten, nach dem süßsauren Karpfen jüdischer Freitagsabende, nach der schalen Oblate aus der ungewaschenen Hand des Pfarrers, nach einer Ente in der 'Tour d'Argent', nach wilden Feigen von Delos" (E 72).[11]

At the root of his suffering lies an incurable, existential boredom, originating from his religiously motivated self-hatred: "Mein Gott, ich bin ja nur ein Kohlestäubchen, und warum vermesse ich mich, dich anzurufen! Mein Leid ist das Leid aller Europäer. Ich sehe immerfort auf die Uhr, verjage die Zeit, langweile mich und fürchte mich doch zu sterben" (E 72–3).[12] Boredom is also one of the key words that Benjamin associates with urban modernity. It makes up the ideological superstructure of the (aristocratic and bourgeois) upper classes, predicated upon the economic base of the working class suffering from the endless torture of the industrial process of production and its mechanical sameness (D 2a,4; P 162, AP 106). In this context it makes sense that Goll's bored protagonist feels incapable of joining the ordinary world of working people because to occupy himself would be to forget himself (E 73). As Benjamin argues, sameness, objectified in the dreariness of rainy weather, turns boredom into something that we feel when we do not know what we are waiting for, whereas if we think we do know what we are waiting for, we only reveal our own shallowness and distracted mindset (D 2,7; P 161, AP 105). Boredom is the unimaginative counterpart to the world of dreams and the unconscious, which is why it appeared elegant to the dandy (D 2a,2; P 162, AP 106). His blasé attitude and ostentatious boredom is a rebellion against the speed of technological modernity (for instance, by parading tortoises and lobsters on a leash in the shopping arcades and grand boulevards (M 3,8; P 532, AP 422). One of the dandy's modern successor figures is Benjamin's ragpicker, a grumpy and tipsy fellow who roams the streets at daybreak picking up the verbal scraps of Western civilization, such as "humanity", "inwardness", or "contemplative absorption". For Benjamin, the ragpicker's activity is the allegory of the politicization of the intellectual, which is why the ragpicker heralds the daybreak of the (proletarian) revolution.[13] Goll's narrator, too, sees himself as a ragpicker browsing in the past of Europe's dead cultural treasures, but he lacks the revolutionary potential of Benjamin's figure, instead experiencing his activity as a condition resembling asphyxiation under collapsed works of Dorian and Cubist art (E 73).

Benjamin regards the *flâneur* as a historical precursor to the detective because both feign indolence as a mask concealing the concentrated pursuit of an unsuspecting criminal (M 13a, 2; P 554, AP 442). Goll reverses this concept: one reason why his protagonist cannot pursue the leisurely stroll of the classical *flâneur* is that he believes he is one of the three bandits who, the newspapers report, have just ransacked the first-class coach of the Marseilles express train. The police caught two of the killers, but the chief bandit got away; his description in the newspapers, including his yellow gloves, seems to fit the protagonist perfectly (E 89–93). As his paranoid fear of being caught grows, he feels everyone's eyes resting on his gloves; escaping into a café, he attracts the attention of an elderly gentleman, who investigates his gloves with a pocket microscope, exclaiming: "Ich habe ihn! Den Eurokokkus!" (E 96).[14]

Introducing himself as a Professor of Chemistry from the University of Philadelphia, the stranger tells the protagonist that the eurococcus bacillus is hollowing out the entire cultural substance of the continent. It has turned Notre Dame Cathedral into an imaginary building void of God and faith; it empties classical books of their intellectual contents; and it transforms a poor donkey pulling a laborer's cart into a mere skeleton covered with its mangy coat. According to the professor, the protagonist is the first human being diagnosed with carrying the bacillus. His hollow physiology is merely the symptom of his spiritual emptiness; as the chemist tells him, he has no ambition, no belief, no sense of love and duty, no respect, no reason, no self-discipline and no goal in life any longer (E 97–109). Now it dawns upon the protagonist why he is suffering so immensely: He is not so much trying to escape the police as fleeing from himself, since nobody has inhaled the pain of the city and the times as much as he has; nobody is infected as much as he is with doubt, boredom and egotism. All of Europe is afflicted with the disease; "das letzte Stadium der Zivilisation war angebrochen: die Seele, das Gewissen, der Instinkt und das Bild Gottes waren gemeinsam schadhaft geworden" (E 112).[15] Like Benjamin's notion of boredom, the eurococcus disease is but the reverse side of the illusion of technological progress: ordinary people are like innocent children; in their back lanes reeking of cheap booze, they play "mit blinkenden Puppen des Fortschritts, mit silberweißen Maschinen voll pfeifender Elektrizität" (E 114).[16] As the protagonist realizes, the eurococcus is not transmitted directly through human touch, but across distances through words and mere gazes (E 115); it is, ultimately, not a (metaphorically) medical disease but, more fundamentally, a semiotic problem, a breakdown in authentic communication, a metaphysical loss of absolute truths and moral values.

At five o'clock in the afternoon, the protagonist reaches the Bar de l'Ennui, where he meets the three daughters of the owner, an Armenian named Dr Syrianx, and discovers the overwhelming, transfiguring power of love. His mentor, the nihilistic dandy Henry d'Anglade, also shows up to give a kind of philosophical summary of the malaise of European modernity. He claims that the age of Europe is in the process of being extinguished, that it is useless trying to save anything, and that even decay and dissolution are as voluptuous as any process of becoming. Now the protagonist suddenly begins to fight these assumptions, asking whether the eurococcus could not be fought with the help of the *Amerikoon*, the remedy of American civilization (E 129–31). Here, Goll's novel reflects the popular discourse of *Amerikanismus* of the early-twentieth century, which constructs the distant continent's capitalist-technological culture as Europe's other, as an idealizing projection of social progress or as a nightmare of alienation, exploitation and superficial values. This movement finds its most radical expression in Kafka's novel *Der Verschollene* (*The Castaway*, 1911–13), which portrays the United States as a hallucinatory mix of fake redemptive promises and real high industrial and entrepreneurial misery. D'Anglade unmasks the American sense of technological advances (hygiene, radio, tennis, petroleum, the flight to the moon) as a quack's remedy, as yet another simulacrum arising from the decay of modern civilization. Dying Europe, he claims, is fighting its final, and fatal, heroic struggle against the transatlantic spiritlessness, the American will to colonize Europe culturally (E 131–2). As La, Dr Syrianx's daughter, points out sarcastically, even love, the protagonist's last hope, proves to be useless. Instead of technological progress and the redemptive power of Eros, universal boredom rules the modern world (E 133).

For Benjamin, boredom is an expression of Friedrich Nietzsche's notion of the eternal recurrence of the same, according to which the illusory newness of modernity is actually only the phantasmagoric reappearance of primordial history in the present (D 8a, 2; P 174, AP 116). Hence the nineteenth-century belief in historical progress and infinite perfectibility and the idea of eternal recurrence are complementary expressions of mythic thinking (D 10 a, 5; P 178, AP 119). Goll's novel proves even more pessimistic than Benjamin's philosophy of history, which, despite its deconstruction of the illusory notion of progress by the trope of the eternal return of the same, believes that the collective may awaken from the mythic dreamworld of capitalism through the force of reason ruthlessly cutting through the jungle and undergrowth of delusions and myth (N1,4; P 570–1, AP 456–7). By contrast, Goll's protagonist must learn that even critical rationality is no remedy for boredom, the other epidemic ruin of Europe. As d'Anglade explains, boredom is not only the final stage of any civilization, but also a theological category: "Immer kommt ein Moment, wo selbst Gott, heiße er Zeus, Zebaoth oder Zoroaster, sich nach der Erschaffung seines Universums fragt: 'Eigentlich, wozu das alles?' Er gähnt und schmeißt alles zusammen. Das Gleiche tut der Mensch mit seiner Zivilisation" (E 134).[17] Boredom, d'Anglade summarizes, reflects the slow devaluation of all virtues and talents: "Langeweile ist die lebenslängliche Verdammnis zu einer Daseinsform, die an sich erschöpft ist" (E 134).[18]

In this situation, d'Anglade's last resource is to cultivate the attitude of idleness. He calls it an ascetic kind of self-torture because it is a painful revolt against work, which serves the ordinary masses as an escapist way of forgetting the emptiness of human existence. Work is a mechanical production of bad commodities for little gain, a pseudo-religious practice, where at the end of six holy workdays one sleeps through an unholy Sunday to escape the infectious sense of boredom (E 135–6). But ultimately d'Anglade's idleness is merely the reverse side of work, being as ineffectual as what it opposes, except that it is self-consciously and proudly ineffective, whereas work deceptively believes in its own productive value. Benjamin traces the historical and socioeconomic origins of idleness (*Müßiggang*) by differentiating it from leisure (*Muße*). Whereas leisure gives meaning and stability to human life, idleness falls victim to the vicissitudes and unpredictability of historical change because it is the purely illusory pursuit of vacuous, isolated chance encounters disconnected from the continuity of genuine experience resulting from work: "Die Erfahrung ist der Ertrag der Arbeit, das Erlebnis ist die Phantasmagorie des Müßiggängers" (m 1a,3; P 962).[19] In feudal society, Benjamin argues, leisure, as the freedom from work, was a privilege that has been lost in bourgeois society because it was associated with two feudalistic practices: religious contemplation and representative court life. These attitudes indirectly benefitted the work of the poet, who in feudalistic times enjoyed leisure as a recognized privilege (m2 a,5; P 964, AP 802). In modernity, however, as Charles Baudelaire shows, the poet meets the dandy-*flâneur* idling away his time through the imaginary city of arcades and their commodity spectacles (m 5,4; P 969, AP 806). Whereas Goll associates the leisurely Sunday with the culmination of wasteful work, Benjamin interprets Sunday as the day of an idle God resting from his creation; this deity serves as a legitimating model for the bourgeoisie's own idleness. In Benjamin's theological view, *flânerie* turns into a kind of sacrilegious *imitatio dei*: "In der Flanerie verfügt er [der Bürger] über dessen Allgegenwart; beim Spiel über dessen Allmacht und im Studium über seine Allwissenheit" (m 4,6; P 967).[20] This attitude corresponds to d'Anglade's cynical celebration of idleness as the nihilistic rejection of all ideals leading to absolute liberation: "Wir müssen als unser Ideal aufstellen, kein Ideal zu haben. Die Ideallosigkeit aber bringt uns das höchste Gut auf Erden, zu dessen Erlangung eigentlich sämtliche Ideale der Menschheitsgeschichte aufgestellt worden sind. Nämlich: die Freiheit, die absolute Freiheit" (E 139–40).[21]

Facing this lesson in nihilism, the protagonist decides to explore the last refuge from the disease of existential vacuity, pure nature, where one does not think or interpret the world but simply follows God's eternal will (E 140). Here Goll evokes the Romantic *topos* of nature as the divinely inspired, morally pure site of genuine love, passion and human freedom, which constitutes the antithesis of the city, seen as the breeding ground of social misery, political corruption and ill health. But when the protagonist reaches the Forest of Saint-Cloud on the outskirts of Paris, he is horrified to discover that, like the trees, statues and lanterns around him, he casts no shadow, making him a modern successor to Adalbert von Chamisso's Peter Schlemihl: "Ich war wesenlos, nicht mehr verbunden mit Raum und Erde, unecht, unwahr."[22] He muses: "War auch die gesamte Natur nur noch Staffage, Kulisse, Täuschung? Das Musée Grévin einer vermoderten Welt?" (E 143–4).[23] The reference to the Musée Grévin, a famous Parisian wax museum founded in 1882, evokes Benjamin's nineteenth-century world of panoramas, wax figure cabinets, museums and other sites of the phantasmagoric dream-world of Paris. Benjamin notes: "Man war unermüdlich, durch technische Kunstgriffe die Panoramen zu Stätten einer vollkommenen Naturnachahmung zu machen" (P 48).[24] Accordingly, panoramas attempted to reproduce faithfully natural sceneries, complete with changing daylight, the rising of the moon and the rush of the waterfalls. If for Benjamin nature intrudes into urban space through the medium of its multifaceted imitations, Goll's novel stages the opposite effect: here, the artificiality and vacuous façade culture of the city permeates its original Other, the realm of organic nature. The effect is entirely unsettling, as it dislocates the protagonist's sense of identity, based on the unity of mind and body. He questions whether he still exists at all because when he touches his forehead and limbs, he no longer senses himself (E 144).

Devastated by this experience, and almost looking forward to what he imagines to be his imminent arrest for the train heist, the protagonist ends up at the Bar de la Mort, a typical *Neue Sachlichkeit* establishment, whose denizens indulge in *Weltschmerz*, cynicism, androgyny and cultural decadence, attitudes deliriously evocative of Gottfried Benn and of Christian Schad. Here Henry d'Anglade finishes up his philosophical treatise on absolute freedom as the product of the absence of ideals, explaining that the only two weapons against mass civilization are smiling, the diplomatically smooth concealing of one's inner being, and lying. This d'Anglade loves because he takes neither himself nor life seriously, as he fears the seriousness of life. It is here that the novel ends abruptly: policemen enter the bar in order to arrest the narrator, but the inspector lets him go free for the arrest warrant was issued in error.

The literary value of Goll's novel has remained an object of considerable controversy. In his afterword to the Argon edition, Joachim Sartorius highlights the "sharply edged snapshots, reminiscent of Expressionism and yet thoroughly concrete", as well as the "acid criticism of the intellectual tendencies of its time and of European mass civilization", which he regards as the text's main merits.[25] In her afterword to the Wallstein reissue, Barbara Glauert-Hesse compares *Die Eurokokke* and Goll's other novels—among them *Le Microbe de l'Or* and *Der Mitropäer*—favorably to such classical texts as Louis Aragon's *Le Paysan de Paris* (1926), Henry de Monterlant's *Les Bestiaires* (1926), André Breton's *Nadja* (1928) and even James Joyce's *Ulysses* (1920), whose German translation by Georg Goyert was facilitated by Goll, who acted as the Paris representative of Rhein Verlag in Basel.[26] By contrast, Marcel Beyer, in his review of the Wallstein edition, flatly dismisses *Die Eurokokke*'s ambitions as a radical novel of metropolitan life. His protagonist does not amount to being a genuine *flâneur*; he remains a mere pretentious talker (*Schwadroneur*), who never attains the former's penetrating gaze at reality. Goll, in Beyer's opinion, always came too late; he was a belated Expressionist, a belated Surrealist, and with his *Eurokokke*, he was merely the creator of a belated, decadent dandy (*Endzeitdandy*). The themes of Goll's novel, Beyer concludes—the fascination with exotic personages, apocalyptic boredom, European melancholia, and petty neuroses—had already been anticipated in perfect form by T. S. Eliot's truly innovative poem *The Wasteland* (1922), published five years before Goll's novel.[27]

Although it is probably true that Goll's novel as a whole cannot compete with the more famous novels of metropolitan modernity, it does share many of their preoccupations: social alienation, the loss of traditional morality, the dissolution of the human self, the uncanny subjectivization of inanimate objects, the fragmentation of external reality and the crisis of representational language. Goll's novel also participates in its competitor texts' formal innovations: montage effects, surrealistic metaphors, a discontinuous stream of consciousness and shock-like engagements of the reader's imagination. More specifically, Goll's narrative technique employs a radically subjective way of recording the disparate surface spectacles of modern metropolitan life that, when read by themselves, within the slim novel's covers as it were, may seem insubstantial when compared to other *Großstadtromane* of high modernism. But as I have tried to show, the surface aesthetics of Goll's novel reveals surprisingly multilayered depth and intellectual complexity when decoded through the analytic apparatus of Benjamin's philosophical reading of urban modernity. It is then that Goll's themes—topographic façades, ruined cityscapes and urban decay; *flânerie*, idling and ragpicking; boredom, nihilism and despair—reflect their origins in particular intellectual traditions—a post-Nietzschean universe marked by the death of God, the revaluation of inherited morality, and the bankruptcy of the ideal of historical progress—as well as material circumstances—high capitalist modes of industrial production, social alienation and commodity fetishism. Herein lies the hermeneutic power of the *Passagen-Werk*: it speaks not only in a truly universal sense about the emergence of European modernity in the cultural topography of nineteenth-century Paris, but it lends the conceptual categories of that analysis to a new reading of a text like Goll's. This novel, in turn, fleshes out in its fictional metaphors and narrative plot scenarios some of Benjamin's most salient themes, even though it was not directly influenced by any of his works. In this way, Benjamin's and Goll's writings supplement one another, each revealing thematic and formal aspects that the other leaves underdeveloped, thus enriching our understanding of the inherent complexity of the as yet unfinished project of European urban modernity.

Bibliography

Benjamin, Walter. "An Outsider Makes His Mark". Vol. 2. of *Selected Writings*, edited by Michael W. Jennings, Howard Eiland and Gary Smith, 305–11. Cambridge, MA: Belknap Press of Harvard University Press, 1999.
—*Das Passagen-Werk*. Vols. 5.1 and 5.2 of *Gesammelte Schriften*, edited by Rolf Tiedemann and Hermann Schweppenhäuser. Frankfurt am Main: Suhrkamp, 1982.
—"Ein Außenseiter macht sich bemerkbar. Zu S. Kracauer, 'Die Angestellten'". Vol. 3 of *Gesammelte Schriften*, edited by Hella Tiedemann-Bartels, 219–25. Frankfurt am Main: Suhrkamp, 1972.
—*The Arcades Project*. Translated by Howard Eiland and Kevin McLaughlin. Cambridge, MA: Belknap Press of Harvard University Press, 1999.
Beyer, Marcel. "Mit Beinen, Brüsten, Bauch. Yvan Goll, befallen mit Eurokokken, will tanzen wie Neger". *Süddeutsche Zeitung*, 20 March 2002. www.buecher.de/shop/ buecher /die-eurokokke/goll-yvan/products_products/content/prod_id/10262704/.
Buck-Morss, Susan. *The Dialectics of Seeing: Walter Benjamin and the Arcades Project*. Cambridge, MA: MIT Press, 1989.
Bürger, Jan. "'Paris brennt': Iwan Goll's Überrealismus im Kontext der zwanziger Jahre". In *Surrealismus in der deutschen Literatur*, edited by Friederike Reents, 87–98. Berlin: de Gruyter, 2009.
Glauert-Hesse, Barbara. Nachwort to Yvan Goll. *Die Eurokokke*. 1927, 159–76. Reprint, Göttingen: Wallstein, 2002.
Goebel, Rolf J., ed. *A Companion to the Works of Walter Benjamin*. Rochester, NY: Camden House, 2009.
Goll, Yvan. *Die Eurokokke*. Berlin: Argon, 1988.
—*Die Eurokokke*. 1927. Reprint, Göttingen: Wallstein, 2002.
Hanssen, Beatrice, ed. *Walter Benjamin and the Arcades Project*. London, New York: Continuum, 2006.
Kafka, Franz. *Der Verschollene*. Edited by Jost Schillemeit. In *Schriften, Tagebücher, Briefe: Kritische Ausgabe*, edited by Jürgen Born, Gerhard Neumann, Malcolm Pasley and Jost Schillemeit. Frankfurt am Main: Fischer; New York: Schocken, 1983.
Rilke, Rainer Maria. *Die Aufzeichnungen des Malte Laurids Brigge*. Bibliothek Suhrkamp, no. 343. Frankfurt am Main: Suhrkamp, 1976.
Robertson, Eric and Robert Vilain. Introduction to *Yvan Goll—Claire Goll: Texts and Contexts*, edited by Robertson and Vilain, 1–8. Amsterdam: Rodopi, 1997.
Sartorius, Joachim. Nachwort to Yvan Goll, *Die Eurokokke*, 119–25. Berlin: Argon, 1988.

Notes

1 Goll, *Die Eurokokke* (Göttingen: Wallstein, 2002). Citations in the text are to this edition, hereafter cited as E followed by page numbers. Translations from the novel are mine. This is a facsimile reprint of the original edition (Berlin: Martin Wassermann Verlag, 1927). Another edition was published by Argon in Berlin in 1988. It has an excellent afterword by Joachim Sartorius (119–25) which situates the novel in the intellectual climate of technological advances and the social crisis of the late 1920s. From 1931 onwards, Goll worked on a revised version of the text, which was never published and must be

considered lost. Goll's French translation of this manuscript appeared under the title *Lucifer Vieillissant*. See Barbara Glauert-Hesse's afterword to the Wallstein reissue, 159–76. She stresses the text's autobiographical references, questioning its status as a novel (159).

2   Benjamin, *Das Passagen-Werk*. Benjamin, Eiland and McLaughlin, *The Arcades Project*. See also Buck-Morss, *The Dialectics of Seeing* and Hanssen, *Walter Benjamin and the Arcades Project*.

3   Robertson and Vilain, introduction to *Yvan Goll—Claire Goll*, 1–2.

4   Ibid., 1–8. For an account of Goll's surrealism, see Bürger, "Paris brennt", 87–98. The essay does not cover *Die Eurokokke*.

5   For various explorations of Benjamin's actuality and translatability into new contexts, see the essays in *A Companion to the Works of Walter Benjamin*.

6   See especially the first Exposé (1935) for the *Passagen-Werk*, "Paris, die Hauptstadt des XIX. Jahrhunderts", P 45–59; "Paris, the Capital of the Nineteenth Century", AP 3–13.

7   "The more […] I retreated into myself, the closer the external world encroached on me, intruding into myself […]. From all the rooms around me flowed the secret feelings of their inmates, their longings, hopes, fears, all their suffering. In Paris, no extant being can shut itself hermetically off from the outer world."

8   Citations in the text to *Das Passagen-Werk* (*The Arcades Project*) provide the convolute number (e.g., K1a,8) followed by page references for the German edition (abbreviated as P) and the English translation (abbreviated as AP).

9   "A construction cane digs like a toothpick in the festering mouth of the sky."

10   "WE DO NOT KNOW."

11   "I long for everything: for the watery rice of the Buddhist, for the sweet and sour carp of Jewish Friday evenings, for the stale oblate from the unwashed hand of the priest, for a duck in the 'Tour d'Argent', for the wild figs of Delos."

12   "My God, after all I am only a speck of coal dust, and why am I arrogant enough to call upon you! My misery is the misery of all Europeans. I constantly look at my watch, chase away time, am bored, and am yet afraid to die."

13   Benjamin's example of the ragpicker here is Siegfried Kracauer, whose book *Die Angestellten: Aus dem Neuesten Deutschland* (*White-Collar Workers: The Latest from Germany*) he reviewed in 1930. See "Ein Außenseiter macht sich bemerkbar", 225 ("An Outsider Makes His Mark", 310).

14   "I got it! The eurococcus!"

15   "The final stage of civilization has begun: the soul, conscience, instinct and the image of God have been damaged altogether."

16   "With glittering puppets of progress, with silvery white machines full of whistling electricity."

17   "There always comes a moment when even God, be he named Zeus, Zebaoth or Zoroaster, asks himself after having created his universe: 'Actually, what's the purpose of it all?' He yawns and smashes everything together. Man does the same with his civilization."

18   "Boredom is the life-long damnation to endure a form of existence that in itself has been exhausted."

19   "[Historically saturated] Experience [*Erfahrung*] is the outcome of work; immediate [presentist] experience [*Erlebnis*] is the phantasmagoria of the idler" (AP 801).

20 "In flânerie, he [the bourgeois] has the omnipresence of God; in gambling, the omnipotence; and in study, it is God's omniscience that is his" (AP 805).
21 "We must declare as our ideal not to have any ideal. It is the absence of ideals that brings us the highest good on earth, actually attained only by the erection of all the ideals of human history. Namely: freedom, absolute freedom."
22 "I was without essence, no longer connected to space and the earth, false, untrue."
23 "Was even nature in its entirety nothing but façades, stage props, deception? The Musée Grévin of a withered world?"
24 "One sought tirelessly, through technical devices, to make panoramas the scenes of a perfect imitation of nature" (AP 5).
25 Sartorius, *Die Eurokokke*, 121 (my translation).
26 Glauert-Hesse, *Die Eurokokke*, 165–6.
27 Beyer, "Mit Beinen, Brüsten, Bauch".

III Narrative Theory

6. Else Meets Dora: Narratology as a Tool for Illuminating Literary Trauma

Gail Finney

It is known that the trauma victim does not assimilate or even fully register the traumatic moment at the time it occurs. Hence accounts of trauma must inevitably reconstruct past experience, and trauma theory, in synthesizing the features of such accounts, confronts a comparable challenge. Similarly, narratology or narrative theory, in talking systematically about the discourse of fiction and film, typically seeks to analyze art of the past (as opposed, for example, to a sociological study of contemporary phenomena). Furthermore, the narratological practice of describing literary and cinematic works in terms of structural categories or types can be seen as analogous to the psychoanalytic dissection of traumatic experience. In this essay I will examine instances of literary trauma through the lens of narrative theory to suggest the ways in which narratology might be useful in elucidating traumatic experience as depicted in literature.

As exemplary texts I will treat two works with a similar thematic focus, Sigmund Freud's *Fragment of an Analysis of a Case of Hysteria* (1905), his account of his therapeutic work with "Dora" (his case name for Ida Bauer), and Arthur Schnitzler's *Fräulein Else* (1924).[1] The case study and the novella both analyze the figure of a late adolescent woman who experiences the trauma of being used as a sexual pawn by her family. The project of this essay is to employ narrative theory to present Freud's case study symbolically as the theoretical counterpart of Schnitzler's text in order to illuminate the intersection between theory (both psychoanalytic and narrative) and literature in representing traumatic experience.[2] The similar traumatic syndrome is depicted here through two divergent narrative modes: the autonomous monologue of *Else*, which renders trauma without external narrative mediation, and the largely indirect discourse of the case study, in which traumatic experience is externally interpreted and recounted by Freud as analyst and author. Symbolically, *Else* can be seen as the continuation of *Dora*, insofar as the bartered, exploited female is taken to the utmost point of desperation, culminating in suicide. The failure to come to terms with trauma is reflected in the dissolution of the narrative in both texts.[3]

The contrast between the narrative modes of *Dora* and *Else* parallels Dominick LaCapra's distinction between writing about trauma and writing trauma. He associates writing about trauma with historiography, which seeks to reconstruct the past as objectively as possible. Literary texts are better vehicles for writing trauma, historiographical or theoretical texts for writing about trauma. LaCapra writes: "Literature in its very excess can somehow get at trauma in a manner unavailable to theory [...] it writes (speaks or even cries) trauma in excess of theory";[4] "Literature [...] may provide a more expansive space [...] for exploring modalities of responding to trauma, including the role of affect and the tendency to repeat traumatic events."[5] According to LaCapra, writing trauma is a metaphor, since it is impossible for the individual to identify the precise moment at which traumatic experience occurs. Instead, trauma is perceived retrospectively in the belated effects of the radical break which it constitutes.[6] Even though *Dora* possesses literary traits, its genre is that of a case study.[7] Whereas Schnitzler seeks to *write trauma* through his ventriloquization of Else as she disintegrates psychologically, Freud *writes about trauma* in his case study of Dora.

The pairing of Freud and Schnitzler is, of course, justified for many reasons. The affinity between the two thinkers as writers and medical doctors has often been pointed out, inspired to a significant extent by Freud's famous letter to Schnitzler in 1922, which was written to congratulate the author on his sixtieth birthday. In this letter Freud asks himself why he has never attempted to meet Schnitzler, even though they have long traveled in the same circles in Vienna, and concludes that he has avoided Schnitzler because of a kind of reluctance to meet his *Doppelgänger*.[8] The parallels are indeed striking: Schnitzler was only six years younger than Freud; both were highly educated, upper-middle-class, secular Jews; both resided in Vienna and knew many of the same people; and both were medical doctors with an avid interest in psychology. Although Schnitzler became a laryngologist, he learned hypnosis, studied its use in treating hysterical symptoms, and memorialized it in his literary oeuvre. His works demonstrate an interest in other facets of the human psyche as well, such as dreams. Though the two men are far from doubles, each existing as a distinct and autonomous presence, Schnitzler arrived as a writer at many of the same psychological insights that Freud achieved through analysis and experimentation.[9]

An overview of the history of trauma studies will serve as a backdrop against which to explore the ways in which narratology may be used to elucidate literary and theoretical portrayals of trauma such as we encounter in Schnitzler's novella and Freud's case study. The term "trauma" originally referred to a surgical wound and derived from the belief that the body is surrounded by a protective envelope, so that a rupture in the skin resulted in a disastrous reaction in the entire organism.[10] The concept came to embrace emotional or psychic as well as physical shock to the system, and the belief that trauma affects the entire organism has persisted. Because the traumatic event is not fully assimilated at the time it occurs, it can only be recognized, understood and represented—for example in a narrative—retrospectively. In the words of Cathy Caruth, whose work essentially launched the contemporary discussion of trauma, "Trauma seems to be much more than a pathology, or the simple illness of a wounded psyche: it is always the story of a wound that cries out, that addresses us in the attempt to tell us of a reality or truth that is not otherwise available."[11] LaCapra's pithy description of the effects of trauma is likewise useful: "Trauma brings about a dissociation of affect and representation: one disorientingly feels what one cannot represent; one numbingly represents what one cannot feel."[12]

We live in traumatic times. Ann Kaplan observes that trauma is often linked to modernity and that modernity, intertwined with imperialism, consumerism and Fascism, "is seen to produce basic twentieth-century experiences, such as the catastrophic event and global cross-cultural conflict."[13] Through technological advances in international and local warfare, a rise in the number of natural disasters, a heightened degree of familial abuse, ongoing racial and religious persecution, and growing exposure to violence and sensationalism in the media, traumatic experience has become an intimate reality for many of us. Accordingly, a body of theoretical literature on trauma, some of it indebted to Freud, has proliferated, and recent literature and film increasingly depict traumatic subjects, whether drawn from the personal, familial or social realm, or from the context of war.

If the twentieth century can be described as the traumatic century, that century begins with the 1880s. For any exploration of trauma must proceed from the work of Freud, the *primum mobile* of trauma studies, and it was in the 1880s that Freud and his friend and patron Dr Josef Breuer, a prominent Viennese neurologist, began studying the etiology of symptoms they encountered in a series of young, primarily upper-middle-class Jewish women in Vienna. Confronted with afflictions which did not respond to medical treatment, ranging from shortness of breath, chronic coughing or sneezing, loss of voice, hallucinations, overexcitement, somnolence and eating disorders to temporary paralysis or loss of sensation in various parts of the body, Freud and Breuer labeled these ailments hysterical. They began treating the young women by means of a technique which one of the patients herself, Anna O. (Bertha Pappenheim), dubbed the "talking cure", the foundation of psychoanalysis. After many of the young women revealed to Freud that they had been sexually molested as children, either by their fathers or by another adult male belonging to or close to their families, Freud deduced that the cause of hysteria was sexual trauma. These analyses culminated in the *Studies on Hysteria*, jointly authored by Freud and Breuer and published in 1895.

In the often-quoted claim made by Freud and Breuer in their 1893 paper "On the Psychical Mechanism of Hysterical Phenomena: Preliminary Communication", "*Hysterics suffer mainly from reminiscences.*"[14] According to Freud's concept of *Nachträglichkeit*, or "deferred action", hysteria is made up of a dialectic between two events: an early incident that was not necessarily traumatic because the child was too young to assimilate it, and a second event that evoked a memory of the first event which was then given traumatic meaning and therefore repressed.[15] In late nineteenth-century Austria, these sexual transgressions had to remain hidden, often buried in the unconscious minds of Breuer's and Freud's patients until they were unearthed through narration.

The second phase of Freud's trauma studies is motivated by his observations of the psychological afflictions of many World War I veterans. As he writes in *Beyond the Pleasure Principle*, "A condition has long been known and described which occurs after severe mechanical concussions, railway disasters and other accidents involving a risk to life; it has been given the name of 'traumatic neurosis'. The terrible war which has just ended gave rise to a great number of illnesses of this kind, but it at least put an end to the temptation to attribute the cause of the disorder to organic lesions of the nervous system brought about by mechanical force."[16] The latter disorder, which was labeled "shell shock" during the war, also afflicted soldiers during combat, but Freud's investigations of the syndrome focus on postwar manifestations. This research was illuminated by his studies on hysteria, in which the repercussions or afterlife of traumatic events could serve as a key to unlock the trauma itself. Just as hysterics demonstrate "fixations to the experience which started the illness",[17] the patient with a traumatic neurosis is frequently haunted by dreams in which he relives the traumatic event. Caruth illustrates the "compulsion to repeat", so central to traumatic experience,[18] through the figure of Tancred in

Torquato Tasso's *La Gerusalemme liberata* (*Jerusalem Delivered*): "The actions of Tancred, wounding his beloved in a battle and then, unknowingly, seemingly by chance, wounding her again, evocatively represent in [*Beyond the Pleasure Principle*] the way that the experience of a trauma repeats itself, exactly and unremittingly, through the unknowing acts of the survivor and against his very will. As Tasso's story dramatizes it, the repetition at the heart of catastrophe—the experience that Freud will call 'traumatic neurosis'—emerges as the unwitting re-enactment of an event that one cannot simply leave behind."[19] In what Freud calls the "dark and dismal subject of the traumatic neurosis", a phenomenon which, as he recognizes, is caused not by bodily but by psychological factors, lie the seeds of what is today termed post-traumatic stress disorder, or PTSD.[20]

The third phase of Freud's studies of trauma, which Kaplan characterizes as his "most significant, and most complete discussion of trauma", is embodied in his last finished work, *Moses and Monotheism* (1939).[21] The primary intention of this iconoclastic book is to hypothesize that Moses was not a Jew but an Egyptian who transmitted his monotheistic religion to the Jews, and that, because of his domineering nature, Moses was eventually murdered by the Jews and his religion was abandoned. Yet Freud postulates that the Jews eventually took up the monotheistic religion of Moses again, thus paralleling on a collective level the phenomenon which in individuals Freud terms the "return of the repressed". Interpreting this history in psychoanalytic terms, Freud writes of the traumatic experience through which an entire people passed.[22] But included in this narrative is a section entitled "The Analogy", in which Freud synthesizes and clarifies his thoughts on individual trauma.[23] Here he writes again of the "fixation to the trauma" and the "repetition compulsion", in which the behavior of the traumatized individual unwittingly recapitulates the early trauma, e.g. a girl who was molested in early childhood becomes promiscuous as an adult. But he elaborates on and refines his earlier beliefs about the role of repetition in trauma, writing that traumatic experiences occurring in early childhood are typically forgotten; they are followed by a latency period and they later manifest themselves in the form of neurotic sexuality or aggressiveness.

These concepts have remained central to the exploration of trauma up to the present day. I have already mentioned Freud's role with regard to the syndrome of post-traumatic stress disorder, which achieved widespread recognition through diagnoses of Vietnam War veterans. Other areas of trauma studies which have been illuminated by Freud's thinking include the attention to child sexual abuse and recovered memories which burgeoned in the United States in the 1980s, the numerous memoirs by Holocaust survivors that have appeared during the past several decades, and recent analyses of trauma in cinema. Studies of psychological trauma are still unthinkable without the work of Freud.

Trauma theorist Ruth Leys observes that "in the economic terms associated with Freud's ideas, the traumatic experience involves a fragmentation or loss of unity of the ego resulting from the radical unbinding of the death drive."[24] This description encapsulates with striking accuracy Schnitzler's rendering of the psychological disintegration of the title character in his *Fräulein Else*, which can be elucidated by narrative theory.

The term "narratology" is commonly used as a synonym for "narrative theory", the theory of narrative structure, or in Patrick O'Neill's concise formulation, "the narrative of narrative".[25] Narratology as a field originated in France during the 1960s. The term *narratologie* was coined by Tzvetan Todorov in 1969 to designate "a systematic study of narrative structure firmly anchored in the common intellectual tradition of the Russian and Czech formalism of the early twentieth century and the French structuralism and semiotics of the sixties."[26] As we will see, the field has since become considerably more global in both scope and national orientation. For example, the American scholar Seymour Chatman elaborates a distinction basic to narratology in his 1978 study *Story and Discourse: Narrative Structure in Fiction and Film*. Somewhat similar to the dichotomy established in Aristotle's *Poetics* between *mythos* and *logos*, the title duality basically refers to the what and the way or how of narrative: to the content or sequence of events, on the one hand, and the means through which these are conveyed or represented on the other.[27]

The "story" of Schnitzler's *Fräulein Else*, set at the turn of the century, is fairly simple: a nineteen-year-old woman from a middle-class family in Vienna, on vacation in northern Italy, receives a letter from her mother informing her that her father, who is fond of gambling and playing the stock exchange, is in danger of being arrested if he does not repay a large debt. Else's mother implores her to speak with the wealthy Herr von Dorsday, a well-to-do and considerably older gentleman who is staying at the same hotel as Else. The implication is clear. After Dorsday agrees to repay the loan on the condition that Else present herself naked to him, she becomes psychologically unhinged and winds up appearing naked in public. Her subsequent derangement leads her to take an overdose of the barbiturate Veronal.

What is of interest to us here is the way in which the "discourse" of *Fräulein Else*—the writing of trauma, to return to LaCapra's term—parallels and facilitates the "story", the trauma itself. The nature of Else's trauma is succinctly described by Robert Weiss. Demonstrating the sophistication of Schnitzler's understanding of psychosis in light of late twentieth-century knowledge, he characterizes Else's illness as a "psychotic break", which he defines as a "sudden transition from relatively normal behavior or even from an established neurosis to an acute state of frank psychosis."[28] He lists her etiological factors as "schizoid personality, prepsychotic; insoluble conflicts; anxiety and guilt neurosis", and her symptomatology as "incident of exhibitionism; hysteric paralysis; suicide to escape insoluble conflicts."[29] Seen from this perspective, *Fräulein Else* resembles a case study, but it is, undeniably, a literary one.

Käte Hamburger's landmark study *Die Logik der Dichtung* (1957) (translated as *The Logic of Literature*, 1973), to which the field of narratology is significantly indebted, shows that only fictional narratives offer a window into the mental world of the characters.[30] As Monika Fludernik observes, the principal focus of narratology has been the presentation of thought in the novel, particularly in the type of narrative called the "novel of consciousness". She notes that this genre reaches a heyday in modernist writers such as Virginia Woolf, James Joyce, Marcel Proust, Franz Kafka and Hermann Broch.[31] To this list should be added the name of Arthur Schnitzler, since *Fräulein Else* could be characterized as a "novella of consciousness". It exhibits the narrative situation designated by Gérard Genette as "internal focalization", in which the point of view is restricted to a single character.[32] Taking Genette's work further, Mieke Bal writes:

> Focalization is the relationship between the "vision", the agent that sees, and that which is seen. [...] The subject of focalization, the focalizor, is the point from which the elements are viewed. That point can lie with a character (i.e., an element of the fabula), or outside it.
>
> If the focalizor coincides with the character, that character will have an advantage over the other characters. The reader watches with the character's eyes and will, in principle, be inclined to accept the vision presented by that character. [...] When focalization lies with one character which participates in the fabula as an actor, we could refer to internal focalization.[33]

Genette makes the key point that internal focalization is fully realized only in the narrative of "interior monologue",[34] and Dorrit Cohn further refines this category by distinguishing between quoted interior monologue and autonomous interior monologue, or simply autonomous monologue.

It is to the latter narrative type that *Fräulein Else* belongs. The category of the autonomous monologue has been rigorously and perceptively analyzed by Cohn, who defines it as "that singular narrative genre entirely constituted by a fictional character's thoughts."[35] Autonomous monologue exists wholly without external narration or mediation. Else's thoughts range from commentary to narration to experience to the registering of her bodily actions. On the last of these Cohn comments: "When monologists become much more enterprising they begin to sound much less convincing; forced to describe the actions they perform while they perform them, they tend to sound like gymnastics teachers vocally demonstrating an exercise."[36] "It is the statement-quality of first-person pronouns combined with present action verbs that mars the mimesis of self-address."[37] A few examples from *Fräulein Else* will convey a sense of the contrived nature of these self-narrated performative acts: "Ich bleibe wirklich stehen. Warum denn? Da stehen wir uns gegenüber"; "Da unten lehn' ich den Brief hin, an die Tür. Da muß er ihn gleich sehen. Es wird ihn doch keiner stehlen? So, da liegt er ..."; "Ich bewege die Hand, ich rege die Finger, ich strecke den Arm, ich sperre die Augen weit auf. Ich sehe, ich sehe. Da steht mein Glas [of Veronal]."[38]

Alongside the heterogeneous and at times contrived elements comprising *Fräulein Else*, which serve to underscore her mental disintegration through their seemingly discordant and random quality, the repetition of obsessive themes and phrases in the fashion of a leitmotif lends the narrative a degree of unity and cohesion. Yet her compulsive repetition of these motifs, reflecting the tendency to repeat traumatic events, also signals her mental breakdown. Examples of these are the Matador and the Filou, two male types who are of erotic interest to Else; the simile "Die Luft ist wie Champagner";[39] the phrase "Adresse bleibt Fiala", referring to the person to whom Dorsday is to deliver the money owed by Else's father;[40] and above all references to the barbiturate Veronal and to Else's own death, both of which increase as the novella progresses, conveying her growing desperation and climaxing in their conjunction with her fatal overdose of the drug. At this point the narrative dissolves into fragments and then simply ends: an innovative portrayal of death from the perspective of the dying subject.

The autonomous monologue form, focused as it is on the inner workings of the perceiving consciousness, is especially well-suited to the depiction of a narcissistic personality. Numerous facets of Else's behavior evoke associations to this syndrome. In her thoughts she characterizes herself and various parts of her body (her shoulders, legs and breasts) as beautiful. Else's self-directed eroticism reaches its height in the scene where she stands naked before a mirror, an image which has served as a symbol for narcissism ever since the mythological Narcissus gazed at his reflection in a pool of water: "Bin ich wirklich so schön wie im Spiegel? Ach, kommen Sie doch näher, schönes Fräulein. Ich will Ihre blutroten Lippen küssen. Ich will Ihre

Brüste an meine Brüste pressen. Wie schade, daß das Glas zwischen uns ist, das kalte Glas. Wie gut würden wir uns miteinander vertragen. Nicht wahr? Wir bräuchten gar niemanden andern. [...] Leb wohl, mein heißgeliebtes Spiegelbild."[41] As Cohn comments on this scene, "Here the schizoid split between ego and alter ego that always suggestively attends direct self-address is objectified and literally mirrored."[42]

Else's self-directed eroticism is strikingly similar to Freud's theoretical description of the syndrome in his 1914 paper titled "On Narcissism: An Introduction". In his definition the term denotes "the attitude of a person who treats his own body in the same way as otherwise the body of a sexual object is treated"; "Strictly speaking, [narcissistic] women love only themselves with an intensity comparable to that of the man's love for them."[43] For Freud the origin of narcissism is the transferral of libido from the external world to the ego, resulting when the individual has taken as the love object not their mother but their own selves. In employing autonomous monologue, the writer Schnitzler again gives appropriate narrative form to ideas that resemble those of the psychologist Freud.

An observation of Fludernik's is useful in further exploring the suitability of Schnitzler's narrative style in *Else* to the writing of Else's trauma: "A psychologically unstable first-person narrator may undermine the normal continuum we automatically assume to exist between narrating and experiencing selves."[44] This insight is linked to a key concept in narrative theory, that of the unreliable narrator, first elaborated by Wayne Booth in *The Rhetoric of Fiction*. His observation about the unreliable narrator of "inside views" is particularly relevant to *Else*: "All authors of stream-of-consciousness narration presumably attempt to go deep psychologically, but some of them deliberately remain shallow in the moral dimension. We should remind ourselves that any sustained inside view, of whatever depth, temporarily turns the character whose mind is shown into a narrator; inside views are thus subject to variations in [...] the degree of unreliability. Generally speaking, the deeper our plunge, the more unreliability we will accept without loss of sympathy."[45] In its association of the stream-of-consciousness technique with the device of the unreliable narrator, Booth's claim further supports the effectiveness of autonomous monologue for conveying Else's traumatic experience and her resulting mental instability and disintegration.

One of the dominant emotions recurring in Else's interior monologue is her feeling of being exploited or for sale. Imagining herself as a character in a novel, she ruminates: "Die edle Tochter verkauft sich für den geliebten Vater."[46] The theme of the daughter's exploitation by the father is the key link between *Else* and *Dora*. The main difference between the two is that Else's literary traumatic experience is articulated as it happens. This phenomenon is rare, since trauma is usually not registered and certainly not written at the moment it occurs. The autonomous monologue form facilitates the immediate recounting of traumatic experience. By contrast, in *Dora* we are presented with the mediation of Dora's traumatic victimization in the past by the voice of patriarchal authority. We will explore the extent to which Freud is omniscient about this case. How much does he know or think he knows? My claim that *Dora* can be read as the symbolic psychoanalytic theorization of *Else* is elucidated by an insight of Caruth's: "[It] is indeed at the specific point at which knowing and not knowing intersect that the language of literature and the psychoanalytic theory of traumatic experience precisely meet."[47]

A brief summary of *Dora* is in order. Compelled by her father, the eighteen-year-old "Dora" entered into therapy with Freud in 1900. Freud was already acquainted with Dora, her father and other members of her family because of previous ailments of theirs that he had been called in to treat. Dora had experienced afflictions similar to many of Freud's earlier hysterical patients, such as difficulty breathing, loss of voice, chronic coughing, migraines and symptoms resembling appendicitis. Not long before she undertook treatment, her parents found a suicide note written by her. By the time Dora began therapy, she had become depressed and dissatisfied with her family, especially her father.

In the course of his sessions with Dora, Freud gradually learned the sordid tale behind her physical ailments: when Dora was a child her parents had become friends with a couple at a health resort, to whom Freud refers in his case study as Herr and Frau K. Both Dora's parents and the K.s are unhappily married, and eventually an affair develops between Frau K. and Dora's father. Meanwhile Herr K. takes a growing interest in Dora. For him to be occupied with her is convenient for her father and Frau K., since it facilitates their liaison. At the same time Dora becomes friendly with Frau K., who imparts to her what might be called sex education. Things take a decisive turn when Herr K. kisses the fourteen-year-old Dora, which she says disgusted her; two years later, during a walk by a lake, he propositions her, whereupon she slaps him. Dora's resentment of her father grows in proportion to her awareness that she is a sexual pawn in this foursome (Dora's mother, whom Freud famously describes as suffering from "housewife's psychosis",[48] is largely left out of the picture); in Freud's formulation, Dora felt that she had been "handed over to Herr K. as the price of his tolerating the relations between her father and his wife" (D 50).

The similarity to Else, also used as a sexual pawn for the benefit of her parents, is clear. But in contrast to Else, who, as it were, "writes" her own trauma through her unmediated, autonomous monologue,

Dora's traumatic experience is filtered through Freud's perceptions and "written about" by him, to invoke LaCapra's distinction again. The case study thus leaves it up to the reader to determine the "truth" of the narrative. In Freud's view, Dora is hysterical either because she is disgusted by Herr K.'s overtures or because she feels shame at being aroused by his advances and at being stimulated by her sexual discussions with Frau K. Two years before Dora began therapy with Freud, he had characterized her as "unmistakably neurotic" (D 34). He concludes that Dora is at least to some degree in love with Frau K. and that she sexually desires both her father and Herr K.

Yet the attentive reader, reading between the lines, recognizes that Dora is, in fact, traumatically victimized and exploited by all these characters: her father, so that he can pursue his affair with Frau K.; her mother, who tolerates this; Frau K., who sexualizes her; Herr K., who makes advances to her as a teenage girl; and Freud, her analyst, who interprets her story through the lens of the patriarchal sexual repression of turn-of-the century Austria.[49] Just as Dora is "handed over" to Herr K. in return for his tolerance of the relationship between his wife and Dora's father, Dora is "handed over" to Freud for psychotherapeutic treatment (D 34). The text contains several other parallels between Freud and Dora's father, the two most authoritarian figures in her life. This is decidedly not a milieu in which two fathers are better than one. Dora's case represents such a classic example of paternal and psychotherapeutic abuse that Robin Lakoff and James Coyne use it as a means of illuminating non-egalitarian practices between patient and therapist in present-day psychotherapy: "We suggest [...] that a non-egalitarian power dynamic is unavoidable if therapeutic change is to occur; but that, as a result of its existence, abuse of the less by the more powerful member of the dyad becomes (as illustrated by Freud's treatment of Dora) an omnipresent threat, to be guarded against zealously by both participants (but with the therapist, as the more powerful member, bearing the major responsibility)."[50]

Freud recounts the history of Dora's case in the first-person imperfect, primarily in indirect discourse, a narrative mode which reinforces the authority of the speaking voice. Dora's voice is rarely heard; for the most part he speaks for her rather than quoting her directly. Just as she lacks power in her life, she lacks power over its narration. To strengthen his authority, Freud often invokes scientific data or generalizations which reinforce his claims. Even when he employs direct discourse and quotes Dora's dialogue, he succeeds in burying her views beneath his own. For example, in the first dream Dora recounts to Freud, which she relates in the first person, a jewel-case appears. Continuing in first-person direct discourse, Freud interprets this detail as a symbol for the female genitals and deduces that Dora felt sexually threatened by Herr

K., since he had given her a jewel-case as a gift not long before she had the dream. Freud's interpretation is typical of his views throughout the case history: "The dream confirms once more what I had already told you before you dreamed it—that you are summoning up your old love for your father in order to protect yourself against your love for Herr K. But what do all these efforts show? Not only that you are afraid of Herr K., but that you are still more afraid of yourself, and of the temptation you feel to yield to him. In short, these efforts prove once more how deeply you loved him" (D 88). He goes on to remark, "Naturally Dora would not follow me in this part of the interpretation" (D 88). Such manipulations of Dora's case history render Freud an unreliable narrator, as does the fact that he writes this case study from memory after Dora ends the therapy.

As we have seen, in the autonomous monologue form of *Else*, we find no such narrator but only Else's voice, shaping the entire narrative. Since this voice is largely internal, however, it is ultimately as ineffective as Dora's. Without acknowledging the kind of sexual exploitation that both these figures experience, Freud's account, written from a perspective external to Dora, can be seen to theorize the hidden trauma experienced by the literary figure Else, by the psychotherapeutic patient Dora, and by countless women like them at the turn of the century.

Bibliography

Bal, Mieke. *Narratology: Introduction to the Theory of Narrative*. 3rd ed. 1985. Toronto: University of Toronto Press, 2009.
Booth, Wayne C. *The Rhetoric of Fiction*. Chicago: University of Chicago Press, 1961.
Caruth, Cathy. *Unclaimed Experience: Trauma, Narrative, and History*. Baltimore: Johns Hopkins University Press, 1996.
Chatman, Seymour. *Story and Discourse: Narrative Structure in Fiction and Film*. Ithaca, NY: Cornell University Press, 1978.
Cohn, Dorrit. *Transparent Minds: Narrative Modes for Presenting Consciousness in Fiction*. Princeton, NJ: Princeton University Press, 1978.
Decker, Hannah S. *Freud, Dora, and Vienna 1900*. New York: Free Press, 1991.
Finney, Gail. *Women in Modern Drama: Freud, Feminism, and European Theater at the Turn of the Century*. Ithaca, NY: Cornell University Press, 1991.
Fludernik, Monika. *An Introduction to Narratology*. Translated by Patricia Häusler-Greenfield and Monika Fludernik. London: Routledge, 2009.
Freud, Sigmund. *Beyond the Pleasure Principle*. 1920. Translated and edited by James Strachey. New York: Norton, 1961.
Furst, Lilian R. "Girls for Sale: Freud's Dora and Schnitzler's Else". *Modern Austrian Literature* 36, no. 3/4 (2003): 19–37.
Genette, Gérard. *Narrative Discourse: An Essay in Method*. 1972. Translated by Jane E. Lewin. Ithaca, NY: Cornell University Press, 1980.
Hamburger, Käte. *The Logic of Literature*. 2nd ed. 1957. Translated by Marilynn J. Rose. Bloomington, IN: Indiana University Press, 1973.

Kaplan, Ann E. *Trauma Culture: The Politics of Terror and Loss in Media and Literature.* New Brunswick, NJ: Rutgers University Press, 2005.
LaCapra, Dominick. *Writing History, Writing Trauma.* Baltimore: Johns Hopkins University Press, 2001.
Lakoff, Robin Tolmach and James C. Coyne. *Father Knows Best: The Use and Abuse of Power in Freud's Case of Dora.* New York: Teachers College Press, 1993.
Leys, Ruth. *Trauma: A Genealogy.* Chicago: University of Chicago Press, 2000.
Marcus, Steven. "Freud and Dora: Story, History, Case History". 1975. In: *In Dora's Case: Freud—Hysteria—Feminism*, edited by Charles Bernheimer and Claire Kahane, 56–91. New York: Columbia University Press, 1985.
Nehring, Wolfgang. "Schnitzler, Freud's Alter Ego?". *Modern Austrian Literature* 10, no. 3/4 (1977): 179–94.
O'Neill, Patrick. *Fictions of Discourse: Reading Narrative Theory.* Toronto: University of Toronto Press, 1994.
Schnitzler, Arthur. *Fräulein Else.* In *Casanovas Heimfahrt: Erzählungen,* 245–99. Frankfurt am Main: Fischer, 1979.
—*Fräulein Else.* In *Desire and Delusion: Three Novellas,* translated by Margret Schaefer. Chicago: Dee, 2003.
Schnitzler, Henry, ed. "Briefe an Arthur Schnitzler". *Die Neue Rundschau* 66 (1955): 95–106.
—*Dora: Fragment of an Analysis of a Case of Hysteria.* 1905. Edited by Philip Rieff. New York: Collier, 1963.
—*Letters of Sigmund Freud.* Edited by Ernst L. Freud. Translated by Tania and James Stern. New York: Basic Books, 1960.
—*Moses and Monotheism.* 1939. Translated by Katherine Jones. New York: Vintage, 1967.
—"On Narcissism: An Introduction". 1914. Translated by Cecil M. Baines. In *General Psychological Theory*, edited by Philip Rieff, 56–82. New York: Collier, 1963.
—"On the Psychical Mechanism of Hysterical Phenomena: Preliminary Communication". 1893. Vol. 2 of *The Standard Edition of the Complete Psychological Works of Sigmund Freud*, translated and edited by James Strachey, 1–17. London: Hogarth, 1955.
Weiss, Robert O. "The Psychoses in the Works of Arthur Schnitzler". *The German Quarterly* 41 (May 1968): 377–400.

Notes

1. These works will henceforth be designated as *Dora* and *Else*, respectively.
2. I describe Freud's reading as symbolic because he is obviously not dealing specifically with *Else*, which appeared nineteen years after *Dora*.
3. These two texts have been discussed comparatively by Furst. Her focus, however, is on thematic parallels between the two works and on biographical and medical similarities and differences between Freud and Schnitzler rather than on narratological perspectives or the treatment of traumatic experience as such.
4. LaCapra, *Writing History*, 183.
5. LaCapra, *Writing History*, 185.
6. LaCapra, *Writing History*, 186.
7. Several critics have pointed out *Dora's* novelistic characteristics. For a detailed reading of this kind see Marcus.

8 Freud, "Briefe an Arthur Schnitzler", 96–7; English translation in *Letters of Sigmund Freud*, 339.
9 See Finney, *Women in Modern Drama*, 25–9, and Nehring, "Schnitzler, Freud's Alter Ego?".
10 Leys, *Trauma*, 19.
11 Caruth, *Unclaimed Experience*, 4.
12 LaCapra, *Writing History*, 42.
13 Kaplan, *Trauma Culture*, 24.
14 Freud and Breuer, "On the Psychical Mechanism of Hysterical Phenomena", 7; in italics in original.
15 See Leys, *Trauma*, 20.
16 Freud, *Beyond the Pleasure Principle*, 6.
17 Freud, *Beyond the Pleasure Principle*, 7.
18 For details on Freud's term "compulsion to repeat", see Freud, *Beyond the Pleasure Principle*, 12–17.
19 Caruth, *Unclaimed Experience*, 2.
20 Freud, *Beyond the Pleasure Principle*, 8.
21 Kaplan, *Trauma Culture*, 31.
22 Freud, *Moses and Monotheism*, 64–5.
23 Freud, *Moses and Monotheism*, 90. Freud indicates that the title of this section represents an analogy "to the remarkable process which we have recognized in the history of Jewish religion."
24 Leys, *Trauma*, 34.
25 O'Neill, *Fictions of Discourse*, 13.
26 O'Neill, *Fictions of Discourse*, 13.
27 See Chatman, *Story and Discourse*, 43–262.
28 Weiss, "The Psychoses", 379.
29 Weiss, "The Psychoses", 397.
30 See Hamburger, *Die Logik der Dichtung*, 55–231.
31 Fludernik, *An Introduction to Narratology*, 79.
32 Genette, *Narrative Discourse*, 189–90.
33 Bal, *Narratology*, 149–50, 152.
34 Genette, *Narrative Discourse*, 193.
35 Cohn, *Transparent Minds*, 218.
36 Cohn, *Transparent Minds*, 222.
37 Cohn, *Transparent Minds*, 236.
38 Schnitzler, *Fräulein Else*, 266, 286, 296 (hereafter cited as *Else* followed by page numbers). "I'm actually staying here. Why? Here we are standing face to face"; "I'll leave the letter leaning against the door here. That way he can't help but see it right away. Nobody will steal it, will they? So there it is ..." [suspension points in original]; "I'm moving my hand, I'm moving my fingers, I'm stretching out my arm, I'm opening my eyes wide. I can see, I can see! There's my glass" (Schnitzler, *Fräulein Else*, transl. by Margret Schaefer, 220, 245, 260). English translation hereafter cited as Schaefer followed by page numbers.
39 *Else*, 247, 253, 254, 256–7, 260 [twice], 268, 272. "The air is like champagne" (Schaefer, 196, 203, 204, 207, 212 [twice], 222–3, 227).
40 *Else*, 280 [twice], 281 [three times], 282, 283, 284, 285, 287, 288, 292, 298. "Address remains Fiala" (Schaefer, 237, 238 [three times], 239, 241, 242, 243, 245, 247, 252, 262).

41 *Else*, 284, 286. "Am I really as beautiful as I look in the mirror? Oh, won't you please come closer, beautiful Fräulein? I want to kiss your blood-red lips. I want to press your breasts against mine. Too bad there's this glass between us, this cold glass. We'd get along so well together, don't you think? We wouldn't need anyone else. [...] So long, dearly beloved image in the mirror" (Schaefer, 242, 244).
42 Cohn, *Transparent Minds*, 246.
43 Freud, "On Narcissism", 56, 70.
44 Fludernik, *An Introduction to Narratology*, 86–7.
45 Booth, *The Rhetoric of Fiction*, 163–4.
46 *Else*, 254. "The noble daughter sells herself for her beloved father" (Schaefer, 203).
47 Caruth, *Unclaimed Experience*, 3.
48 Freud, *Dora*, 34 (hereafter cited in text as D, followed by page numbers).
49 See Decker, esp. 14–40, for an in-depth study of *Dora* within the sociohistorical context of turn-of-the-century Vienna.
50 Lakoff and Coyne, *Father Knows Best*, 2.

7. "Das kleine Ich": Robert Menasse and Masculinity in Real Time*

Heidi Schlipphacke

> "*Genau dasselbe Leben noch einmal, nur anders*"
> —Fernando Pessoa

The Austrian author and essayist Robert Menasse has famously called Austria a "Land ohne Eigenschaften"[1] echoing and complicating Robert Musil's seminal novel *Der Mann ohne Eigenschaften*. Whereas Musil had explored the limits of the self and the fragility of masculinity in his interwar novel, the contemporary Jewish-Austrian author Menasse moves from "Mann" to "Land", masculine subject to nation, underscoring the fraught parallels between these two ideology-laden constructs. Menasse, one of the leading literary and critical voices of his generation, offers a differentiated perspective on Austria that follows from those of his "anti-Heimat" predecessors, such as Thomas Bernhard and Elfriede Jelinek; however, Menasse's critique of Austria is less explicitly fixated on the Nazi past. Menasse sees Austria as anomalous within a globalizing Western landscape not only due to the involvement of many of its citizens in Nazi crimes during World War II, but also due to its unique lack of "qualities". As a nation, according to Menasse, Austria resembles Musil's hyper-modern Ulrich in its postmodern ability to shift positions in what Menasse refers to as a method of transvestism. Here we see Menasse elegantly linking a critique of nation with a nuanced exploration of contemporary masculinity.

In an essay entitled "Die Verösterreicherung der Welt" (The Austrianization of the World), Menasse articulates what he sees as an Austrian national identity that, in its consistent ability to remake itself on the surface without effecting any real change, engages in a mode of transvestism that enables the nation to adapt seamlessly to global changes:

> Never in history has the population of a country had to change its identity so often in such a short period of time as the Austrians: from the monarchy to the First Republic, from the First Republic to the Austro-fascist class society (*Ständesstaat*), from the class society to National Socialism, from National Socialism to the Second Republic—within only a single generation. And from this the desire for the acquisition of a real identity did not result, but rather the desire for the acquisition of a final transvestism: the Social Partnership in which each individual takes on the appearance of his social opposite, in order to anticipate in this guise yet another change and, hence, definitively to block it.[2]

For Menasse, the metaphor of transvestism embodies the mechanisms of borrowing, appropriation and harmonizing that characterize the various "clothing changes" of Austrian political identity in the twentieth century. Here we have a metaphor of gender bending that is not radical hyperperformance along the lines famously laid out by Judith Butler.[3] We do *not* have the celebrated drag performance that reveals the unnaturalness and performativity at the root of all gendered identities. Rather, Menasse's notion of transvestism is much more banal, calling forth the cross-dressing straight man who enjoys wearing women's underwear under his everyday trousers. Menasse's musings on Austrian identity are, in this sense, both mundane and startling, calling into question the future of gender in a postmodern world as he playfully dissects the hallowed relationship between the male body and the national body.

In his essay linking Austria's literary history to its political history, "Die Ohnmacht des Machers im Literaturbetrieb: Zu Tod und Werk von Gerhard Fritsch" (The Impotence of the Maker in the Literary Business: On the Death and Work of Gerhard Fritsch), Menasse uses the metaphor of transvestism to analyze the literary works and publishing history of Gerhard Fritsch, who committed suicide in 1969 at the age of 45. For Menasse, "this Austrian transvestism is redemption and salvation without heroes."[4] The constant borrowing and appropriation (selective cross-dressing) that characterize the *Sozialpartnerschaft* policies of Austria's Second Republic have produced a mode of redemption but no heroes. This is a particularly interesting facet of Menasse's reading of Austrian history. The heroes are not, as the psychotherapist Horst-Eberhard Richter has argued about contemporary German masculinity, "clueless" (*ratlos*). For Richter, German men are given the impossible task of serving as replacements for their fathers who either fell in the war or were tarnished by the guilt of the Nazi past.[5] Richter's understanding of contemporary German masculinity reflects a yearning for redemption and for a healing of the "clueless" heroes of today. In contrast, Menasse's model for Austria demotes redemption to a pragmatic exercise, foreclosing the possibility of heroes in this post-dialectical nation.

In this essay, I will explore Menasse's notion of transvestism as metaphor and its repercussions for national and gendered identities. Reading through and across his interlinked essays and prose works, I will focus in particular on Menasse's most recent prose writings, the novel *Don Juan de la Mancha, oder die Erziehung der Lust* (2007) and the short story collection *Ich kann jeder sagen: Erzählungen vom Ende der Nachkriegsordnung* (2009).[6] These works are not only mercilessly focused on drifting male figures in the midst of crises that are not fully realized, but they are also written from the perspective of a narrative "I" that seems to present one and the same figure (who resembles the author quite closely) from subtly shifting perspectives. In this sense, Menasse's newest prose works reflect both on contemporary masculinity and on the identity of the "I" as transvestite, as an entity that embodies elements of the other without fully performing otherness. A fitting image of this kind of identity is pictured in the play with coffee mugs in *Don Juan de la Mancha*. Nathan, a young college student, moves into a stale basement apartment (though the details prove later to be fabrications of the narrator for the benefit of his psychoanalyst) in which two coffee mugs have been left by the previous tenant: one says "Du" and the other "Ich". The constant play with these mugs (various figures in Nathan's life drink from both mugs) underscores the irrelevance of this dialectic for the narrator of the novel: sometimes Nathan is "Ich", sometimes "Du". When a fortune teller reads Nathan's astrological fortune as a "Grenzfall" (borderline case) between shifting astrological constellations, Nathan interprets this in terms of the "Ich" and "Du" mugs: "I was the border. The borderline case. I will be, according to Piroska, regardless of what I do, simultaneously the other. The one with the 'Du' mug, so to speak, who, while he says I, looks at another, who has the 'I' mug."[7] This experience of identity is not the modernist encounter with the Other; rather, it enables the self both to look at a distorted version of itself from the outside and to crossdress as an other in a manner that undermines simple dichotomies. In this sense, Menasse depicts an Austria that has retreated from a dialectical mode of history, and literary figures such as Nathan experience a crisis of masculinity that is not only postmodern, but also post-dialectical.

The Social Partnership: Either-and-Or

Menasse's novels and short stories focus on Jewish-Austrian male characters who experience their own "Ich" as an unheroic alienation from the self. These figures (with names like Leo, Roman and Nathan) resemble Austrian-Jewish variations on Philip Roth's American anti-heroes. Like Roth's "Zuckerman" novels, which feature the self-hating and self-aggrandizing Nathan Zuckerman, Menasse's prose narratives feature male figures that are at once narcissistic and paralyzed by self-doubt. Whereas Roth's figures revel in their abjection, Menasse's anti-heroes tend to drink out of the "Du" mug that disallows any exaggerated notion of self, even in humiliation. Menasse's central characters embody a self-conscious mode of masculinity that structurally mirrors the appropriative practices of the Austrian *Sozialpartnerschaft* in the early years of the Second Republic. Through claiming the characteristics and policies of one another as their own, the Austrian *Volkspartei* and the Social Democratic Party worked together to create a stagnating harmony in the Second Republic. What Steven Beller calls the "Austrian Way" is emblematized in the secret dealings between these two parties, who did not much like one another but who wanted to exclude the Communists from power. Hence the parties engaged in a mode of co-operation based on the concept of *Proporz*, "proportionality reflecting party strength."[8] Each minister was balanced by an undersecretary of the other party so that coalitions were formed on a micro- as well as on a macro-scale. This mode of partnership was then mirrored in the relationship between capital and labor in the Second Republic. Agriculture and business were allied with the Austrian *Volkspartei* while labor was allied with the Social Democratic Party. These bodies then co-operated behind closed doors along the lines laid out by the two parties. As Beller points out,

> this co-operative corporatist approach ensured a remarkable level of industrial peace, and was a major boost to prosperity. The "social partnership" of capital and labour formed a parallel economic complement to the political Grand Coalition that made parliamentary politics, at most, secondary. The Second Republic resembled more a corporation, Austria Inc., than a parliamentary democracy.[9]

The relationship between traditionally oppositional groups is stabilized through what might be seen as political and economic cross-dressing, that is, the borrowing of certain qualities from the other in order to pre-empt opposition and create harmony. This is the sense in which Menasse points to a "Verösterreicherung der Welt": a world system in which co-operation between historically situated opposites produces a harmony that we might see exemplified in the multinational corporation.¹⁰

As Guillaume van Gemert writes in his analysis of Menasse's essay collection *Überbau und Underground: Die sozialpartnerschaftliche Ästhetik. Essays zum österreichischen Geist* (1997), "The Austria of the Social Partnership, and also its literature, withdraws from—one could summarize Menasse's essay this way not lastly also with relation to the ironizing closing point—the dialectic."¹¹ Here, Menasse describes a structure not of "either/or" but of "either and or" (*Entweder-und-Oder*):

> The signs are increasing. Vienna, the capital city of the Social Partnership, was chosen as the seat of the international Institute for Conflict Avoidance, as the center of a Social Partnership of an international layout, as the location for the plan for an either-and-or system of former world powers. Austria is, of course, already a former world power. Not the demise of the real world, as the Greens are murmuring, but rather the demise of the world of realities is the future of the world.¹²

The *Sozialpartnerschaft* model for social and cultural structures creates, according to Menasse, the field of possibility "either-and-or" that resembles Ulrich Beck's "both/and" understanding of the globalizing world system.¹³ Oppositional structures are situated in a manner so as to undermine a traditional dialectic. Menasse lays out the parallels between the politics of *Sozialpartnerschaft* and Austrian literary production. In his essay on Gerhard Fritsch, he points to Fritsch's role in 1960s Austrian literary culture as a harmonizer of all contradictions ("die Harmonisierung aller Widersprüche").¹⁴ Fritsch's novel *Moos auf den Steinen* (1956) reflects this harmonizing tendency since

> [...] the polarities that thus arise never become productive contradictions that could then make possible a dialectical synthesis. Rather, the polarities and contradictions into which Fritsch's novel collapse are aligned in such as way that they simply mutually annihilate one another and in this way render irrelevant the parts as well as the whole.¹⁵

Here, Menasse is not simply describing a "universeller Verblendungszusammenhang" or a kind of arrested dialectic.¹⁶ To my mind, what makes Menasse's "either-and-or" model of thought particularly provocative are the ways in which binary categories, including gender, might be thought beyond the performative politics of Judith Butler.¹⁷

"Das kleine Ich"

Within Menasse's prose works, masculine identity is represented in a non-dialectical manner that reflects the "either-and-or" world of the *Sozialpartnerschaft* system, as a masculine crisis that does not produce postmodern performance but rather, awkward scenes of transvestism. *Don Juan de la Mancha* ends with a scene of cross-dressing, in which Nathan is dressed as a woman by his lover, Christa, while she plays the masculine role with a horseradish root. Though we might speak of "drag" here, Menasse's notion of transvestism is probably more useful. It is clear that Nathan is not engaging in a "hyperperformance" of femininity; he is, rather, appropriating elements of femininity while retaining characteristics associated with traditional masculinity. In this sense, this scene of intimacy cannot be read as an undoing of gender, just as it does not signify the deconstruction of naturalness that Butler's drag performances should embody. In the age of the virtual, that is, a world in which much is similar and nothing is the same, the relation between gender and nature is almost beside the point.

The national body's retreat from a dialectical understanding of history, then, is revealed symptomatically and in the same time span in the body of the "average" Austrian male as simultaneously sexual prowess, impotence, boredom, self-hatred and exaggerated self-love. As the difference between "Ich" and "Du" becomes distorted, a subjective perspective becomes both a kind of limiting prison and an impossibility. Here, we might say, is the post-dialectical crisis of masculinity: the loss of a stable subject position vis-à-vis stable objects and the loss of a philosophical worldview that serves as the proof of (male) subjectivity and genius. Peter Bürger has summarized the essence of Menasse's *Trilogie der Entgeisterung* project along these lines. What I am calling the post-dialectical/postmodern crisis of masculinity could be reformulated as the crisis of the death of the philosopher. Bürger imagines a dialogue between a modernist and Menasse, whom he characterizes as an author writing the tale of modernism from a postmodern perspective. In response to the accusation from the "modernes Ich" that postmodernism is of necessity based on historical processes, the postmodern author (Menasse) in Bürger's aphorism responds:

> I don't deny that at all, answers the postmodern author, but I do believe I have recognized that nothing else stands behind the great words of theory (situation, prehistory, composition of the future) than the small I with his boundless desire for recognition, whereby the point lies in this: that the small I disdains those from whom it wants recognition.[18]

As Bürger suggests, Menasse's prose works tell the narrative of the "kleines Ich" with his limitless desire for recognition, a desire that can never be realized. The awareness of his reduction to a small "I" is unbearable to the modern male self, a self mercilessly ironized in many of Menasse's most recent prose works.

Menasse's central novel in the *Trilogie der Entgeisterung* is *Selige Zeiten, brüchige Welt* (Blessed Times, Fragmented World, 1991),[19] a narrative of just such a small "I", Leo Singer, who spends the novel trying to write his masterpiece, a reconceptualization of Hegel's *Phänomenologie des Geistes* as degeneration. Yet this work of "genius" is ultimately only produced by Judith, Leo's former lover, who has recorded Leo's rambling ideas on paper in the attempt to produce her own monograph. In a drugged state, Judith unwittingly includes Leo's ideas in her writings on *Tristram Shandy*, ideas that Leo has repeatedly espoused in the "Bar jeder Hoffnung" ("Bar of every hope" or "Without any hope") in Sao Paolo, Brazil, where he and Judith meet with other Austrian expatriates (both Jews and Nazis). The work of "genius", published after Leo murders Judith and erases all signs of her own writing, ends with the following sentence: "'In the beginning is the copy.' That's how I see it."[20] Leo Singer's reformulation of Hegel's dialectic as regression for contemporary times necessitates that, in the end, the author will have arrived at the point of "sinnliche Gewissheit" (sensual certainty), the first stage in Hegel's *Phänomelogie des Geistes*. *Sinnliche Gewissheit* is also the title of the first novel in Menasse's trilogy. The author enters the pre-dialectical state of the "kleines Ich": radical perspectivism without a stable Other.[21]

That this small "I" is male is clear to Bürger, who likens this figure to Don Quixote,

> [...] who, with the knight's armor of a great philosophical theory, embarks on the misadventure of thought in order to create the work that changes the world; who can arrange nothing else in life other than a seduction that should keep him from his work; who therefore sees in woman the windmill of life that he must conquer in order to be able to work.[22]

Woman stands in as the phantom seducer and "windmill" that must be overcome and, simultaneously, as the impetus for production. But while Menasse refers to Don Quixote in the title of his most recent novel, *Don Juan de la Mancha*, his most recent figures are much too conscious of their own limitations to aspire to philosophical genius. *Don Juan de la Mancha*'s Nathan is keenly aware of the clichéd nature of "Männerphantasien" and is unable to assign subject and object positions in his post-dialectical world: "Male fantasies? My fantasy was arrested back then and who objectifies whom—oh, what's the point of this discussion? It wasn't there anymore. Object? Everything became so subjective."[23]

Not only Menasse, but also his most recent literary figures, are keenly aware of the limited subjective nature of their positions. The shift to a narrative "I" ("das kleine Ich") in his most recent prose works reflects this awareness.[24] Menasse is deeply concerned with the pitfalls of the "I", what he calls "das hypertrophierte Ich"[25]:

> The names that the "I"s call themselves should result in a history whose kernel is the retrospective to a time in which names still meant something. But this history never comes to be, since every "I" that—somehow insisting, hoping, feeling—gives itself over remains in the no-man's-land between exclusivity and generic value.[26]

The no-man's-land between exclusivity and generality is the space in which the small "I" stumbles in a post-dialectical world. As the narrator in *Don Juan de la Mancha* remarks, it is a "Kleinbürgersyndrom" to think "that everything is somehow exemplary—what one is and how one is and why one is so."[27] Menasse's recent focus on a narrative "I" dovetails with the intertextual and almost autobiographical nature of these recent works. Born in 1954 to Jewish-Austrian parents in Vienna, entering the student movements of the late 1960s a little too late, Menasse himself embodies a kind of "Grenzfall". Menasse's narrators are likewise often born around 1954 (usually in 1955, perhaps due to its historical importance as the year of the signing of Austria's *Staatsvertrag*) to Jewish parents, often stemming from the petit bourgeois class, often engaged in some alienated manner with the student movement, etc. In this way, a kind of virtual repetition with minor changes is performed. The narratives in his recent prose works are often called up again in essays, and vice versa,[28] so that a web of interweaving narratives is created with the small "I" located somewhere in the vicinity of the center. The epigraph at the end of *Don Juan de la Mancha* is a citation from the Portuguese poet and critic Fernando Pessoa, "Genau dasselbe Leben noch einmal, nur anders."[29]

And this is, indeed, what Menasse gives us in his most recent prose works: shifting versions of the narrative of the "kleines Ich". In the short story "Die blauen Bände", the narrative "I", the owner of an academic bookstore, considers getting rid of all autobiographies in his store after being unable to recall clearly the face of a petty criminal whom he observed committing a crime: "definition of autobiography: dialectical lie of life."[30] The narrator of "Romantische Irrtümer", a similarly pensive and bookish man who travels to Germany for business, likewise calls into question the problem of narrative, the inability of one small "I" to tell, in essence, more than one story:

> It was on the return trip from Dresden that it suddenly became clear to me that the abundance that I distributed through storytelling was a lie. That I had actually always told the same paltry story. Only the "plot" was different each time, the so-called experiences, and in this way it became clear how arbitrary that which was experienced, life, was.[31]

Later, he likewise mourns the fact that his stories are "always a variation of the same story", the attempt to give meaning to "a disfigured life" through "phantom pains".[32] Here, the narrator refers not only to his own crippled life as the son of a Jew who lived in England during the war but also to the false pregnancy of the narrator's girlfriend in another story, "Die amerikanische Brille", a narrative that ends with the "phantom pains" of the narrative "I" himself, as he suffers from stomach aches that he interprets as "the constricted desire. For a child. That I used to be."[33] To become an adult "I" is to return to childhood, to retell the story of one's life in a slightly altered fashion.[34]

The Longing for Normality

Menasse's figures are self-conscious small "I"s, aware of their corporeality and alienated even from their own desire. These figures are, in a word, average, and they strive to be nothing less or more than average and "normal". These characters are neither complete failures nor geniuses; they obsess about the quotidian, about eating and their bodies. In "Romantische Irrtümer" the narrative "I" eats out of boredom and feels self-loathing as a result. But the act of eating is "the attempt to give meaning to meaninglessness",[35] and it creates the context of normality: "The human must eat. One torments oneself, but while one eats one at least torments oneself in the appearance of normality."[36] Yet to admit to the "normal" desire to eat (in order to create the sense of normality) is not traditionally masculine, and the narrative "I" in "Romantische Irrtümer" tells of his compulsive eating in the German hotel:

> Then I went to my room and looked at the bombardment of Dresden. I ate nuts while doing this because I simply can't resist it when I find some in the minibar of a hotel room. I hated myself. It was completely irrational. I had just eaten dinner, wasn't hungry, and still shoved in these nuts that senselessly ravage my body.[37]

The narrator's description of his self-hatred for his banal lack of self-control constitutes yet another moment of cross-dressing in Menasse's work. The masculine narrator admits to a quotidian hatred for his own body in a manner normally only articulated by female writers in what is considered to be "trivial" literature.

The narrative "I" in *Don Juan de la Mancha* describes himself similarly in terms of his "Mittelmäßigkeit" (averageness), and he is aware of his longing for normality when his mistress calls him after a period of silence: "Finally normal relations again. I have such a desire for normality."[38] Menasse's little "I"s long for averageness and mourn their limitations at the same time. In the story "Anekdoten mit Toten", the narrator visits the grave of his father's English foster parents who had cared for him during the Nazi regime in Austria. In this graveyard he sees a stone with his own name on it:

> I remembered a life that was so grand... and so average that I didn't know why the tears came to me now. Maybe exactly for this reason. A life that—I suddenly had to laugh—was so grotesque in its eternally and diligently hidden banality, that—and now I had to cry.[39]

Menasse's figures both long for and fear normality, and they more likely inspire laughter in the reader than tears or disgust. The story that follows upon the narrator's visit to the grave of his namesake is called "Schluss machen" (Coming to a Close), an impossible task in a non-dialectical world, as Menasse makes clear. Here the first sentence reads: "He had a face that straightaway said nothing"[40]: normality as a sad fact and a goal, as a kind of prison and a refuge.[41]

The fixation with normality and averageness on the part of Menasse's narrators poses an interesting contrast to the historical question of "normalization". In post-fascist Germany discourses surrounding "normalization" have circulated widely. The notion of a "normal" Germany, one no longer defined by its abnormal past, is simultaneously desirable and unnerving to Germans. The goal of being normal, just like the others despite the infamous Nazi history, cuts across the contemporary German political spectrum. When asked by Serge Schmemann of the *New York Times* after the fall of the Berlin Wall about his goals for Germany, Chancellor Helmut Kohl expressed the desire that "things will normalize. That's the most important thing for us, that we become a wholly normal country, not 'singularized' in any question [...] that we simply don't stick out. That's the important thing."[42] The goal of normalcy is, certainly, a schizophrenic one for a nation and it reflects Germany's anomalous position amongst the European nations. As George Mosse has shown, nation and masculinity are allegorically allied in European modernity. According to Mosse, the masculine body has stood in for Western conceptions of nation since the eighteenth century. Visual representations of masculine beauty have symbolized national ideals as manifested in the neoclassical revival of the European Enlightenment and its perverse reappropriation by the Nazis in the twentieth century.[43] Within a German context, then, the masculine body is in crisis, called upon to represent a "normalcy" that would destabilize the link between the male body and fascism while ultimately undermining the power associated with the trope of masculinity.

The question of "normalization" becomes even more complex when translated onto the Austrian landscape. Despite Austria's unique modern history—the fall of the Habsburg Empire, the First Republic, Austro-fascism and the "Anschluß" (annexation) and subsequent Nazification—Austria has famously avoided the kind of international scrutiny that Germany experienced after 1945. Poised somewhere between perpetrator and victim, Austria's "normalcy" is a kind of disciplined sublimation. As Herbert Eisenach put it in 1964: "Austrian is firstly once and for all the struggle for distance. [...] Austrian is, then, the voluntary renunciation of real effectuality [...]. Austrian is further the aversion to everything grand, to everything loud, to everything powerful, to every forced change [...]."[44] This is exactly the sense in which Robert Menasse imagines Austria. As Guillaume van Gemert puts it, Austria is, for Menasse, "the embodiment of equilibrium, of the middle, of neutrality and therefore essentially like a museum. [...] Austria is for Menasse, as the birthplace of what he calls 'Austrianization' and as the lived Social Partnership, plainly a cipher for postmodern non-commitment."[45]

Whereas a hard-won stasis stands as a political and cultural goal in post-Nazi Germany, Menasse sees Austria and, in particular, Vienna, as a cultural space blindly intent on preserving a kind of stale "normalcy". Vienna is one of two world cities at the center of *Selige Zeiten, brüchige Welt* (the other being São Paolo, Brazil), and the city is represented as the space of paralysis early in the novel:

> His ideas sounded odd in a city so particularly and stolidly ignorant of any notion that things could be different from what they were, a city that seemed so set in its ways that the expression "Vienna will always be Vienna" came across as a lie only because it sounded too much like a euphemism: the verb "be" was far too dynamic.[46]

As Menasse has articulated in his essays on Austria, modern Vienna has, to his mind, not changed at all despite monumental historical events such as the fall of the Habsburg Empire, fascism, and its defeat. As the city of stasis and *Sozialpartnerschaft*, Vienna is petrified in its ahistorical historicism.

The citation from *Selige Zeiten, brüchige Welt* is reminiscent of Thomas Bernhard's tendency to compare Vienna to a graveyard. Menasse's narrator cites Bernhard's fondness for Vienna's cemeteries in the story "Anekdoten mit Toten", noting that Bernhard called Vienna "by nature a pure zombie dance."[47] In the narrative "Lange nicht gesehen", a homeless man is arrested in Vienna for pretending to be blind and encouraged to register under the category: "invalidity" (*Invalidität*). He refuses: "I know, he said, that invalidity is the most desired privilege in Austria and therefore the life goal of every Austrian."[48] Once again, Austria is the space of paralysis in which the identity of the invalid, in all senses of the word, is desirable as one in which action is not required. In "Aufklärung kommt vor dem Fall" (Enlightenment Comes Before the Fall), the narrator wins tennis games by simply avoiding action. Named "die Wand" (the Wall) he makes no points; rather, "I lived off of the mistakes of the opponents."[49]

These text passages reveal the close link between Menasse's essayistic writings on Austrian identity and his literary depictions of Austrian men. Menasse's representations of masculinity offer ironized images of a "national body", one that is weighted down by its own paralysis. *Don Juan de la Mancha, oder die Erziehung der Lust*, which appeared in 2007, is a first-person narrative about a modern day Don Juan who is relatively successful with women but not always potent. In a word, Nathan is "average", and he aspires to this averageness. Toward the end of the novel, the narrative shifts briefly to the third person as we are given an excerpt from Nathan's parodical autobiography which he has written for his psychologist:

> One has to imagine Nathan as a happy man. He was attractive, though attractive in the case of a man generally doesn't have to mean much more than that he has straight limbs, is not very overweight, doesn't have too massive hair loss yet. In his life he had not yet had any success worthy of mention, but he had also never had larger problems or pressing cares. Already this mediocrity gave him apparently the appearance of a privileged man.[50]

Here is Viennese masculinity in a nutshell, the bodily representation of a static culture, averageness *par excellence*. Nathan is aware that the masculine body, while standing in for a national body, is often not beautiful. His insecurity is also reflected in the words "apparently" (*offenbar*) and "appearance" (*Anschein*): "this mediocrity gave him apparently the appearance of a privileged man." "Normal" masculinity is represented here as an empty shell, easily approximated but signifying little.

A Modern Nathan

Citing not only Roth's Zuckerman, but also Cervantes' Don Quixote and Lessing's Nathan, the protagonist of *Don Juan de la Mancha* represents a particular post-fascist and globalizing Austrian mode of masculinity. Menasse's Nathan is certainly not a model citizen in the vein of Lessing's paradigm for tolerance and reason. He is, rather, obsessed with himself and with sex. Unlike Cervantes' Quixote, he is not driven by higher ideals. Rather, he is a successful Don Juan who, in the end, nevertheless rejects the structures of desire. He engages in Freudian psychoanalysis while still skeptical of its value. In the novel, the half-repressed recent Nazi past coexists with a globalized culture of apathy and post-national desires. Nathan writes an article about the fact that the university library has forgotten to lift the ban on books forbidden by the Nazis, an article he then neglects to publish. Representing a mode of contemporary masculinity that is simultaneously exemplary and empty, vacillating between radical particularism and generalization, Nathan borrows characteristics from all of the Nathans that precede him in a manner that only enhances his normality.

The figure of Nathan is reminiscent of the Jewish American antiheroes in Philip Roth's novels, and Menasse's Nathan even reads Roth's *Everyman* after quitting his job as a managing editor for the "Leben" section of the newspaper. Yet he is critical of Roth's "old man literature" (*Altmännerliteratur*),[51] and considers Roth's representations of masculine sexuality "lies". Indeed, Menasse's *Don Juan de la Mancha*, while clearly influenced by novels such as Roth's *Everyman*, succeeds, it seems to me, in ironizing masculinity in a manner never attempted by Roth. Like Roth's characters, Menasse's Nathan is primarily concerned with sex and his own masculinity; but Menasse's Nathan resists the nostalgia that allows for a kind of intact masculinity to be imagined. He is often nakedly vulnerable in particularly unglamorous ways. The novel ends with the cross-dressing sex scene between Nathan and his lover Christa that feminizes him in a manner that, perhaps surprisingly, does not completely undermine his post-dialectical mode of subjectivity. Here, the resilience of the *Sozialpartnerschaft* might have a productive potential for contemporary gendered identities.

In an essay on Austrian culture from the collection *Das Land ohne Eigenschaften*, (1992), Menasse puts the question of perspective at the center of his reflections on Austria's fraught relationship to history and time. Menasse uses the metaphor of the window to advocate a loosening of what he elsewhere describes as the "petrified conditions" (versteinerte[n] Verhältnisse) of contemporary Austria.[52]

> "Austrian identity"—this term is reminiscent of a dark and musty room where, if one enters for some reason, one immediately

wants to move the curtains apart and open the window to let in some air and light. But what if the window has no view and the room therefore wants to brighten only slightly?[53]

In contrast to the petrified nature of Austrian identity, Menasse calls for an "airing out", a destabilization of the Austrian "normal". Throughout his narratives, the figures look longingly to windows. In *Don Juan de la Mancha* there are indications that Nathan desires to "open the windows", both literally and allegorically. As a student, he lives in a basement apartment. Here, he is obsessed with the windows at street level. Staring at the calves of the passers-by he feels like a prisoner— "How can I get out of there?"[54] He is fixated on another student named Anne, who lives in a bourgeois apartment filled with doors that seem to open up myriad possibilities: "exit doors out of the lower classes."[55] When Nathan feels stifled by his girlfriend, he stands at the window, insisting: "I want out! I want to get away!"[56] Anne's apartment, on the other hand, via its many openings, offers escape: "So many doors. Open double-wing doors that opened the view on to suites of rooms [...]. Now I believed I loved Anne. I was crazy about her. She would open doors, suites, unlock new spaces in my life."[57]

Entrapment is perceived as a product of stasis, of the inability to open the windows of history. Yet Menasse's characters live in a space in which history is not dialectical, so that a symbolic opening of windows would probably be met with the harmonizing mechanism of the *Sozialpartnerschaft*. The impetus for writing the article about the residues of Nazi laws in Austria is coincidence and not political engagement: "Weeks earlier I had discovered by chance that the literature that had been forbidden by the Nazis still could not be borrowed, simply because after 1945 they forgot to lift this ban."[58] Inaction is perceived as a form of perpetration, yet Nathan never publishes the article. The "kleines Ich" that is Nathan mirrors the "either-and-or" of the transvestite Austrian state, embodying traditionally feminine characteristics, such as the non-activity of waiting and entrapment, in concert with traditionally masculine traits such as the ability to seduce multiple women.

Like the self-critical characters in *Ich kann jeder sagen*, Nathan is unsatisfied with his own relatively static mode of masculinity. After losing his job at the newspaper, Nathan retreats to his weekend house where he becomes obsessed with baths that mimic the maternal "amniotic fluid" (*Fruchtwasser*),[59] where absolutely nothing happens and one just needs to exist. Yet after ordering special products that are supposed to recreate the *Fruchtwasser* and spending days in the bathtub (to his wife's horror), Nathan becomes repulsed by his own solipsism and returns to Vienna.

Throughout the novel Nathan is aware of his complicity in his own static identity, comparing himself to a "centuries-old turtle, just as much handicapped as protected by a hard armor."[60] From his father, a playboy who took him on business trips where he read books while his father enjoyed himself, he learned to wait: "My father had enjoyed himself in an exemplary manner, and I had to wait so long. And so I learned to wait from him, of all people."[61] Nathan is feminized by his father in his role as passive attendant, yet he has also learned to anticipate the privilege traditionally afforded the adult male:

> I wanted the world to remain for a while just as I had gotten to know it. Only the fathers were at some point, soon, to leave. But otherwise the world was to stay as I knew it. How else should I have taken over its domination, if everything constantly became different?[62]

Nathan's understanding of masculine privilege is based on a resistance to change, a contradictory position, since no Oedipal shift is possible without change. Nathan's resistance to action is informed by the mistakes of history, by a sense that any action could result in crimes. In his job as managing editor for the "Life" section of a newspaper, Nathan makes a point of simply staying out of the way of his co-workers:

> "So I am not effective?" I said. "What I am doing here has no effect? Not the smallest?"
> Franz looked at me.
> "Wonderful! Then I am innocent!"[63]

This mode of masculinity is informed by the assumption that action is always potentially accompanied by guilt. Yet inaction is potentially emasculating. Early in the novel, Nathan marries for the first time after having known a woman for two weeks. During the wedding ceremony he panics and stakes his masculinity on being able to say "no" for once: "If I am a man, then I will now say no."[64] Instead of pulling off this rebellion, however, he rather hesitates, asking the civil servant, "Can you please repeat the question?"[65] In response to the shocked families and the anger of his bride, Nathan capitulates: "And I, in the meantime completely exhausted, said with my last ounce of energy: Yes."[66]

In *Don Juan de la Mancha* masculinity is a dance between non-action and avoidance of the perpetrator role, a dialectic that is revealed to be false: "I would then not be the asshole if I succeeded in being the victim."[67] In his conversations about sex with the feminist Alice during his university days, penetration becomes the site of oppression. But even here, Nathan attempts to walk a line between the role of the masculine oppressor and a desexualized emasculated wimp: "When one lay in bed and first engaged in the penetration debate, one could patiently wait to see if an erection developed at all. If yes, then there was always the chance of an exception. If not, then one simply remained emancipated."[68] Nathan's lover Christa even makes fun of him at some point for being the only man she has ever met "who pretends to have an orgasm."[69] In anticipation of the penultimate transvestite scene in the novel, Nathan borrows traditionally feminine characteristics without completely undermining his masculinity.

The intimate linkage between gender, sex and history is underscored when Nathan goes looking for porno films to revive his waning libido. Next to the "Sex-Tempel" he sees a poster for a discussion at the "Gedenkzentrums Knochenfabrik" (Memorial Center's Bone Factory) on the topic: "CAN ONE TEACH THE HOLOCAUST?"[70] The list of speakers includes a variety of academics and a rabbi as well as someone named "Susanne Lemberg, Survivor. The only woman on the podium was 'survivor'. In the list of names and professions the professional categorization of 'survivor' was so grotesque, so obscene, that this fear of entering overtook me at the temple."[71] Here, once again, Menasse reveals the complexity of his male narrators: Nathan is buying pornography, generally considered to be an industry that objectifies women; yet he is likewise moved to a mode of feminist criticism when he reads the list of speakers planned for the Holocaust discussion. Nathan is chauvinist pig and feminist sympathizer in one "small I".

Like most of Menasse's characters, Nathan is presumably Jewish, with a Jewish "Mamme" and an aunt in Tel Aviv, but this identity is not emphasized in the novel. Rather, this mode of alterity is seemingly subsumed under a kind of "normalizing" transvestism. In a fully feminine manner, Nathan obsesses about his body, for example his hands, which he does not like: "I have hands like a butcher."[72] It is precisely the hyper-masculine nature of his hands that repulses Nathan, and the text here offers a twist on the trope of the stereotypical, feminized Jewish body.[73] In terms of gender identity, the "either-and-or" model might open up more interesting possibilities than a hyperperformance of gender would. The traditionally feminized Jewish body is "clothed" with the hyper-masculine proletariat hands of a slaughterer, and it is precisely these hands that cause Nathan to fixate on his body in a feminine manner, reminiscent of the multiple vacillations between "Ich" and "Du" that ultimately undermine clear dichotomies.

Transvestism in Real Time

So what do we make of the literal scenes of transvestism in Manasse's texts? In his article on Menasse and Austrian identity, Jaime Feijoo highlights a number of these scenes in the novels of *Trilogie der Entgeisterung*: for example, Leo's rebirth in Venice via the necessity of wearing new clothes due to his fall into the canal in *Selige Zeiten, brüchige Welt* and, in the same novel, the suicide of Judith's lover Michael while wearing her dress. In stark contrast to the drag performer who makes sure that every aspect of the performance is perfect, Michael resembles the everyday cross-dresser, someone who appropriates certain feminine attributes while still remaining an "average" man. "Underneath Michael had a bra that he had not been able to close in the back, and one of her stockings."[74] The image of Michael in Judith's clothes, unable to fit into her bra, is neither glamorous nor campy. Feijoo also points to the scene of cross-dressing in the final novel of the trilogy, *Schubumkehr*, in which the mayor's son is murdered while dressed in the clothes of a foreign girl.[75]

Menasse links the transvestism motif not only to Austria's mode of self-presentation but also to the history of literature in the Second Republic. As he writes in his essay on Fritsch, "Transvestism is the running metaphor in the novel *Fasching*",[76] the last novel written by the author. The notion of borrowing and appropriation is threaded throughout Menasse's works, and these appropriations are not limited to clothing from the opposite sex. In *Don Juan de la Mancha*, Nathan compares men with beards to children with ape masks: "Beards are ape masks with children's faces."[77] The image is, of course, highly complex, as it is the beards, the prop of the travesty, that seem to own the children's faces. Hence, while the men wearing the beards are usually understood to be enhancing their masculinity, Menasse sees these men as doubly weakened, through the animal mask and the very fact that the mask controls the face of the child that is the man. Indeed, Nathan meets his wife at a cloakroom, where his wife takes his coat, revealing to him that she works in fashion: "*Fashion* is the flimsy clothing in which the Zeitgeist wraps itself. That is exciting. One can understand the time in which one lives."[78]

The cross-dressing scenario at the end of *Don Juan de la Mancha* offers yet another variation on the non-dialectical relationship between "Ich" and "Du". Whereas Menasse's notion of the "Austrianization of the world" is primarily critical, his use of the notion of tranvestism for gender identity is potentially productive. The players do not engage in a performative deconstruction but rather borrow and appropriate in a seemingly arbitrary fashion. In the scene, Nathan is shaved all over, given a new feminine hairstyle, made up and dressed as a woman, while Christa is made up as a man. They then engage in a sexual game in which Christa literally performs the masculine role with a horse-radish. "If this were a film, I thought, it would now have to freeze this image. Freeze-frame and cut! I in miniskirt and stockings. In front of me Chris in a suit. Open pants. Horseradish. I in skirt and stockings. Fluttering lashes. In front of me Chris with an erect horseradish. I. You."[79] Menasse invites us to consider here the dialectical image, a moment that is historically significant. Yet we have been taught as readers throughout *Don Juan de la Mancha* not to trust our narrator and to expect constant fluctuations between identities that are perceived as fixed. The presumed dialectic of "asshole/victim"(Arschloch/Opfer) is not reversed but rather opened up here as Menasse cracks the windows of the "dark, musty room" (dunkles, muffiges Zimmer) of gender and history.

Yet we have also learned that Menasse is not comfortable with endings. The final story in *Ich kann jeder sagen*, "Schluss machen", makes this clear, as the narrator confronts the issue of narrative and the difficulty of producing endings in a post-dialectical world. The final, eighty-third chapter in *Don Juan de la Mancha* functions much like credits at the end of a film: we find out about the lives of the characters in the novel in the "present". To varying degrees, they all are living "normal", productive lives, even Nathan himself, who has been rehired by the newspaper that fired him and who is happily unhappy with his wife, Beate. The only deviation from this stasis is the fate of Christa's husband: "Georg, Christa's husband, took his life with sleeping pills after he had written a love letter with lipstick on his stomach."[80] These are the last words of the novel, reminiscent of the suicide of Judith's lover Michael in *Selige Zeiten, brüchige Welt*. We know little about Georg, except that Christa leaves him at the end of the novel to take a position in Berlin, and that he speaks incessantly about competition, "above all with China."[81] Georg's cross-dressing suicide, then, is the act of a man probably caught in rigidified notions of masculinity that are linked to competition and racial superiority. Whereas Nathan can engage in cross-dressing play with Christa (and be left by her) without any damage to the self, Georg represents an older mode of masculinity that cannot survive the humiliation of being left by one's wife.

The waning of a dialectical notion of history is, of necessity, accompanied by a shift in temporalities. Outside of the dialectic, it is not only gender that begins to expand beyond confines of the traditional binary; the process of becoming an adult is ultimately a return to one's childhood, creating figures such as the "ancient child" (greises Kind), Leo Singer, in *Selige Zeiten, brüchige Welt*. In the phase of "sinnliche Gewißheit", the "I" has an unreflected and unmediated relationship to the here and now. In this sense, a non-dialectical world system informed by the logic of *Sozialpartnerschaft* could offer more than simply stasis: it could produce the conditions for a less rigidified understanding of gender and for a return to the time of the present. This is precisely the goal Menasse mentions in his interview at the

Frankfurt Book Fair in 2007: *Don Juan de le Mancha* should offer a sense of thrown-ness into the present. As Menasse explains, his work attempts to say something about the "spirit of the time" (Geist der Zeit): "In telling stories I want to secure my place in the contemporary. I tell the time of life." [82] This mode of experience is depicted perhaps most beautifully in the story "Ewige Jugend" (Eternal Youth), in which the narrator and his bride spend their wedding night in the storied Bad Ischl, resort home to the Habsburg emperors and former home of the narrator. The two spend the evening watching the events of the fall of the Berlin Wall on television, yet another mediated experience. The next day, they take a walk in the snow, and this walk represents a life in "real time" (*Echtzeit*), a mode of experience in which the past and the present coexist and in which the actions of the present are more important than the traces of the past:

> It had snowed heavily in the night, and we tramped along the pier, not in slow motion and also not with the deliberateness of veterans, but rather in real time over to the "Kaiserpromenade", and everything had lost its meaning or taken on another. We tramped through the snow from yesterday—and were the first who left their impressions therein.[83]

Above and beyond the "Austrianization of the world" lies the possibility for "the trace of the better" (die Spur des Besseren)[84] which, for Menasse, is embodied in the random play between the small "Ich" and the small "Du" in the real time of the present.

Bibliography

Arnds, Peter. "The Fragmentation of Totality in Robert Menasse's *Selige Zeiten, brüchige Welt*". In *Transforming the Center, Eroding the Margins: Essays on Ethnic and Cultural Boundaries in German-Speaking Countries*, edited by Dagmar C. G. Lorenz and Renate S. Posthofen, 215–26. Columbia, SC: Camden House, 1998.

Beck, Ulrich. *What is Globalization?* Translated by Patrick Camiller. Cambridge, MA: Polity, 2000.

Beller, Steven. *A Concise History of Austria*. Cambridge, MA: Cambridge University Press, 2006.

Brockmann, Stephen. "'Normalization': Has Helmut Kohl's Vision Been Realized?". In *German Culture, Politics, and Literature into the Twenty-First Century: Beyond Normalization*, edited by Stuart Taberner and Paul Cooke, 17–31. Rochester, NY: Camden House, 2006.

Bürger, Peter. "Ein Abgesang auf die kritische Theorie". In *Die Welt scheint unverbesserlich: Zu Robert Menasses "Trilogie der Entgeisterung"*, edited by Dieter Stolz, 178–80. Frankfurt: Suhrkamp, 1997.

Butler, Judith. *Gender Trouble: Feminism and the Subversion of Identity*. New York: Routledge, 1990.

Eisenach, Herbert. *Das schöpferische Mißtrauen oder Ist Österreichs Literatur eine österreichische Literatur*. Gütersloh: Mohn, 1964.
Feijoo, Jaime. "Verkehrte Geschichte(n): Erkundung eines österreichischen Grundmotivs in Robert Menasses 'Trilogie der Entgeisterung'". *Modern Austrian Literature* 34, no. 3/4 (2001): 63–78.
Fritsch, Gerhard. *Moos auf den Steinen*. Graz: Styria, 1985.
Gemert, Guillaume van. "Die Kehrtwendung des Engels der Geschichte: Zu Robert Menasses Österreich-Bild". In *Hinter den Bergen eine andere Welt: Österreichische Literatur des 20. Jahrhunderts*, edited by Anke Bosse and Leopold Decloedt, 307–28. Amsterdam: Rodopi, 2004.
Gilman, Sander. *The Jew's Body*. New York: Routledge, 1991.
Hardt, Michael and Antonio Negri. *Empire*. Cambridge, MA: Harvard University Press, 2000.
Hegel, Georg W. F. *Phänomenologie des Geistes*. Vol. 3 of *Werke*. Frankfurt am Main: Suhrkamp, 1970.
Horkheimer, Max and Theodor Adorno. *Dialektik der Aufklärung*. Frankfurt am Main: Fischer, 1988.
Jameson, Fredric. *The Prison-House of Language: A Critical Account of Structuralism and Russian Formalism*. Princeton, NJ: Princeton University Press, 1972.
Menasse, Robert. *Das Land ohne Eigenschaften: Essays zur österreichischen Identität*. Frankfurt am Main: Suhrkamp, 1995.
—*Das war Österreich: Gesammelte Essays zum Land ohne Eigenschaften*. Edited by Eva Schörkhuber. Frankfurt am Main: Suhrkamp, 2005.
—*Don Juan de la Mancha, oder Die Erziehung der Lust*. Frankfurt am Main: Suhrkamp, 2007.
—*Ich kann jeder sagen: Erzählungen vom Ende der Nachkriegsordnung*. Frankfurt am Main: Suhrkamp, 2009.
—Interview. Frankfurter Buchmesse, 2007. archiv.literadio.org/get.php?id=766pr951.
—*Phänomenologie der Entgeisterung: Geschichte des verschwindenden Wissens*. Frankfurt am Main: Suhrkamp, 1995.
—*Selige Zeiten, brüchige Welt*. Frankfurt am Main: Suhrkamp, 1994.
—*Sinnliche Gewißheit*. Frankfurt am Main: Suhrkamp, 1996.
—*Überbau und Underground: Die sozialpartnerschaftliche Ästhetik. Essays zum österreichischen Geist*. Frankfurt am Main: Suhrkamp, 1997.
—"Vortrag: Strukturwandel der Innerlichkeit der Öffentlichkeit". *Permanente Revolution der Begriffe: Vorträge zur Kritik der Abklärung*, 69–82. Frankfurt am Main: Suhrkamp, 2009.
—*Wings of Stone*. Translated by David Bryer. New York: Calder Publications/Riverrun Press, 2000.
Mosse, George. *The Image of Man: The Creation of Modern Masculinity*. Oxford, NY: Oxford University Press, 1996.
Musil, Robert. *Der Mann ohne Eigenschaften*. Reinbeck: Rowohlt, 1992.
Richter, Horst-Eberhard. "Die Helden sind ratlos". *Der Spiegel* 40 (2006): 150–4.
Roth, Philip. *Everyman*. Boston: Houghton Mifflin Harcourt, 2006.
Schlipphacke, Heidi. "Fragmented Bodies: Masculinity and Nation in Contemporary German Cinema". In *Mysterious Skin: Male Bodies in Contemporary Cinema*, edited by Santiago Fouz-Hernández, 27–43. London: IB Tauris, 2009.

Notes

* I would like to thank Michael Boehringer and his graduate seminar on masculinity at the University of Waterloo for their engaged feedback on an earlier version of this essay.
1. See the title essay in the following volume: Menasse, *Das war Österreich*, 29–120.
2. Menasse, *Das war Österreich*, 259. "Noch nie in der Geschichte hat die Bevölkerung eines Landes so oft in kurzer Zeit ihre Identität wechseln müssen wie die Österreicher: von der Monarchie in die Erste Republik, von der Ersten Republik in den austrofaschistischen Ständestaat, vom Ständestaat in den Nationalsozialismus, vom Nationalsozialismus in die Zweite Republik—im Lauf nur einer einzigen Generation. Mit dem Ergebnis, daß daraus nicht das Bedürfnis nach der Erlangung einer wirklichen Identität stand, sondern das Bedürfnis nach der Erlangung eines endgültigen Transvestismus: der Sozialpartnerschaft, in der jeder den Anschein seines gesellschaftlichen Gegenteils annimmt, um in dieser Verkleidung eine weitere Änderung vorwegzunehmen und eben dadurch definitiv zu verhindern." Unless otherwise noted, all translations are mine.
3. See Butler, *Gender Trouble*, especially chapter 3: "Subversive Bodily Acts".
4. Menasse, *Das war Österreich*, 221. "Dieser österreichische Transvestismus ist Erlösung und Rettung ohne Helden."
5. Richter, "Die Helden sind ratlos". See also my essay, "Fragmented Bodies", in *Mysterious Skin*, 27–43.
6. The title of Menasse's short story collection, *Ich kann jeder sagen*, engages with a post-dialectical model for subjectivity in interesting ways.
7. Menasse, *Don Juan de la Mancha*, 227. "Ich war die Grenze. Der Grenzfall. Ich werde, so Piroska, was immer ich mache, zugleich der andere sein. Der mit dem 'Du'-Häferl sozusagen, der, während er Ich sagt, auf einen anderen blickt, der das 'Ich-Häferl' hat."
8. Beller, *A Concise History of Austria*, 255.
9. Ibid., 255.
10. See, for instance, Michael Hardt and Antonio Negri's critique of a post-national "imperial" world in *Empire*. See, in particular, part 3, "Passages of Production", in which they link their critique of a post-national world order to capitalism.
11. Gemert, "Die Kehrtwendung des Engels der Geschichte", 314. "Das Österreich der Sozialpartnerschaft, und somit auch seine Literatur, entziehe sich—so könnte man Menasses Essay nicht zuletzt auch mit Bezug auf die ironisierende Schlusspointe zusammenfassen—der Dialektik."
12. Menasse, *Das war Österreich*, 259. "Die Anzeichen mehren sich. Wien, die Hauptstadt der Sozialpartnerschaft, wurde zum Sitz des internationalen Institutes für Konfliktvermeidung erkoren, zur Zentrale einer Sozialpartnerschaft internationalen Zuschnitts, zur Planungsstelle eines Entweder-und-Oder Systems ehemaliger Weltmächte. Österreich ist ja bereits eine ehemalige Weltmacht. Nicht der Untergang der wirklichen Welt, wie die Grünen raunen, sondern der Untergang der Welt der Wirklichkeiten ist die Zukunft der Welt."
13. See, for example, Beck, *What is Globalization?*, 26. "In research associated with 'cultural theory', the linearity assumption and the Either-Or of national

axiomatics are replaced by Both-And postulates: globalization *and* regionalization, linkage *and* fragmentation, centralization *and* decentralization, are dynamics that belong together, as two sides of the same coin."

14 Menasse, *Das war Österreich*, 215.
15 Menasse, *Das war Österreich*, 218. "Daß die so entstehenden Gegensätze nie zu produktiven Widersprüchen werden, die dann eine dialektische Synthese doch ermöglichen könnten. Vielmehr ordnen sich die Gegensätze und Widersprüche, in die Fritschs Roman zerfällt, in einer Weise an, daß sie sich gegenseitig einfach auslöschen und auf diese Weise sowohl die Teile als auch das Ganze nichtig machen."
16 Fredric Jameson uses this term in *The Prison-House of Language*: "It would not perhaps be too far-fetched to see in [the binary] a kind of arrested dialectic [...]. The binary opposition is dialectical insofar as it is dynamic, insofar as it involves differential perceptions" (120).
17 I am thinking here of the ways in which Butler lays out the productive function of gender "performance", a critical practice that has seen been taken up by postcolonial theorists such as Homi Bhabha.
18 Bürger, "Ein Abgesang auf die kritische Theorie", 179. "Das leugne ich gar nicht, antwortet der postmoderne Autor, nur glaube ich, erkannt zu haben, daß hinter den großen Worten der Theorie (Situation, Vorgeschichte, Gestaltung der Zukunft) nichts anderes steht als das kleine Ich mit seinem grenzenlosen Verlangen nach Anerkennung, wobei die Pointe darin liegt, daß es die verachtet, von denen es anerkannt sein will."
19 The novel has been translated into English as *Wings of Stone*, but this title does not render the citational nature of Menasse's original title.
20 Menasse, *Phänomenologie der Entgeisterung*, 87. "'Im Anfang ist die Kopie.' So sehe ich das."
21 Gemert points out another problem with Leo's thesis, namely: "Wer soll das lesen?" Gemert, "Die Kehrtwendung des Engels der Geschichte", 319.
22 Bürger, "Ein Abgesang auf die kritische Theorie", 178. "Der die Ritterrüstung der großen philosophischen Theorie angelegt, sich auf die Irrfahrt des Gedankens begibt, um das Werk zu schaffen, das die Welt verändert; der im Leben nichts anderes auszumachen vermag als eine Verlockung, die ihn abhalten soll vom Werk; der in der Frau daher die Windmühle des Lebens erblickt, die er besiegen muß, um fähig zu werden zum Werk."
23 Menasse, *Don Juan de la Mancha*, 210. "Männerphantasien? Meine Phantasie hatte damals ausgesetzt und wer wen zum Objekt macht—ach, wozu diese Diskussion? Es gab sie nicht mehr. Objekt? Es wurde alles so subjektiv."
24 See Gemert, who also points to the fact that *Sinnliche Gewissheit* is the only one to be written from the perspective of a narrative "I", hence reflecting the initial stage in Hegel's philosophy in which the unreflected relationship of the "I" to the here and now is central (Gemert, "Die Kehrtwendung des Engels der Geschichte", 321).
25 Menaasse, *Überbau und Underground*, 105.
26 Ibid., 106. "Die Namen, die die Ichs sich zurufen, sollen eine Geschichte ergeben, deren Kern die Retrospektive auf eine Zeit ist, in der Namen noch etwas bedeutet haben. Diese Geschichte kommt aber nie zustande, da jedes Ich, das—etwas meinend, hoffend, empfindend—sich preisgibt, im Niemandsland zwischen Exklusivität und allgemeiner Geltung bleibt."

27 Menasse, *Don Juan de la Mancha*, 27. "[…] dass alles irgendwie exemplarisch ist, was man ist und wie man ist und warum man so ist."
28 See, for example, the essay "Strukturwandel der Innerlichkeit der Öffentlichkeit", in which Menasse discusses the epochal change located in the global experience of the death of John F. Kennedy. The details of Menasse's engagement with this moment are similarly presented in his short story "Die amerikanische Brille" that appears in *Ich kann jeder sagen*, 96–113.
29 "Exactly the same life once more, only different."
30 Menasse, *Ich kann jeder sagen*, 54. "Definition von Autobiographie: dialektische Lebenslüge."
31 Ibid., 128. "Es war auf der Rückreise von Dresden, als mir plötzlich klar wurde, dass der Reichtum, den ich erzählend ausbreitete, eine Lüge war. Dass ich im Grunde immer dieselbe dürftige Geschichte erzählt hatte. Nur die 'Handlung' war jedes Mal eine andere, die sogenannten Erlebnisse, und ebendadurch zeigte sich, wie beliebig es war, das Erlebte, das Leben."
32 Ibid., 129. "Variante immer derselben Geschichte"; "ein verstümmeltes Leben"; "Phantomschmerzen."
33 Ibid., 111. "Die eingeschnürte Sehnsucht. Nach einem Kind. Das ich gewesen bin."
34 In *Don Juan de la Mancha*, the narrator reflects upon the concept of adulthood after the death of his parents, concluding that "Erwachsen zu sein heißt, Herrschaft antreten" (198) which, in the end, means that one has the means to create an environment for oneself that is a recreation of the environment of one's childhood (199).
35 Menasse, *Ich kann jeder sagen*, 134. "Der Versuch von Sinngebung im Sinnlosen."
36 Ibid. "Essen muss der Mensch. Man quält sich, aber essend quält man sich immerhin im Anschein von Normalität." In the next paragraph of this story, the narrator reflects on the fact that he comes from a family that had experienced hunger (Jews under the Nazi regime), another seemingly incompatible aspect of the particular identity of this narrative "I".
37 Menasse, *Ich kann jeder* sagen, 137. "Dann ging ich in mein Zimmer und schaute mir die Bombardierung Dresdens an. Ich aß dabei Nüsschen, weil ich einfach nicht widerstehen kann, wenn ich in der Minibar eines Hotelzimmers welche finde. Ich hasste mich. Es war völlig irrational. Ich hatte eben erst abendgegessen, war ohne Hunger, und stopfte dennoch diese Nüsschen in mich hinein, die meinen Körper sinnlos verwüsten."
38 Menasse, *Don Juan de la Mancha*, 82. "Endlich wieder normale Verhältnisse. Ich habe solche Sehnsucht nach Normalität."
39 Ibid., 183. "Ich erinnerte mich an ein Leben, das so großartig… und so durchschnittlich war, dass ich nicht wusste, warum mir nun die Tränen kamen. Vielleicht ebendeswegen. Ein Leben dass—ich musste plötzlich lachen—so grotesk in seiner ewig mühsam vesteckten Banalität war, dass—und jetzt musste ich weinen."
40 Menasse, *Ich kann jeder sagen*, 184. "Er hatte ein auf Anhieb nichtssaggendes Gesicht."
41 In the story "Chronik der Girardigasse" from *Ich kann jeder sagen*, the narrator describes the apartment building in which he lives in Vienna, a former brothel that is both a theater and a prison, resembling the character of the city of Vienna itself: "Denn wie kann man den Eindruck, den diese Stadt

macht, anders beschreiben als mit einem Reigen dieser Begriffe: Theater und Gefängnis und verdrängte oder vergessene Geschichte. Schöner Schein, unklares Sein. Ein Publikum, das sich am liebsten selbst beobachtet und sich selbst applaudiert, und dabei das Gefühl nicht los wird, in Wahrheit weggesperrt zu sein, nicht hinauszukönnen in das freie, das wirkliche Leben" (For how can one describe the impression that this city makes other than with a row of these concepts: theater and prison and repressed or forgotten history. Beautiful appearance, unclear being. A public that most likes to watch itself and that applauds itself and that can yet not get rid of the feeling of, in reality, being locked away, not able to get out into the free and real life.) Menasse, *Ich kann jeder sagen*, 72.

42 Cited in Brockmann, "Normalization", 17.
43 See Mosse, *The Image of Man*.
44 Eisenach, *Das schöpferische Mißtrauen*, 84. "Österreichisch ist zuerst einmal und überhaupt das Bemühen um Distanz. [...] Österreichisch ist sodann der freiwillige Verzicht auf aktuelle Wirksamkeit [...]. Österreichisch ist ferner die Aversion gegen alles Große, gegen alles Laute, gegen alles Gewaltsame, gegen jede erzwungene Veränderung [...]."
45 Gemert, "Die Kehrtwendung des Engels der Geschichte", 323. "Die Verkörperung des Ausgleichs, der Mitte, der Neutralität, und somit wesenhaft museal. [...] Österreich ist bei Menasse, als Geburtsstätte der Verösterreicherung und als gelebte Sozialpartnerschaft, schlechthin Chiffre für postmoderne Unverbindlichkeit."
46 Menasse, *Wings of Stone*, 8. "Seine Thesen klangen bizarr in einer Stadt, die so besonders abgebrüht ignorant war gegenüber allen Ideen, daß etwas anders sein könnte, als es war, die so besonders erstarrt erschien in ihrem Sein, daß der Satz 'Wien bleibt Wien' nur deshalb als Lüge empfunden wurde, weil er zu euphemistisch klang: das Verbum 'bleiben' war schon viel zu dynamisch" (Menasse, *Selige Zeiten, brüchige Welt*, 16).
47 Menasse, *Ich kann jeder sagen*, 174. "Naturgemäß ein einziger Zombietanz."
48 Ibid., 21. "Mir ist bekannt, hat er gesagt, dass Invalidität das begehrteste Privileg in Österreich und daher das Lebensziel jedes Österreichers ist."
49 Ibid., 163. "Ich lebte von den Fehlern der Gegner."
50 Menasse, *Don Juan de la Mancha*, 242. "Man muss sich Nathan als einen glücklichen Mann vorstellen. Er war gut aussehend, wobei gut aussehend bei einem Mann in der Regel nicht viel mehr bedeuten muss, als dass er gerade Glieder, wenig Uebergewicht und noch keinen allzu starken Haarausfall hat. Er hatte in seinem Leben noch keinen nennenswerten Erfolg, aber auch nie größere Probleme oder drückende Sorgen gehabt. Schon diese Mittelmäßigkeit gab ihm offenbar den Anschein des Privilegierten."
51 Ibid., 235.
52 Ibid., 13. See also Peter Arnds, who argues that Menasse's project of "depetrification" is the desire to rid Austria of its "ethnocentricity and to shape its self-understanding, since according to Hegel's dialectic, one gets to know oneself better by getting to know the other" (Arnds, "The Fragmentation of Totality", 224).
53 Menasse, *Das Land ohne Eigenschaften*, 7. "'Österreichische Identität'—dieser Begriff hat etwas von einem dunklen und muffigen Zimmer, in dem man, wenn man aus irgendeinem Grund eintritt, sofort die Vorhänge beiseite schieben und das Fenster öffnen möchte, um etwas Luft und Licht

hereinzulassen. Doch wenn das Fenster keine Aussicht hat und sich der Raum daher nur wenig erhellen will?"
54 Menasse, *Don Juan de la Mancha*, 70. "Wie kam ich da raus?"
55 Ibid., 55. "Ausgangstüren aus den kleinen Verhältnissen."
56 Ibid., 72. "Ich will da raus! Ich will weg."
57 Ibid., 44. "So viele Türen. Offenstehende Flügeltüren, die den Blick freigaben in Zimmerfluchten [...]. Jetzt glaubte ich Anne zu lieben. Ich war verrückt nach ihr. Sie würde Türen öffnen, Zimmerfluchten, neue Räume in meinem Leben erschließen."
58 Ibid., 52. "Ich hatte Wochen zuvor durch Zufall festgestellt, daß Literatur, die von den Nazis verboten worden war, noch immer nicht entlehnt werden durfte, bloss weil nach 1945 vergessen wurde, dieses Verbot wieder aufzuheben."
59 Ibid., 203.
60 Ibid., 202. "Jahrhundertalte Schildkröte, ebenso behindert wie geschützt von einem schweren Panzer."
61 Ibid., 21. "Mein Vater hat vorbildlich genossen, und ich musste so lange warten. So habe ich, ausgerechnet von ihm, das Warten gelernt."
62 Ibid., 24. "Ich wollte, daß die Welt noch eine Zeit lang so blieb, wie ich sie kennen gelernt hatte. Nur die Väter sollten irgendwann, bald, abtreten. Aber sonst sollte die Welt bleiben, wie ich sie kannte. Wie sollte ich sonst in ihr die Herrschaft übernehmen, wenn ständig alles anders wurde?"
63 Ibid., 120. "'Ich bin also nicht wirksam?' sagte ich. 'Was ich hier tue, hat keine Wirkung? Nicht die geringste?'
Franz schaute mich an.
'Wunderbar! Dann bin ich unschuldig!'"
64 Ibid., 64. "Wenn ich ein Mann bin, dann sage ich jetzt nein."
65 Ibid., 65. "Können Sie die Frage bitte wiederholen?"
66 Ibid. "Und ich, mittlerweile völlig erschöpft, sagte mit letzter Kaft: Ja."
67 Ibid., 72. "Ich würde dann nicht das Arschloch sein, wenn es mir gelang, das Opfer zu sein."
68 Ibid., 157. "Wenn man im Bett lag und erstmal die Penetrationsdebatte führte, konnte man in Ruhe abwarten, ob sich überhaupt eine Erektion einstellte. Wenn ja, gab es immer die Chance, eine Ausnahme zu machen. Wenn nein, blieb man eben emanzipiert."
69 Ibid., 268. "Der einen Orgasmus vorspielt."
70 Ibid., 229. "KANN MAN DEN HOLOCAUST UNTERRICHTEN?"
71 Ibid., 230. "Susanne Lemberg, Überlebende. Die einzige Frau auf dem Podium war 'Überlebende.' In der Liste der Namen und Berufbezeichnungen war die Berufbezeichnung 'Überlebende' so grotesk, so obszön, dass mir dies die Schwellenangst vor dem Tempel nahm."
72 Ibid., 114. "Ich habe Hände wie ein Metzger."
73 See Mosse, *The Image of Man*. See also Gilman, *The Jew's Body*.
74 Menasse, *Selige Zeiten, brüchige Welt*, 259. "Darunter hatte Michael einen BH, den er am Rücken aber nicht verschließen hatte können, und eine ihrer Strumpfhosen."
75 Feijoo, "Verkehrte Geschichte(n)", 74.
76 Menasse, *Das war Österreich*, 220. "Der Transvestismus ist die durchgehende Metapher im Roman *Fasching*."
77 Menasse, *Don Juan de la Mancha*, 24. "Bärte sind Affenmasken mit Kindergesichtern."

78 Ibid., 252. "*Mode* ist der fadenscheinige Rock, in den sich der Zeitgeist hüllt. Das ist spannend. Man kann die Zeit verstehen, in der man lebt."
79 Ibid., 273. "Wenn das ein Film wäre, dachte ich, müsste er nun einfrieren in diesem Bild. Standbild und aus! Ich in Minirock und Strümpfen. Vor mir Chris im Anzug. Offene Hose. Meerretich. Ich in Rock und Strümpfen. Flatternden Wimpern. Vor mir Chris mit erigiertem Meerrettich. Ich. Du."
80 Ibid. "Georg, Christas Mann, nahm sich mit Schlaftabletten das Leben, nachdem er mit Lippenstift einen Liebesbrief auf seinen Bauch geschrieben hatte."
81 Ibid., 11. "Vor allem mit China."
82 Menasse, Interview. "Ich will mich erzählend meiner Zeitgenossenschaft vergewissern. Ich erzähle Lebenszeit."
83 Menasse, *Ich kann jeder sagen*, 127. "Es hatte stark geschneit in der Nacht, und wir stapften den Kai entlang, nicht in Zeitlupe, auch nicht mit der Bedächtigkeit von Veteranen, sondern in Echtzeit, hinüber zur 'Kaiserpromenade', und alles hatte seine Bedeutung verloren, oder eine andere bekommen. Wir stapften durch den Schnee von gestern—und waren die Ersten, die darin ihre Eindrücke hinterließen."
84 Horkheimer and Adorno, *Dialektik der Aufklärung*, 151.

8. Sebald's Encounters with French Narrative

Judith Ryan

Sebald's scholarly writings on literature tend to focus on themes and issues rather than on narrative technique. In his book on Döblin from 1980, for example, his main concern is to trace the representation of power and violence in Döblin's novels. To be sure, he can hardly avoid addressing the issue of montage, but he does so primarily in order to move beyond it.[1] When he touches upon Döblin's use of language, his aim is to demonstrate its tendency toward mythic abstractions rather than to engage in close stylistic analysis.[2] Although he cites Döblin's 1928 essays "Vom Bau des epischen Werkes" and "Das Ich über die Natur", he reads them as evidence of Döblin's tendency toward historical monumentalism. Sebald's essayistic writings on literature—his two collections of essays on Austrian literature, *Beschreibung des Unglücks* (1985) and *Unheimliche Heimat* (1991), as well as his volume of essays *Logis in einem Landhaus* (1998)—focus on writing as a response to lived experience. Here again, his interest is mainly thematic: at the center of these essays are such topics as disorientation caused by disaster, displacement or psychological disturbance.

We know, of course, that Sebald was not only a scholar and a writer but also a practicing translator who founded the British Centre for Literary Translation in 1989. Good translation cannot be achieved without close attention to style. In the manuscripts of his own literary works, now housed at the Deutsches Literaturarchiv in Marbach, we can observe him working on style, especially on word choice and sentence rhythm.[3] Similarly, his responses to drafts of the English translations of his own works are meticulously detailed and accompanied by occasional notes of explanation.[4] Still, his work in this area cannot tell us what he knew about the inner workings of narrative. In this essay, I aim to trace one filiation in his understanding of narrative theory by following his reading of three French authors: Michel Butor, Gustave Flaubert and Marcel Proust.

Michel Butor's novel, *L'emploi du temps* (1957), provides important clues to Sebald's early acquaintance with a narrative structure that recurs in different forms in *Die Ringe des Saturn* and *Austerlitz*. During his first year in England, while teaching as an assistant lecturer at the University of Manchester, Sebald read *L'emploi du temps* with distinctly personal attention. He read the book in the French original and marked it up closely.[5] Set in an oppressive English industrial town reminiscent of Manchester but bearing the fictional name Bleston, the novel is narrated by a young man, Jacques Revel, who is spending a year as an intern in a bank. The novel takes the form of a diary, although as it turns out, an extremely complicated one. Revel hates every moment of his life in Bleston: at every turn, he expresses his animosity toward the place. Against Revel's observation that his writing feels "comme une petite vengeance" against the town, Sebald makes a small "x", and in the bottom margin of the page Sebald writes a footnote in what looks like rather thick brown felt-tipped pen: "J'ai commencé à lire *L'emploi du temps* pour cette raison."[6] In addition to the repugnance that the town evokes in him, Jacques Revel is handicapped by his lack of fluency in English. For some time, he can only negotiate the language by constant translation into his native tongue: "traduisant, toujours traduisant".[7] In the upper margin of the blank page at the front of the novel, Sebald copies these words in brown felt-tipped pen; further down on the same page, he adds in the same pen: "De plus/en plus…" (More and more). Most newcomers to a foreign country have exactly the opposite experience, gradually putting translation behind them and learning to think directly in the foreign language. On the first page of the narrative itself, Sebald writes:

Sunday night 12^h
13th November 66
Chorlton/Bleston

1966 was the year Sebald joined the University of Manchester, having received his licence ès lettres from the University of Fribourg in the preceding year. Chorlton is a place not far from Manchester. Later in the novel, he inserts a similar notation, no longer indicating the place but still giving the day of the week and the date: against Revel's diary entry for "lundi 26 mai" Sebald writes "Tuesday 15 Nov. 66" (he has now read 65 pages). At least at the beginning of Butor's novel, then, Sebald is mapping the dates of his reading in 1966 against the chronology of Revel's diary. Is he reading it as a parallel to his own experiences in Manchester? Yet at the point when he inscribes the two dates from November 1966 in his copy of Butor's novel, he cannot have had much time to settle in the city. Just over halfway through the novel, Sebald underlines Revel's description of his writing table: "cette table qui était déjà mon rampart contre Bleston."[8] It would go too far to suppose that Sebald identifies with Revel's belief that writing can protect him from the hostility of the city, but he is certainly tracing the theme as it unfolds in the novel. Other underlinings and marginal lines show that Sebald is reading the book attentively, following the connected motifs of fire and smoke, the theme of irrational action, and the narrator's notion that he can assuage his distress by burning his original copy of the city map and continuing to work laboriously at the text of his diary.

Unlike most diary-novels, *L'emploi du temps* is constructed as a curious kind of multiple record-keeping: having arrived in Bleston on 1 October, Revel does not begin his diary until 1 May. Instead of recounting only what happens on the days of these entries, he also looks back at his experiences during the previous months of his stay. Thus each entry covers a dual time period. As he gains new insights into his previous impressions and experiences, his account of earlier dates expands, but these insights still fail to provide explanations, causing him to double back repeatedly to revisit episodes on which he has already reported. These digressions, as well as the fact that he only writes in his diary on weekdays, dooms to failure his original hope of bringing the two main temporal levels together in the course of writing. Ultimately, his narrative proliferates into five different angles of perception. Butor, of course, has developed these temporal complications with great care, but they can be quite dizzying for the reader. It is not surprising that Sebald rapidly gives up mapping his own experience against that of the increasingly complex time-structure of Revel's narrative.

Still, the gloomy and forbidding city that forms the novel's backdrop, its labyrinthine character, and the narrator's sense of being imprisoned within the confines of its complicated streets are elements that Sebald repeatedly marks in his copy. Jacques Revel's desire to escape by visiting areas outside the city proves impossible because the urban sprawl of the area makes it difficult to gain access to anything like open countryside. The labyrinth, in the first instance a metaphor for the disposition of the city and the fears it evokes, is also connected with Revel's attempt to uncover hidden truths through the act of revisiting his experiences in writing. In this regard, he follows a traditional expectation about writing as a guide to understanding. He sees his diary as an equivalent to Ariadne's thread, a guide that will lead him out of darkness into light. Sebald underlines the passage where Revel makes this point.[9] Although the labyrinth is a motif that appears in several of Sebald's prose works (notably *Die Ringe des Saturn*, with its photo of the labyrinth at the Somerleyton estate),[10] the somber, smoky atmosphere of Bleston finds its most striking parallel in *Austerlitz*,[11] where the theme of imprisonment is most extensively treated. Revel's nighttime wanderings in Bleston are a precursor, as it were, of the unnamed narrator's night-time wanderings in *Austerlitz*. Yet the divagations, physical and mental, of Sebald's narrators do not yield the truth they are seeking. However much he believes he has discovered about his past, Austerlitz is still convinced that he also needs to find traces of his father and his former friend Marie de Verneuil. The unnamed narrator who passes on Austerlitz's stories also comes to no clear conclusion: we do not even know if he ever finishes the book by Dan Jacobsen, part of which he reads while visiting the former concentration camp Breendonk.

Both *L'emploi du temps* and *Austerlitz* pose serious questions about the value of narration. Jacques Revel alternates between belief in the power of narrative to uncover the truth and despair at the complications that it introduces: writing as a way to salvation comes to appear highly questionable. Perhaps most tellingly, *L'emploi du temps* explores the question of the narrator's implication in the troubling atmosphere of the city. One critic writes on this connection: "Rhetoric is a powerful tool used by first-person narrators to make confessions, perpetuate narrative indeterminacy and vindicate themselves."[12] Revel uses various types of narrative slippage to imply that the fires that keep springing up in various parts of Bleston have been started by others and have nothing to do with him. Yet his impetuous burning of the map of Bleston is a destructive act that puts him, so to speak, on the same level as the fiery city, even if it does not lead to more actual fires. Since the city remains a mystery to him, he is obliged to purchase another copy of the map the following day. Unable to admit that he deliberately burned the first map, he finds himself trapped in a lie.

In an article on the relation of *L'emploi du temps* to the detective novel, Laura R. Kubinyi argues that its structure forms the narrative equivalent of a labyrinth without a center.[13] Lorna Martens connects the "empty center" of *L'emploi du temps* with the ambiguity of the novel's ending.[14] She shows how language takes over in Revel's writing, expanding his descriptions of Bleston into overwrought, fanciful metaphors that "give the prose its peculiar heavy, sonorous quality."[15] Revel assigns this power to the city itself rather than to the runaway effects of his own language. In a passage that Sebald underlines in brown felt-tipped pen, Revel compares Bleston with such American cities as Pittsburgh and Detroit:

Il me semble qu'elle, Bleston, pousse à l'extrême certaines particularités de ce genre d'agglomérations, qu'elle est, de toutes, celle dont la sorcellerie est la plus rusée et la plus puissante.[16]

"Agglomérations" is a pertinent word, one that describes not only the expansion of the city into adjoining areas but also the proliferation that marks Revel's record-keeping and continual retracing of events already narrated. The more one tries to escape from such a structure, the more one feels trapped in its mesh. A few pages later, Revel feels lost in its "filaments" even as he attempts to examine "cette énorme cellule cancéreuse dont chaque encre d'imprimerie, comme un colorant approprié, faisait ressortir un système d'organes."[17] On one level, the magic power ("sorcellerie") that emanates from the agglomerative city is negative, but it also has a positive aspect. In the ancient myth that subtends this motif in Butor's novel, the maker of the labyrinth, Daedalus, was an artist. For Revel, the story of Theseus and the minotaur, depicted in the tapestries of Bleston, is connected with the myth of Cain, depicted in the stained-glass windows of the old cathedral. "Il faut vous rappeler que c'est une oeuvre de la Renaissance; l'artiste honorait en Caïn le père de tous les arts."[18]

Thinking of Sebald's maze-like narrative structures as labyrinths without a center may help us to identify the extraordinary effect his writing exerts on the reader. On one level, in experiencing Sebald's texts as labyrinths, we often find ourselves undertaking a surprising amount of detective work, without necessarily finding a key that brings the works into coherent focus. On the other hand, life itself is disorderly and resistant to systematic ordering. The two opposing desires—to find an articulable truth and to represent the chaos of actual experience—come together in Sebald in a manner that is at once fascinating and frustrating. In contrast to Butor in *L'emploi du temps*, Sebald does not use the detective-novel model as a methodological meta-level within his narratives, but he does allude to related models that allow an investigator to follow traces and solve puzzles: those of the scholar, the essayist and the collector.[19] In *Die Ringe des Saturn*, for example, we see the narrator following up on a television program which he fell asleep watching: the program tells the story of Roger Casement, at first knighted for his exposure of abuses of native workers in South American rubber plantations but later executed for treason in his attempt to provide German armaments to the Irish rebels. The narrator follows the case as it is revisited in the British media and debated by handwriting specialists and other experts. In *Austerlitz*, the fictive protagonist travels to Prague in an attempt to find what he believes are his own family origins. In *Die Ringe des Saturn*, the narrator seems to arrive with undue haste at the conclusion that Casement really did write the "black diaries" that turned public opinion against him; and in *Austerlitz*, the protagonist seems even more hasty in deciding that he has really found his old nanny in Prague. Mysteries that cannot be satisfactorily solved abound in Sebald's literary writings.

It is instructive to compare the assiduous reading that Sebald gave to *L'emploi du temps* in 1966 with his markings in the 13-volume Suhrkamp Taschenbuch edition of Proust in German translation that he purchased and read in 1964/65.[20] The first and last volumes are heavily marked; markings continue to be fairly frequent in volume 2, the second half of *In Swanns Welt* (Swann's Way),[21] but in subsequent volumes they occur at increasingly lengthy intervals. Only rarely does he note aspects of the novel's composition, as when he writes in the second volume: "über 100erte von Seiten sind die Vergleiche gespannt: selten aber!"[22] The sheer length of Proust's novel makes it much more difficult for the reader to perceive its fine structure than is the case with Butor's *L'emploi du temps*, where motivic repetitions and variations are dense and flamboyantly displayed. Nonetheless, Sebald's markings betray a degree of uncertainty about what to notice that may simply reflect the fact that he was a young student who may not yet have had extensive practice in close reading. Often, his markings draw attention to the narrator's reflections on problems of subjectivity or memory—two of the best-known themes in Proust's novel.[23] In the middle volumes, he often marks generalizations in the "we" or "one" form, in other words sentences that announce themselves explicitly as insights into human behavior. That is not to say that some of his markings are not perceptive: examples are his underlining in black crayon of the phrase "der Vorraum der Erinnerung" and the sentence, "Er bewunderte die furchtbare, immer neue Produktivität seiner Erinnerung" in the second volume.[24] In the first volume, he marks a passage about the relation between fiction and reality: "Hätten meine Eltern mir erlaubt, den Schauplatz eines Buches, das ich las, selber aufzusuchen, so hätte das meiner Meinung nach einen unschätzbaren Fortschritt in der Eroberung der Welt bedeutet."[25] In the final volume, he begins to notice the motif of optical instruments, as when the narrator describes the work of a writer as "lediglich eine Art von optischem Instrument, das der Autor dem Leser reicht, damit er erkennen möge, was er in sich selbst vielleicht sonst nicht hätte erschauen können."[26]

Whatever impulses he may have received from his reading of Proust in the mid-1960s, Sebald appears to have all but forgotten about the *Recherche* for some time. Still, French literature is never far from Sebald's mind. An essay that first appeared in the *Neue Rundschau* in 1989 and was later included in Sebald's essay collection *Unheimliche Heimat* bears a title that alludes to Aragon: "Le Paysan de Vienne: Über Peter Altenberg".[27] Sebald's copy, now in the archive at Marbach, contains numerous markings; it is not clear, however, when he made them. Many of the marked passages have to do with the atmosphere of the Paris arcades: their mysterious, phantasmic and almost religious effects, the glimpses they afford of the sheen on women's clothing, their bizarre perversions of nature and reason. Repeatedly, he marks phrases suggesting that for the flâneur the cityscape has become a substitute for open nature, to which he has no access. At the same time, Sebald seems also taken by the reaction the arcades inspire in the urban wanderer: "Cette conscience exquise d'un passage est le frisson dont je parlais."[28] Regardless of when Sebald actually marked up Aragon's *Le Paysan de Paris*, he was clearly thinking of it while writing his essay on Altenberg. This connection between wandering and narrative precedes *Die Ringe des Saturn*, where the narrator explores open countryside rather than Aragon's urban landscape.

In the 1990s, Sebald turns his attention to Flaubert, perhaps as a result of conversations with a colleague at the University of East Anglia, Janine Dakyns's, a Flaubert enthusiast. In *Die Ringe des Saturn*, the narrator devotes several pages to Janine Dakyns's, detailed knowledge of the French author's letters, from which she recites at length.[29] In Sebald's *Korsika* manuscripts about Corsica, Flaubert's travel report on the island forms the backdrop against which the narrator views his experiences there.[30] In a hotel where the narrator is staying, a Pléiade edition of Flaubert amusingly turns up in the drawer of the night table as if it were a Bible. The volume includes Flaubert's *Trois contes*, from which the narrator reads and then summarizes "La Légende de Saint Julien l'hospitalier".[31] Although Sebald's personal library as contained in the Marbach archives includes several volumes of Flaubert in various languages and editions, none of these appears to be marked up, as was Sebald's custom otherwise with any book he read carefully. A two-volume edition of *Madame Bovary* in French and an Everyman edition of the same novel in English are among these volumes. Yet we cannot assume from these unmarked volumes that Sebald did not read Madame Bovary. It is quite likely that Sebald borrowed his reading copy of Flaubert from Janine Dakyns's or the University of East Anglia library (he is known to have marked library books in the same intense way as he did his personal copies).

Sebald owned and carefully underlined Jean de La Varende's Rowohlt monograph on Gustave Flaubert.[32] Most of Sebald's markings in this slender book concern Flaubert's life and psychological constitution (melancholic), but one heavy line down the margin of a page takes note of Flaubert's constant struggle to write the perfect sentence: "immer mehr verwickelte sich der Schriftsteller in seine Entwürfe, änderte um, formte neu, kämpfte mit jedem Satz."[33] Several other markings emphasize related aspects of Flaubert's stylistic methods, including his habit of testing the rhythms of his prose by reading it aloud.[34] Similarly, Sebald's careful reading of an essay on Flaubert by James Wood, "Half Against Flaubert", in *The Broken Estate: Essays on Literature and Belief* (1999), draws attention to a number of passages about Flaubert's stubborn struggle with style, his "obsession with the sentence" and his desire to "impart to prose the rhythm of verse."[35] Wood also discusses questions of realism, notably what he calls the "tyranny of the detail."[36] Sebald's pencil marks this passage, as well as one the following page, where Wood explains how Flaubert made such observations "into a style" by giving as an example the sentence, "A breeze from the window ruffled the cloth on the table...."[37] He also marks a passage where Wood quotes Stephen Heath's observation that "it is with [Flaubert] that literature becomes *essentially* problematic."[38] Yet it is difficult to tell whether Sebald understood what it was about Flaubert's writing that constituted this new quality.

It seems more likely that Sebald's reading of the two texts by Flaubert mentioned in *Campo Santo*, *Voyage aux Pyrénées et en Corse* (1840) and "La Légende de Saint Julien l'hospitalier" (1877), was more significant than either of these secondary sources for his understanding of Flaubert's narrative strategies. Representing the earliest and the latest of Flaubert's writing, the travelogue and the story stand in marked contrast to each other. The travel report was written when Flaubert was nineteen; the story is the result of a gestational period of over thirty years. Whereas *Voyage aux Pyrénées et en Corse* treats violence—the heritage of banditry and the ferocity of Corsican men—with deliberate understatement, the story of Saint Julian is replete with excesses of carnage and ends with an equally excessive account of the saint's final ascension to heaven. Thematically, "Saint Julien" and the *Voyage aux Pyrénées et en Corse* confirm many of Sebald's ideas about violence and destruction in human society and in nature.[39] In terms of narrative strategy, this early travel narrative also confirms something of the method that Sebald had used in *Die Ringe des Saturn*, the book he completed just before setting out on his trip to Corsica. Two aspects of Flaubert's travelogue are significant in this regard: first, he writes the last section of it retrospectively, and second, he does so by reassembling and adding detail to disparate jottings from his notebooks.[40] By retracing Flaubert's Corsican journey, Sebald adds a second level of delay to the narration, taking stock of what has changed and what has remained the same. Characteristically, however, Sebald complicates his repetition of Flaubert's trajectory by introducing material from other sources, such as Edward Lear's journey through Corsica in the summer of 1876 and Dorothy Carrington's *The Dream Hunters of Corsica*.[41] Although his project on Corsica appears to have motivated his reading of and about Flaubert at this point, we can also consider it as part of what was ultimately to become his preparation for *Austerlitz*. It has been described as the "Keimzelle" or germ of the later work.⁴² Part of the reason for his abandonment of the Corsica project was doubtless that it was developing in a way that seemed too close to *Die Ringe des Saturn*.

I would add to that, however, an important piece of reading in which Proust reappears on Sebald's horizon. The turning-point occurs in late 1999, when Sheila Stern gives Sebald a copy of her book, *Proust: Swann's Way* (1989).⁴³ The copy in Sebald's library at Marbach includes a dated dedication: "For Max from Sheila, October 1999." Written from a sophisticated point of view that resists talking down to the audience it addresses, Stern's book gives its readers a good workout in such matters as the difference between "récit" and "discours", problems of the "realist" method, the representation of consciousness, the subtle positioning of the first-person narrator at different moments in the chronology of events, and the relation between the narrator and the reader. Although time is inevitably involved with these narrative elements and strategies—and Sebald registers Stern's comments on such imbrications—it is not the primary focus of her analysis. In order to follow her reading of *Swann's Way*, Sebald is forced to attend closely to her observations about narrative technique.

Much of Sebald's engagement with Stern's book on Proust has to do with finding support for ideas he had already been developing. One of these is the notion of "analogy-seeking". Sheila Stern introduces this idea in her discussion of Proust's allusions to other works of literature. She writes, "Such mental mannerisms as this of literary analogy-seeking, with their remote origins and models in our upbringing, exist in our innermost selves, as cultural traces."⁴⁴ The reason why this search for analogies works is given in a phrase that Sebald marks in the final volume of the German Proust: people contain "noch alle Stunden der Vergangenheit"⁴⁵ and thus all traces of their previous reading. The text itself speaks (in the German version) of "das Wunder der Analogie", a phrase that Sebald circles in pencil in his copy of the Suhrkamp translation.⁴⁶

Sebald also takes careful note of Sheila Stern's analysis of consciousness in Proust. He underlines, for example, a passage about the narrator's ability to "command the recollection of a mental state with its physical conditions" while also being aware of his present situation as he converts the recollection into writing.⁴⁷ Sebald underlines in ballpoint pen an entire passage in Stern's book about the movements of the mind in Proust's first volume:

> Still, the mind which proceeds by intuitive leaps and deductions from observation, to conclusions that are never irrevocable

certainties, and which has always, as the shifting backdrops of its inner vision, scenes from the distant past, as well as objects, tasks, affections and fears that belong to the transient present moment—this mind is after all very familiar to us, because it is our own.[48]

Here is an insight that may help explain the curious effect not only of Proust but also of Sebald on their respective readers. Whereas Proust could count on his readers' familiarity with certain kinds of information (a situation that is rapidly fading away and that was doubtless never entirely the case with readers outside of France), Sebald leaves his readers with much more to puzzle out, even while his narrators are informing us about largely unfamiliar material. It is possible to learn a great deal of history, for example, from Sebald's prose works, even while still remaining caught up in the conundrums posed by both his individual works and his body of work as a whole.

It is not clear to what extent, if any, Sheila Stern's book sent Sebald back to Proust's novel. His dominant use of blue-black ink in many of the volumes suggests that many of the markings were contemporaneous with his purchase of the books, in which he inscribed his name in that medium. It is not clear whether other markings in pencil or black crayon also date from that early period. We simply do not know how often he may have returned to the text at different times. One phase in his reading or re-reading, however, may have been during the lead-up to *Austerlitz*, which includes an unusual passage from volume 13 of the Suhrkamp Proust edition. The passage refers to the behavior of passengers on a steamship crossing the Caspian Sea who become so seasick that they offer no resistance to any suggestion that they might simply be cast into the waters. Sebald underlines the entire passage in pencil and traces a double line against it in the margin of his Proust edition, where it reads as follows:

> [...] so wie hochgradig seekranke Leute, wenn sie auf einem Dampfer über das Caspische Meer fahren, auch nicht den leisesten Widerstand andeuten, falls man ihnen sagt, man werde sie nunmehr ins Wasser werfen.[49]

Sebald borrows the passage almost entirely, making only two tiny changes: inserting the word "etwa" before "Dampfer" and changing "nunmehr ins Wasser werfen" into "jetzt über Bord werfen".[50] In essence, this borrowing is a kind of teasing on the part of Sebald, who participates in postmodernist pastiche throughout his prose works. It is rendered all the more tantalizing because Sebald is working from the German translation of Proust rather than from the French original.

At two different points in his study of Sheila Stern's *Proust*, marginal jottings (rare even in the most heavily underlined of his books) reveal that Sebald is thinking about *Austerlitz*. When Stern describes evenings "half-remembered, half-forgotten" and the narrator's grandmother who likes to roam about in the twilight, Sebald writes at the bottom of the page: "es sei dieser Teresin & die ganze Umgegend selbst heute derart niederdrückend, daß", but does not finish the thought.[51] At the top of the following page he continues to think along similar lines, writing "Auss. in Paris" (possibly referring to the view of Paris from the new national library), and adding in the lower margin, "Truppenübungsplatz".[52] The topic of Stern's discussion here is the striking difference between the earlier and the later Swann, and the way in which we are enabled to put together, in a kind of mosaic, the impressions Swann makes at various times and in many different situations; Stern goes on to explain that, "We do arrive at something resembling a precise knowledge of Swann."[53] In Sebald's *Austerlitz*, we get more than disparate glimpses of the protagonist, yet the lengthy accounts of his life that Austerlitz gives the narrator are separated by considerable temporal gaps: the first meeting occurs in the 1960s in the waiting room at Antwerp station; the second in a bar in London decades later; in a letter to the narrator in the late 1990s, Austerlitz explains that he has sold his house in London and will devote himself to filling in the missing details of his biography. If the reader finds Austerlitz's story mostly continuous, that is largely because it is mediated by the narrator; the sustained voice of the narrator makes the repeated backtracking and circling around in chronology less obvious than it might have been otherwise. The narrator's relation to the protagonist is quite different from that of Proust's narrator to Swann. In Proust, the narrator's observations of Swann are indebted to a perceptual model akin to that of the Impressionists; in Sebald, the narrator does not so much observe Austerlitz as reproduce the latter's own problematic narrative.

One of Sheila Stern's most telling observations concerns the narrator's ability to affect the reader. Proust, she remarks, does so through a certain "intimacy" of tone "that has the effect of an extension of the writing self, which accommodates us, while we read, like an alter ego."[54] It is not surprising that Sebald should register this view of the relation between writer and reader in the midst of composing *Austerlitz*, a novel of alter egos and of the strangely compelling effects of the protagonist's story-telling on the narrator. Yet Sebald's own approach to this and related problems was somewhat different from Proust's: whereas in Proust, the narrator adopts an intimate tone toward the reader, this immediacy is replaced in *Austerlitz* by the intimacy between narrator and protagonist. The point of *Austerlitz* is, after all, to explore the problem of mediation, most particularly with respect to Walter Benjamin's theory about storytelling as a mode of giving counsel.[55]

One question that remains open is that of the relation between Sebald's narrators and his biographical person. Is this relation similar to that between the narrator and the author of the *Recherche*? In the debate about Sebald's narrators, some scholars have decided to use the term "pseudo-Sebald", perhaps in imitation of the related term "pseudo-Marcel".[56] The term owes much to the Albertine section of Proust's novel, in which the notion that the narrator's first name might possibly be "Marcel" is at once suggested and retracted. In *The Distinction of Fiction*, Dorrit Cohn comments that at least in two instances Proust carries the "imbrication of his fictional world in the real world to emphatically elaborate extremes", while at the same time, the narrator insists equally emphatically that the entire book is fictitious.[57] Sheila Stern addresses this question in a judicious formulation that Sebald marked in the margin of her book: contrasting Proust's novel with Dickens' first-person novel *David Copperfield*, she comments: "It would not be candid to pretend that *La Recherche* is fully fictional in that sense [i.e., in the sense of *David Copperfield*], but by means of various transferences and suppressions the author frees himself from autobiographical fact for as long as the design of the novel requires it."[58]

Proust's attempts to disengage his narrator from an identification with the biographical author are in large measure the result of his rejection of Sainte-Beuve's argument that a literary text could only be understood in the context of biographical knowledge about its author. Sebald, in contrast, seems to challenge the now almost unquestioningly accepted notion that the narrator must never be conflated with the author. In endowing his narrators with the same interests as himself, in portraying them as visiting places he visited and as having friendships with people he actually knew, Sebald provokes questions that resist easy answers. By constructing his narrators so that they share key experiences with him, Sebald makes no claim to writing entirely fictitious works. Indeed, the fact that Sebald did not provide a genre designation for three of his prose works, *Schwindel. Gefühle.*, *Die Ringe des Saturn* and *Austerlitz*, suggests that he did not consider them as novels. Furthermore, Sebald seems to have been very conscious of the scholarly attention his works would receive. By partially constructing his *Nachlaß* ahead of time, Sebald reveals something of his working methods while also thumbing his nose at scholarly preoccupations. Revealing some of his sources while concealing others, the folders of photographic and other materials continue the mystifications of his literary texts in his posthumous papers.

I would like to conclude this essay with a brief discussion of what Sebald did not learn from French narrative. Most notably, he does not show any awareness that one of Flaubert's greatest achievements is his brilliant handling of free indirect discourse. Long held to be the touchstone of fine literature, free indirect discourse is now employed by a wider range of authors; it is difficult to imagine a time when the technique could have caused the confusion that it did for readers of *Madame Bovary*, who seem to have believed that the narrator's infiltration into the thoughts of his characters meant that the author accepted those thoughts and their moral implications. One reason why Sebald does not use free indirect discourse may be that his reading of Flaubert during the gestational period of his own fictional writing did not include *Madame Bovary*; at least, there does not appear to be any evidence to this effect (though he may have read it earlier). Another reason is that Sebald's major literary texts are in the first person,[59] a form that does not readily accommodate the technique of free indirect discourse.

By the same token, Sebald does not plumb the depths of his characters' subconscious: the remarkable exploration of time and memory in *Austerlitz*, for example, does not include forays into the deeper recesses of the protagonist's psyche. Several episodes do suggest that there is more than meets the eye: Austerlitz's discovery of the unused waiting room at Liverpool Street Station, his stay at Marienbad, and his travel by train across Germany on his return from Prague, to name some of the most prominent moments in the novel. Yet despite these hints at something that may be concealed, the text remains on the surface of things, crossing vast amounts of terrain both literal and figurative but always stopping short of plumbing the depths. Just as Sebald's first-person narrative focus scarcely lends itself to the use of free indirect discourse, it virtually forbids interior monologue.[60] So too does Proust's use of first-person narration in the *Recherche*, where the narrator sometimes regards himself as a deep-sea diver but in fact never encounters anything other than the fascinating but often deceptive surfaces of his world. Rather than exploring the depths, Sebald is concerned to show us how the mind works at a more conscious level. In *Die Ringe des Saturn*, he demonstrates the fugitive nature of the mind as it establishes associative connections, takes off on digressions, gets side-tracked by chance encounters, and otherwise fails to conform to the requirements of logical thinking.

One formal feature that Sebald's narratives eschew is the combination of description, conversation and action that was a mainstay of the nineteenth-century novel. This structure, which persists in many novels today, creates a space where fictional characters speak in individual voices. Even when a novel is told by a narrator with distinctive habits of speech, the narrator's voice does not usually bleed over into the conversations of other characters.[61] In Sebald's *Austerlitz*, however, narrator and protagonist speak in exactly the same voice. This effect is particularly striking because Sebald uses neither quotation marks nor the subjunctive of indirect speech.[62] In his earlier works, he had already practiced the seamless transition from the unnamed narrator to another source (written or oral), although there are some moments where the subjunctive still occurs, as it does for a brief moment during the conversation between the narrator and Alec Garrard in *Die Ringe des Saturn*.[63] *Austerlitz* is the most consistent example of Sebald's method of rendering the speech of other characters in the indicative without quotation marks. One small exception is the first sentence spoken by Vera, which is represented by double embedding ("sagte Vera, sagte Austerlitz"). Addressing Austerlitz in French, the language they had spoken together in Prague, she sounds very different from either Austerlitz or the unnamed narrator: "Jacquot [...], est-ce que c'est vraiment toi?"[64] After that, however, her words for the most part blend smoothly into the rest of the narrative. By eliminating most markers of direct or indirect speech, the text lulls our skepticism to a considerable extent. This is one reason why many readers are reluctant to entertain the notion that Austerlitz may not "really" have the past that he is convinced he has discovered. Yet what prevents us from thinking that he might be suffering from false memory syndrome? By assimilating the protagonist's voice to the narrator's *Austerlitz* takes the proverbial "suspension of disbelief" to an extreme, using uniformity of tone to create, surprisingly, an effect of narrative credibility.

Sebald's narrative innovations rest on his recognition, first, of the fundamentally digressive nature of the human mind, and second, of its powerfully assimilative mechanisms. While our attention is constantly drawn to things outside us, our understanding of them works continually to bring them into harmony with our existing expectations. This double movement, centrifugal and centripetal, can be partially traced back to the French narratives that Sebald read or read about. Butor, Flaubert and Proust present different versions of the strange loops that characterize Sebald's literary texts. Yet Sebald also strikes out on his own through the challenge he presents to modern tenets about the relation of author to narrator and the problem of credibility in fiction.

Bibliography

Aragon, Louis. *Le Paysan de Paris*. Paris: Gallimard [Poche], 1926.
Bales, Richard. "Home and Displacement: The Status of the Text in Sebald and Proust". In *Schreiben ex patria / Expatriate Writing*, edited by Gerhard Fischer, 461–74. Amsterdam: Rodopi, 2009.
Benjamin, Walter. *Illuminationen. Ausgewählte Schriften*. Frankfurt am Main: Suhrkamp, 1977.
Bray, Joe. "The Source of 'Dramatized Consciousness': Richardson, Austen, and Stylistic Influence". *Style* 35, no. 1 (2001): 18–33.

Bülow, Ulrich von. "Sebalds Korsika-Projekt". In *Wandernde Schatten: W. G. Sebalds Unterwelt*, 211–24. Marbach: Deutsche Schillergesellschaft, 2008. Exhibition catalogue.
——"The Disappearance of the Author in the Work: Some Reflections on W. G. Sebald's *Nachlass* in the Deutsches Literaturarchiv Marbach". In *Saturn's Moons: A W. G. Sebald Handbook*, edited by Jo Catling and Richard Hibbitt, 247–63. Oxford: Oxbow Books, 2011.
Butor, Michel. *"L'emploi du temps" suivi de "L'Exemple" de Georges Raillard*. Paris: Union générale d'éditions, 1957. Translated by Jean Stewart as *Passing Time* New York: Simon and Schuster, 1960.
Catling, Jo. "*Bibliotheca abscondita*: On W. G. Sebald's Library". In *Saturn's Moons: A W. G. Sebald Handbook*, edited by Jo Catling and Richard Hibbitt, 265–98. Oxford: Oxbow Books, 2011.
Cohn, Dorrit. *The Distinction of Fiction*. Baltimore: Johns Hopkins University Press, 1999.
Dakyns, Janine. *The Middle Ages in French Literature 1851–1900*. London: Oxford University Press, 1973.
——"The Nineteenth Century (Post-Romantic)". *Year's Work in Modern Language Studies* 53 (1991): 180–207.
Descombes, Vincent. *Proust: Philosophie du roman*. Paris: Éditions de minuit, 1987.
Flaubert, Gustave. "La Légende de Saint Julien l'hospitalier". Vol. 2 of *Oeuvres*. Paris: Gallimard (Bibliothèque de la Pléiade), 1952.
——*Trois contes*. Vol. 2 of *Oeuvres*. Paris: Gallimard (Bibliothèque de la Pléiade), 1952.
——*Voyage aux Pyrénées et en Corse*. Vol. 2 (*Par les champs et par les grèves; Correspondance 1830–40*) of *Oeuvres complètes*, edited and with preface by Maurice Nadeau. Lausanne: Société Coopérative Éditions Rencontre, 1964.
Heath, Stephen. *Gustave Flaubert: Madame Bovary*. Cambridge: Cambridge University Press, 1992.
Kubinyi, Laura R. "Defense of a Dialogue: Michel Butor's *Passing Time*". *Boundary 2: A Journal of Contemporary Literature and Culture* 4, no. 3 (1976): 885–904.
La Varende, Jean de. *Gustave Flaubert*. Translated by Hans Magnus Enzensberger. 6th ed. Hamburg: Rowohlt, 1996.
Martens, Lorna. "Empty Center and Open End: The Theme of Language in Michel Butor's *L'Emploi du temps*". *PMLA* 96, no. 1 (1981): 49–63.
Mauriac, Claude. *Marcel Proust par lui-même*. Paris: Le Seuil, 1954. Translated by Paul Raabe as *Marcel Proust in Selbstzeugnissen und Bilddokumenten*. (17th ed.) Hamburg: Rowohlt, 1997.
Münchberg, Katharina. "Glückhafte Vergegenwärtigung, unheimliche Wiederkehr. Zwei Formen der Erinnerung bei Proust und W. G. Sebald". *Cahiers d'études germaniques*, 48–49 (2005): 159–72.
Orr, Mary. "Provincial Transfers and French Cultures: Flaubert's *Voyage aux Pyrénées et en Corse*". In *Visions/Revisions: Essays on Nineteenth-Century French Culture*, edited by Nigel Harkness et al., 83–97. Oxford: Peter Lang, 2003.
Proust, Marcel. *Auf der Suche nach der verlorenen Zeit*. Translated by Eva Rechel-Mertens. Frankfurt am Main: Suhrkamp, 1964.
——*À la Recherche du temps perdu*. Vols 1–4. Paris: Gallimard (Bibliothèque de la Pléiade), 1987–89.
——*Finding Time Again*. Edited by Christopher Prendergast. Translated by Ian Patterson. New York: Penguin, 2002.

—*Swann's Way*. Edited by Christopher Prendergast. Translated by Lydia Davis. New York: Viking Penguin, 2003.

Rangaran, Sudarsan. "Lies and Betrayals: Rheoric in Butor's *L'emploi du temps*". *Symposium* (Winter 2007): 247–65.

Sebald, W. G. *Der Mythos der Zerstörung im Werk Döblins*. Stuttgart: Klett, 1980.

—*Beschreibung des Unglücks: zur österreichischen Literatur von Stifter bis Handke*. Frankfurt am Main: Fischer, 1985.

—*Unheimliche Heimat: Essays zur österreichischen Literatur*. Frankfurt am Main: Fischer, 1995.

—"Das Schrecknis der Liebe. Überlegungen zu Schnitzlers *Traumnovelle*". *Merkur: Deutsche Zeitschrift für europäisches Denken* 39, no. 2 (1985): 120–31.

—*Die Ausgewanderten. Vier lange Erzählungen*. Frankfurt am Main: Fischer, 1994. Translated by Michael Hulse as *The Emigrants*. New York: New Directions, 1996.

—*Die Ringe des Saturn: Eine englische Wallfahrt*. Frankfurt am Main: Fischer, 1997. Translated by Michael Hulse as *The Rings of Saturn*. New York: New Directions, 1998.

—*Logis in einem Landhaus*. Frankfurt am Main: Fischer, 2000.

—*Austerlitz*. Frankfurt am Main: Fischer, 2003. Translated by Anthea Bell. New York: Modern Library, 2001.

—*Campo Santo*. Edited by Sven Meyer. Frankfurt am Main: Fischer, 2006. Translated by Anthea Bell. New York: The Modern Library, 2005.

Stern, Sheila. *Proust: Swann's Way*. Cambridge: Cambridge University Press, 1989.

Stifter, Adalbert. *Der Nachsommer*. Vol. 4 of *Gesammelte Werke*. Frankfurt am Main: Insel, 1959.

Walsh, Richard. "Who is the Narrator"? *Poetics Today* 4, no. 4 (1997): 495–513.

Wood, James. *The Broken Estate: Essays on Literature and Belief*. London: Jonathan Cape, 1999.

Notes

1 Sebald, *Mythos der Zerstörung*, 7.
2 Ibid., 136.
3 The manuscripts, materials, and collections of images connected with Sebald's literary writing are housed at the Deutsches Literaturarchiv in Marbach. I am grateful to the archive and its curators and librarians, especially to Ulrich von Bülow, for the opportunity to examine parts of this material.
4 I am grateful to Houghton Library, Harvard, for the chance to consult the typescripts of Michael Hulse's English translations of Sebald, carefully corrected by Sebald himself.
5 This copy is in the collection of books owned by Sebald that is now held at the Deutsches Literaturarchiv in Marbach. I am grateful to the archive, especially to Nikolai Riedel, for the opportunity to examine this and other books from Sebald's personal library. For informative discussions of this collection, see Bülow, "The Disappearance of the Author in the Work"; and Catling, "*Bibliotheca abscondita*".
6 Butor, *L'emploi du temps*, 78. The phrase Sebald marks is rendered "a small private revenge" in Jean Stewart's translation (Butor, *Passing Time*, 55). Sebald comments that he "began to read *L'Emploi du Temps* for that reason", i.e., to take revenge on the city of Manchester, the model for Butor's Bleston. In what

follows, I cite passages from Sebald's reading in the language of the book he owned and marked up; an English translation follows in the text or in a note.
7   Sebald is quoting from p. 267 of the novel, where he has underlined in purple felt-tipped pen the phrase "traduisant, toujours traduisant" (translating, always translating)—these words are omitted in Stewart's translation (Butor, *Passing Time*, 192).
8   Butor, *L'emploi du temps*, 263. "This table which served me as a rampart against Bleston" (Butor, *Passing Time*, 187).
9   Butor, *L'emploi du temps*, 274. "Ce cordon de phrases est un fil d'Ariane parce que je suis dans un labyrinth, parce que j'écris pour m'y retrouve." (That rope of words is like Ariadne's thread, because I am in a labyrinth, because I am writing in order to find my way out of it; Butor, *Passing Time*, 195).
10 *Die Ringe des Saturn*, 206; *The Rings of Saturn*, 173.
11 See also the story "Max Aurach" in *Die Ausgewanderten* (217–35), explicitly set in Manchester; translated as "Max Ferber" (*The Emigrants*, 147–237).
12 Rangaran, "Lies and Betrayals", 27.
13 Kubinyi, "Defense of a Dialogue", 887–8.
14 Martens, "Empty Center and Open End", 58. See also her chapter on the same work in *The Diary Novel* (Cambridge: Cambridge University Press, 1985), 213–32. In this essay, I cite the earlier version.
15 Martens, "Empty Center and Open End", 51.
16 Butor, *L'emploi du temps*, 53. "It seems to me that Bleston exaggerates certain characteristics of such urban centers, that none other is as cunning or as powerful in its witchcraft" (Butor, *Passing Time*, 36).
17 Butor, *L'emploi du temps*, 61; Sebald marks this passage in the margin. "This huge cancerous growth, this organism in which the different systems were picked out in appropriately colored printer's ink" (Butor, *Passing Time*, 41).
18 Butor, *L'emploi du temps*, 105; Sebald marks this passage in the margin with a double line. "You must remember that this is a work of the Renaissance. The artist paid tribute to Cain as being the father of all the arts" (Butor, *Passing Time*, 75).
19 In all three genres, Walter Benjamin is an important precursor for Sebald.
20 The edition, using the 1953 translation by Eva Rechel-Mertens, was published in 1964. In each of the thirteen volumes, Sebald has written "ex libris/ Winfried Sebald" on the blank first page, followed by the month and year. Occasional crossing-out and correction of the year suggest some uncertainty whether the year is 1964 or 1965.
21 When Sebald's reading is at issue, titles are given in the language in which he read (or marked up) the work. In other instances, I use the original titles.
22 "The comparisons extend over hundreds of pages; but they're rare!" (my translation).
23 Building on Rainer Warning, who notes that Proust's *Recherche* begins to undermine the notion of memory as specific to individual "Innerlichkeit" (interiority), Münchberg shows that in Sebald individual memory has been replaced by a socially communicative memory that endangers the structure of individual identity (Münchberg, "Glückhafte Vergegenwärtigung", 160–1).
24 Proust, *Auf der Suche nach der verlorenen Zeit*, vol. 2, 464, 486. "The cloakroom of his memory" (Proust, *Swann's Way*, 364). "He admired the terrible re-creative power of his memory" (Ibid., 381).
25 Proust, *Auf der Suche nach der verlorenen Zeit*, vol. 1, 119. "If my parents had allowed me, when I was reading a book, to go to visit the region it described,

I would have believed I was taking an invaluable step forward in the conquest of truth" (Proust, *Swann's Way*, 88).
26 Proust *Auf der Suche nach der verlorenen Zeit*, vol. 13, 329. "Only a kind of optical instrument which he offers the reader to enable him to discern what without this book he might perhaps see in himself" (Proust, *Finding Time Again*, 220). Sebald also marks a related passage about the book as a magnifying glass for its readers (Proust, *Auf der Suche nach der verlorenen Zeit*, vol. 13, 493; Proust, *Finding Time Again*, 342–3).
27 Sebald, *Unheimliche Heimat*, 65–86.
28 Aragon, *Paysan*, 155. This is one of the passages Sebald marks in his copy.
29 Janine Dakyns was a colleague of Sebald at the University of East Anglia. See *Ringe des Saturn*, 16–19. Her published work was on nineteenth-century literature, including a book on the Middle Ages in late nineteenth-century French literature; she also wrote a book on letters from Tennyson to an ancestor of hers. In her annotated bibliographical report on work in post-Romantic nineteenth-century literature during the year 1991, she shows wide-ranging knowledge and informed judgment (on Flaubert, see Dakyns, *Year's Work*, 95–8). As recorded in *Ringe des Saturn*, she died in 1994.
30 Sebald's manuscripts about Corsica were published posthumously: one selection by Sven Meyer under the title *Campo Santo* (2003), and additional versions assembled and introduced by Ulrich von Bülow (2008).
31 Ulrich von Bülow reports that Sebald had taken Flaubert's "Un Coeur simple" with him on his trip to Corsica (Bülow, "Sebalds Korsika-Projekt", 144). "Un Coeur simple" and "La Légende de Saint Julien l'hospitalier" are the first two stories in Flaubert's *Trois contes*; the third is "Hérodiade".
32 Varende, *Gustave Flaubert*.
33 Ibid., 28. "Increasingly, the writer got caught up in his drafts, made changes, reformulated, struggled with every sentence" (my translation).
34 Ibid., 48.
35 Wood, *Broken Estate*, 48–9. The book includes an essay on Sebald himself, which he also carefully marked.
36 Ibid., 52.
37 Ibid., 53. Countering Wood's suggestion that Flaubert's use of detail is a mannerism, Sebald writes in the margin: "but the change of level or view makes it work."
38 Wood, 59. The italics are Stephen Heath's. See his *Gustave Flaubert*, 145.
39 Mary Orr comments that Flaubert's account of his first trip, *Voyage aux Pyrénées et en Corse*, "sets in place foundational tenets of his oeuvre: that nature is culture and culture nature, and civilization is barbarianism in another guise" (Orr, "Provincial Transfers", 96). The similarity with Sebald's conception of human and natural destruction is apparent.
40 Flaubert, *Voyage aux Pyrénées et en Corse*, 104.
41 Bülow "Sebalds Korsika-Projekt", 198, 217.
42 Ibid., 218.
43 Also in the late 1990s, Sebald seems to have purchased the Rowohlt monograph on Proust by Mauriac, *Marcel Proust in Selbstzeugnissen*. While the volume shows very scant markings, it does testify to Sebald's revived interest in Proust at that time.
44 Stern, *Proust: Swann's Way*, 80.

45 Proust, *Auf der Suche nach der verlorenen Zeit*, vol. 13, 516. "Every hour of the past" (Proust, *Finding Time Again*, 356). Sebald underlines this passage in blue ink in the German.
46 Proust, *Auf der Suche nach der verlorenen Zeit*, vol. 13, 275. "The miracle of an analogy" (Proust, *Finding Time Again*, 180).
47 Stern, *Proust: Swann's Way*, 35.
48 Ibid., 56.
49 Proust, *Die wiedergefundene Zeit*, 506. This is the final (13th) volume of the German Proust translation: its title is a direct rendering of the French volume title, *Le Temps retrouvé*. Prendergast's English title is *Finding Time Again*, which avoids the more familiar but less accurate *Time Regained*. The quoted passage means "just as extremely seasick people, when crossing the Caspian Sea on a steamboat, don't show even the slightest resistance if they are told that they will be thrown into the water" (my translation from the German version that Sebald read).
50 Cf. *Austerlitz*, 182. For a discussion of this textual appropriation, see Richard Bales, "Home and Displacement", 464. Bales compares Sebald's version with the French original, but not with the German translation Sebald owned and marked. Anthea Bell's translation of *Austerlitz* naturally follows Sebald's adapted version: "about to be thrown overboard" (123).
51 In the lower margin of Stern, *Proust: Swann's Way*, 45. "This Terezin and its whole surroundings were, even today, so depressing, that" (my translation). The German verb is in the subjunctive of indirect speech, suggesting that Sebald is sketching part of Austerlitz's narrative (though, in the end, this novel does not use the subjunctive for its characters' narration).
52 These jottings are in Stern, *Proust: Swann's Way*, 46. The phrase "Auss. in Paris", short for "Aussicht in Paris", means "view in Paris"; "Truppenübungsplatz" means "military exercise ground".
53 Ibid., 46.
54 Ibid., 40.
55 See Benjamin's essay "Der Erzähler" in *Illuminationen*, 385–410.
56 See Descombes, *Proust: Philosophie du roman*.
57 Cohn, *Distinction*, 64–5.
58 Stern, *Proust: Swann's Way*, 5–6.
59 Narrative theorists do not agree on whether first-person narratives can include free indirect discourse. Among those who believe it can, Joe Bray argues that "first-person narrators can dramatize their own consciousness when recalling their own past thoughts" (Bray, "The Source of 'Dramatized Consciousness'", 21).
60 One can hardly reproach him for not referring to Dujardin's *Les lauriers sont coupés*, the earliest version of a complete narrative in the form of interior monologue; but he certainly knew its German successors, Schnitzler's "Leutnant Gustl" and "Fräulein Else". As for depth psychology more generally, Sebald did write an essay on Schnitzler's "Traumnovelle". See his essay "Das Schrecknis der Liebe. Überlegungen zu Schnitzlers *Traumnovelle*" (Sebald, *Beschreibung des Unglücks*, 38–60).
61 Richard Walsh points out that just because many characters in *Huckleberry Finn* speak in dialect, we do not assume that the narrator of the novel (Huck himself) is a master mimic (Walsh, "Narrator", 508).
62 Sebald's measured style has often been compared with the characteristically even tone of Adalbert Stifter; yet unlike Sebald in *Austerlitz*, Stifter uses the

subjunctive to indicate indirect speech by a character other than the narrator. It is true, however, that in direct speech, Stifter's individual figures do not tend to differ in their style of expression. See, for example, the conversation between the narrator and his host in chapter 6 of *Der Nachsommer*.

63 In a transition from Garrard's direct speech in English (rendered in italics without the use of quotation marks), an entire sentence uses the subjunctive of indirect speech: "Man müsse die Mischna studieren, fuhr er fort, und sämtliche anderen verfügbaren Quellen [...], denn nur so komme man auf die richtigen Ideen" (*Rings of Saturn*, 291). Garrard's remarks then continue for over half a page in the indicative, again without quotation marks. In the typescript of Michael Hulse's English translation of *The Rings of Saturn*, Sebald changes the name Alec Garrard to Thomas Abrams. The German subjunctive is rendered by the past tense in English: "You had to study the Mishnah" (*Rings of Saturn*, 245).

64 *Austerlitz*, 224.

IV Autobiography

9. Gender, Psychoanalysis, and Childhood Autobiography: Christa Wolf's *Kindheitsmuster*

Lorna Martens

The reception of Freud profoundly changed the genre of childhood autobiography, which originated in Romanticism. Representations of psychic complexity, Oedipal conflict and the deceptiveness of memory succeeded the well-remembered childhood idyll of an earlier era. Historians of childhood autobiography have shown that pre-Freudian writers turned to their childhoods for a variety of reasons: some idealize nostalgically, others analyze psychologically, while yet others, starting with Jules Vallès' *L'Enfant* in 1878, seek to expose the hardships of childhood.[1] Despite this variety, it can nevertheless be said that up to World War I, the genre contributed to formulating and then perpetuating what literary and art historians call the romantic myth of childhood. A romantic conception of childhood persisted—in fact with remarkable strength—in turn-of-the-century authors such as Proust and Rilke. A reader who picked up a childhood autobiography or other narrative of childhood (it is often hard to distinguish between fiction and non-fiction in this genre, nor, for my purposes, useful to do so) prior to World War I could reasonably expect to find that the work confirmed the cultural preconception that childhood is a delightful time in which the poetic vision of the child encounters the simplicity of life of yesteryear.

With the reception of Freudian theory, this conception of childhood was out of date. As early as Walter Benjamin's *Berliner Chronik*, the 1932 draft that eventually evolved into *Berliner Kindheit um Neunzehnhundert*, one sees the imprint of psychoanalytic memory theory on recollections of childhood. Michel Leiris, another author influenced by surrealism, who moreover underwent psychoanalysis in 1929, wrote his first autobiography of childhood and adolescence *L'Age d'homme* (1939) with an attention to sexuality that testifies to the revolution Freud had started to create in the popular vision of childhood. After the Second World War psychoanalytic conceptions invaded accounts of childhood en masse. Especially noticeable is a thematization of the constructed nature of childhood memories that reverses the confident remembering of nineteenth-century childhood autobiographers. Thus Leiris, commenting in *Biffures* on a childhood memory, casts doubt on it as a potential creation of the present.[2] Lip service to doubt in one's memories became habitual in post-World War II childhood autobiography, while in some works the issue is treated with considerable seriousness, for example Mary McCarthy's *Memories of a Catholic Girlhood* (1957), Nathalie Sarraute's *Enfance* (1983) and Christa Wolf's *Kindheitsmuster* (1976).

My purpose is to explore Wolf's debt to psychoanalysis in *Kindheitsmuster* and to relate Wolf's autobiographical novel to the genre of childhood autobiography. It will become apparent that Wolf dislocates the genre paradigm in two ways: she displaces the traditional focus of childhood autobiography from childhood on to memory, a dislocation that motivates a reliance on psychoanalysis, and she uses a personal story, which she strategically fictionalizes, in order to demonstrate, by way of analogy, the collective behavior patterns of the generation of Germans that grew up in the Third Reich. She thus de-centers a self-centered genre. If Rousseau aimed at a self-portrait and Wordsworth at the growth of the poet's mind, Wolf, in her quest for the representation of a mass mentality and mass amnesia, subverts self-portraiture. Turning the spotlight away from the self is not an unknown move in the history of childhood autobiography. Women writers in particular, whether out of modesty or in the pursuit of an ulterior agenda, have frequently, from the genre's inception on to the present day, sidestepped the traditional quest for self. What makes Wolf unique is the way in which she accomplishes her de-centering, namely, through the route of depth psychology.

Childhood autobiography has become a popular women's genre, but women came to it later than men. The earliest examples come from France, where George Sand's Rousseau-inspired *Histoire de ma vie* (1855) was seminal. The first French autobiography entirely devoted to childhood was Athénaïs Michelet's *Mémoires d'une enfant*, published in 1866. Michelet, wife of the famous historian and intimist Jules Michelet, produced a curious blend of local and family history and personal confession. A different, unrelated tradition arose in the English-speaking countries somewhat later in the nineteenth century. There, women's childhood autobiography grew out of children's literature, writing for the young, and writing about children much more than it imitated models of male autobiography. Lucy Larcom in *A New England Girlhood* (1889) barely says "I": instead, she writes about the ancestors, the family and the places where she grew up, opting instead for the personal pronoun "we"—by which she means the siblings and then the girls in the Lowell mills, where she worked starting at age eleven. Frances Hodgson Burnett in *The One I Knew the Best of All* (1893) opts for the third person and writes about "the Small Person", who, she assures us, resembles "any Child with an Imagination."[3] Thus initially women shied away from writing straightforwardly about themselves; to do so would have been to violate modesty and privacy. Yet childhood was easier for them to write about than maturity, since childhood enjoyed the cachet of innocence, and since, moreover, childhood experiences laid a certain claim to universality. Childhood yielded plenty of material to write about that was not terribly intimate.

Prior to the end of World War I, according to Richard N. Coe's bibliography in *Reminiscences of Childhood*, only eight childhood autobiographies by women were published, in contrast to the fifty-two titles by men that had appeared by 1920. Between 1921 and 1939, again according to Coe, twenty-six titles by women appeared. The remaining 142 titles by women listed in Coe's bibliography were published after World War II, and many more have been published since that bibliography appeared in 1984. Coe lists only one title published by a German woman, Ilse Koehn's *Mischling* (1977), but Brettschneider, who devotes a study to "childhood as a topic in autobiographical literature" in the German-speaking countries, lists, along with a few autobiographical works of fiction and posthumously published autobiographical writings on childhood, two women's childhood autobiographies published prior to Wolf's *Kindheitsmuster*: Marie von Ebner-Eschenbach's *Meine Kinderjahre* (1906) and Marieluise Kaschnitz's *Haus der Kindheit* (1956). One could add Hedwig Dohm's *Kindheitserinnerungen einer alten Berlinerin* (1912) and Ricarda Huch's "Mein erstes Jahrzehnt" (1931). But prior to *Kindheitsmuster*, the genre had obviously not yet undergone the boom it experienced starting in the late 1970s. *Kindheitsmuster* is not an early woman's childhood autobiography, but I have not found a German or in fact any other model for it. The work was, however, at the forefront of the wave of Third Reich childhood autobiographies published by non-persecuted writers in the 1970s and 1980s.[4] As so often, Wolf was original and trend-setting.

Rousseau and Wordsworth were important influences on the genre of childhood autobiography. They set the course for works to come, especially those written by men. Rousseau was the first to write about his childhood in detail, while Wordsworth can be taken to be one of the principal founders of childhood autobiography, since he wrote extensively and passionately about his childhood, initiating an influential vision of the intimate connection between childhood, nature and poetic creativity. He justified the novel undertaking of writing about his childhood by declaring that "the child is father of the man."[5] Both Rousseau and Wordsworth viewed childhood as formative. Men who wrote about their childhoods subsequently frequently, though not always, took a developmental approach, scrutinizing childhood for formative influences on adulthood. Both Rousseau and Wordsworth looked back on childhood as a lost paradise. Nostalgia remained a dominant, though not the universal, tone in childhood autobiographies written by men before World War I.

Childhood autobiography written by women developed along somewhat different lines, as is to be expected given women's different upbringing and life patterns. As various as early examples are, they frequently show a fascination with the figure of the mother, with whom the girl sometimes has a conflicting relationship, e.g. Michelet and Hanna Lynch (*Autobiography of a Child*, 1899). The "mother-daughter plot" remained a dominant in women's autobiography. Relatively few women writing prior to the reception of psychoanalysis create an idyllic picture of childhood; Julia Daudet in her "L'Enfance d'une Parisienne" [1982] and Ebner-Eschenbach might come closest. Some make a point of telling of traumatic incidents and negative turns of fate (Michelet, Lynch, Judith Gautier in *Le Collier des jours* [1902], and Marguerite Audoux in *Marie-Claire* [1910]); perhaps precisely these tribulations make the author's story seem worth writing. While self-portraits, even self-portraits of strong personalities, are found (in Lynch and Gautier), the teleological plot line is, not surprisingly, rare, though Burnett, for example, does gently tell the reader how, although she was a girl, she managed to become a writer. I conjecture that the reception of psychoanalysis was propitious to the rise of women's childhood autobiography. With psychoanalysis, the complex, conflicted self came into being; the idea of character ebbed and with it the sense that the life worth writing about was one that brought a career and fame. Psychoanalysis undermined the childhood idyll and the *Bildungsroman* plot and upgraded interest in child-parent conflict and in trauma. It also liberated the tongue.

Christa Wolf's *Kindheitsmuster* is a work in which the appropriation of psychoanalytic theory is particularly pronounced.[6] It is an example of the negative and critical retrospection that overshadows many women's childhood autobiographies; yet Wolf availed herself of the genre in a novel and original way, introducing two significant innovations. First, she sets herself up as an example and witness of something larger. This type of decentering has nothing to do with the self-deprecating modesty of early women childhood autobiographers; rather, her example-and-witness role anticipates more recent childhood autobiographers' use of the "child perspective device" in the service of some agenda. Examples include Fatima Mernissi's sympathetic presentation of Moroccan harem life in *Dreams of Trespass* (1994) and Arundhati Roy's exposé of postcolonial conditions in India in *The God of Small Things* (1997).

Wolf too appropriates the genre of childhood autobiography for didactic purposes, in order to profile the theme of growing up under fascism. Her protagonist's childhood is invoked not for its own sake but for its conformity to a "pattern" out of which so many contemporaneous German childhoods were cut.[7] Nelly stands for a whole generation of Germans who "forgot"—for whom a childhood lived under fascism was lost, inasmuch as it involved a positive interaction with fascism that was later repudiated. Seeking to contribute to cultural memory, Wolf chooses to present her theme as an adventure of *individual* memory. She constructs her book around details from her own childhood not for their own sake, not to achieve particularity, but, according to her own testimony, to lend authenticity to a "typical" account. She stated in 1973: "Ich schreibe ein Buch über eine solche Kindheit zu dieser Zeit. [...] Ich versuche authentisch zu sein dadurch, daß ich mich auf meine Erinnerung stütze und dann diese Erinnerung an Dokumenten überprüfe, die mir zugänglich sind."[8] As Therese Hörnigk confirms, she also fictionalizes, beyond just changing the names: "Obwohl in *Kindheitsmuster* eine mit den Lebensanfängen und biographischen Abläufen der Autorin sehr eng verbundene Kindheit und Jugend erzählt wird, kann das Buch nur bedingt als Autobiographie gelesen werden. [...] Authentische Erfahrungsverarbeitung ist mit fiktiven Elementen durchsetzt."[9] A degree of fictionalization is extremely common in childhood autobiographies. Especially authors who use childhood narrative in the service of an ulterior agenda feel free to retouch, embellish and invent. To take the cited examples, Mernissi admits to fictionalizing by conflating multiple real-life characters, while Roy's work, despite strong autobiographical elements, has a novelistic plot and is a self-declared novel.

Second, Wolf is to my knowledge the first author who wrote about his or her childhood because it exemplified a state of delusion, because as a child she was raised to accept and believe in what she later acknowledged was a pack of lies. Thus this is not a cherished childhood, eagerly remembered; rather, she represents it as a childhood that has been forgotten and can only be remembered with a great deal of pain. It is precisely this forgotten aspect of it that Wolf wants to probe. Why do we forget? How does memory work? Can we forget with impunity?

The inquest into memory holds the narrative together. Acts of recollection in the present of narration, in the four-year period from January 1971 to 2 May 1975 in which both Wolf and her narrator conceived and wrote the book, give the narrative its overarching structure. Reflecting back on her Nazi and wartime childhood and simultaneously on her brief visit in 1971 to the now-Polish town where she grew up, Wolf problematizes remembering from the outset of the book. The theme of memory dominates the first seven chapters, in which the narrator gives an account of her prewar childhood, and persists through the following six chapters, receiving a fresh analysis when the narrator reaches the period of the "Endlösung". Thereafter, when the childhood plot takes up her family's flight westwards after Germany's defeat, the theme of memory is dropped and superseded by another: the teenager Nelly's emotional numbness is paired with a crisis in the present of writing that consists of exhaustion, inability to write, and finally the appearance of puzzling anxiety attacks. Wolf pursues a double agenda: she shows how repression distorts memories, and she strongly suggests that repressed memories fissure the self and make a person sick. My contention is that both dramas, the drama of memory and the drama of anxiety, closely conform to psychoanalytic models.

Wolf represents her narrator as questing not just for memory but for knowledge of memory. The narrator consults many sources, from *Meyers Neues Lexikon* to recent memory theory.[10] Through her own quest for her childhood memories she "discovers" much that is known or commonly postulated about memory. Thus, for example, she implies that memory, which goes back precisely to the moment when the child first says "I" (16), is the basis for selfhood. By staging her narrator's return to her hometown in present-day Poland (a trip Wolf herself made) she demonstrates that memory is indeed triggered by cues, an idea made famous by Proust and accepted today. Her major insight, however, is one that Freud initiated and whose essential idea has been widely recognized (though without Freudian trappings) by modern psychology: that memory is partial, constructive and deceptive. We remember as it suits us to remember: consequently, we forget, repress, distort or refashion the past. The narrator draws this conclusion repeatedly and builds up to the point where she speaks of "die Erinnerung, dieses Betrugssystem" (226).[11]

Later, when the narrative turns to the topic of the extermination of the Jews, the narrator starts to theorize her unwillingness to remember with greater precision. She specifies that consciousness itself is darkening the memories that she had hoped to illuminate with its help (318). She observes that precisely when she thinks back on the Nazi events that Nelly participated in with the greatest degree of engagement, such as mass manifestations in the stadium, details are erased. She concludes: "Der Schwund muß einem tief verunsicherten Bewußtsein gelegen gekommen sein, das, wie man weiß, hinter seinem eigenen Rücken dem Gedächtnis wirksame Weisungen erteilen kann, zum Beispiel die: Nicht mehr daran denken. [...] Weil es nämlich unerträglich ist, bei dem Wort 'Auschwitz' das kleine Wort 'ich' mitdenken zu müssen" (337).[12] It is obvious that Wolf is relying very heavily here on tenets of psychoanalysis, on notions of repression and psychic censorship.

Besides Freud, there are probably other intertexts. Wolf acknowledged having read Mitscherlich.[13] All of her main theoretical points in *Kindheitsmuster* are made in Alexander and Margarete Mitscherlich's *Die Unfähigkeit zu trauern* (1967), a Freudian analysis of why the Germans "forgot" the Holocaust. The Mitscherlichs argue that the Germans collectively repressed a past that would awaken fear, guilt and shame; such repression results in neurosis with various symptoms, including anxiety; people do not remember objectively, but always color history to their advantage.[14] But the Mitscherlichs' analysis draws above all on the later Freud—on the narcissism essay, "Mourning and Melancholia", "The Ego and the Id", and beyond—and is, unsurprisingly, presented at a much higher level of psychoanalytical sophistication than Wolf's. Wolf adopts early Freudian theory: repression, the pathological potential of repressed memories, the notion that the split psyche is pathological; the distorting effect of the force of repression on memory. Arguably, the appearance of Ingeborg Bachmann's stunning novel *Malina* in 1971 may have further encouraged Wolf. Wolf was a great admirer of Bachmann's, and *Malina*, with its Holocaust themes, split protagonist, abundant use of dreams, and allusions to a past trauma that have made her protagonist forget, anticipates some of Wolf's techniques in *Kindheitsmuster* and may have provided Wolf with a model. Yet the parallels especially to early Freudian theory are so sharp that I would conjecture that they are based on a knowledge of relevant works rather than received ideas—especially since Wolf acknowledges having studied Freud "early on" in a letter to Habermas of 7 December 1991.[15]

In *Studies on Hysteria*, the founding work of psychoanalysis, Freud and Breuer assert that memories are responsible for the pathological condition of hysteria. They declare at the outset of their book that "hysterics suffer mainly from reminiscences."[16] Every case of hysteria involves a memory or set of memories that fester, inaccessible to normal consciousness, in a split-off area of the mind. The cure consists of finding out what they are, bringing them to the patient's consciousness and to words, and thereby getting rid of the nefarious *double conscience* that makes her sick. The healthy patient is whole, not split. The idea of pathogenic memories leads Freud to formulate the concept that would become a cornerstone of psychoanalysis: repression. He contends that the hysteric's pathogenic memories are incompatible with her self-conception, in conflict with her normal trains of thought, and so her mind "gets rid of" them, so to speak, by repressing them. They subsequently re-emerge in the form of somatic symptoms. Five years later, when Freud wrote *The Interpretation of Dreams*, he institutionalized repression and overthrew the idea of the normative wholeness of the mind. In *Studies on Hysteria*, however, repression makes the patient sick, and that idea unquestionably appeals to Christa Wolf.

Freud pursued the topic of memory in "Screen Memories", a paper he published in 1899, asserting there that so-called childhood memories are very frequently constructions that are invoked and even created in the service of a present interest. They stand in for something repressed and as such are thoroughly unreliable. Although Freud focused specifically on childhood memories, the fact that he soon thereafter extended the same mechanism to dreams and jokes, both of which show the distorting effects of repression, suggests that the mechanism could be seen to operate in memories generally. Without adopting Freud's notion of repression, twentieth-century psychology has experimentally verified that memory is constructive or reconstructive, starting with Sir Frederick C. Bartlett's milestone 1932 study *Remembering*. It is universally believed today that memory is untrustworthy and easily influenced.

Wolf adopts this entire line of thinking in *Kindheitsmuster*. Her narrator ostensibly queries the working of her memory, but in reality what she wonders is thoroughly given over to a Freudian psychic model. For her, undesirable memories are repressed into "verschlossene Räume in unseren Gedächtnissen" (107), just as they are for Freud and Breuer.[17] For Freud repression is dynamic; it is a force that puts up resistance.[18] For Wolf repression is similarly dynamic; she asserts that Germans have expended great energy on repressing the Nazi atrocities: "Du aber, neunundzwanzig Jahre später, wirst dich fragen müssen, wieviel verkapselte Höhlen ein Gedächtnis aufnehmen kann, ehe es aufhören muß zu funktionieren. Wieviel Energie und welche Art Energie es dauernd aufwendet, die Kapseln, deren Wände mit der Zeit morsch und brüchig werden mögen, immer neu abzudichten" (107).[19] Moreover, Wolf offers several examples of the type of memory displacement that Freud discusses in his essay "Screen Memories", in which a vivid but insignificant memory becomes a placeholder for something important. For example, she remembers the antics the children play behind the altar at her confirmation but is unable to recall the contemporaneous Battle of Stalingrad (374). Her "white ship" memory is similar to a screen memory: Nelly remembers such a "white ship" because (as she pieces together later) it implies war and is

Gender, Psychoanalysis, and Childhood Autobiography 153

closely linked to her contemporaneous anxious fantasy of her mother's death (211–12). Later in the book Wolf includes an admiring description of Dali's psychoanalytically inspired painting, "The Persistence of Memory"—its title, the narrator points out, is ironic—whose representation of memory as a surreal landscape mirrors her own views on memory.

The central theme of the first seven chapters, memory makes a comeback in Chapter 10, where it is a question of Nelly having forgotten events from the Final Solution period, when she was an enthusiastic Hitler youth group leader. The narrator reflects that her failure to remember events from the wartime years after she turned thirteen can no longer be chalked up to childhood amnesia. Rather, it is a case of repression, pure and simple. She elaborates: "Gerade jetzt, da Aufrichtigkeit sich lohnen würde, was ja nicht immer, vielleicht nicht einmal häufig der Fall ist, stößt du auf eine neue Art Erinnerungsverlust, nicht gleichzusetzen mit den Gedächtnislücken, welche die frühe Kindheit betreffen. [...] Jetzt aber scheint das Bewußtsein selber, verstrickt in die Vorgänge, über die es sich erinnernd erheben sollte, einer Teil-Verdüsterung zu unterliegen. Es scheint Mit-Urheber jener Verdunkelung zu sein, die du mit seiner Hilfe erhellen willst" (318).[20] First in *Studies on Hysteria* and then in *The Interpretation of Dreams*, Freud asserts that the psyche has a built-in mechanism to prevent unacceptable thoughts from reaching consciousness: repression. He identifies a psychic "censorship" whose job it is to keep incompatible thoughts out of the conscious mind. Wolf too speaks of a "Selbstzensur" (332).

According to Freud in *The Interpretation of Dreams*, dreams function as a vent for repressed material, which reaches consciousness in distorted form, under a disguise imposed by the censorship. In keeping with this theory, Wolf's narrator has a revealing dream that brings back forgotten material from her teenage years. It shows, in montage style, a Jewish friend, who in real life was shipped to Buchenwald, walking in the company of Nelly's German school friends. The narrator's dream analysis brings home an unpleasant truth. If the Jewish boy had been able to be in her home town at that time (admittedly an impossibility), he would more likely have walked in the company of the other German girls, who came from religious Christian families, than in Nelly's, who strove for social recognition through prominence in the Nazi youth group (she joined the ranks of the "Führeranwärterinnen" at age twelve). "Die Wächter vor den Toren des Bewußtseins abziehen": "Recall the guards from the gates of consciousness",[21] the narrator admonishes herself, unpleasantly reminded of her teenage devotion to the Nazi ideology. Besides blaming a consciousness-protecting censorship for her faulty memory, the narrator suggests that her repression persists into the present day, for, if she had wanted to, she could easily, on the occasion of her visit to G., have taken a look at the building that formerly housed the district headquarters of the Hitler Youth, but "it didn't occur to her" to do so (340).

In Chapter 12, the final chapter on the Nazi period before the tide of the war starts to turn and the plot transitions to the flight, Wolf links Nelly's memory problems to the amnesia of Germans of her generation through a story that allegorizes Hitler's sway over the masses: the story of the confirmation-party hypnotist. This hypnotist figures as a charismatic opportunist. Having been hired as a photographer for fourteen-year-old Nelly's confirmation party, he seizes the opportunity to put on a magic show, gets many of the guests interested, and soon usurps control of the party. He successfully hypnotizes Nelly's cousin, obliging her to do uncharacteristic, embarrassing things. This story not only shows how eerily easy it is to perpetrate a power grab and, thereafter, to get people dancing on one's string, but it also explores the relationship between the mental state of the "puppets" and their subsequent memories. Freud and Breuer practiced hypnosis on their Viennese hysterics in order to access the closed-off "second consciousness" that, in their view, housed the pathogenic kernel.[22] Hypnosis, endorsed as a hysteria treatment by French practitioners including Charcot, Bernheim and Liébeault, was well known to put patients in an "other condition" in which they were susceptible to suggestion but which they would not remember when they woke up. Wolf's narrator, citing present-day psychological tests, observes that novel stimuli produce more eye movements, which are a sign that memory is processing. Yet shoppers in supermarkets, she says, have been shown to blink less. In other words, too much novel information—the overwhelming masses of merchandise—put the shoppers in a state akin to hypnosis, causing them to stare (vacantly) and fail to remember, instead of processing the new information.

Walter Benjamin, theorizing the history of memory, espoused Freud's idea in *Beyond the Pleasure Principle* that consciousness arises in place of a memory trace. For him this implied that becoming conscious of something and committing it to memory are mutually exclusive. He associated the decline of memory in the nineteenth century with the barrage of stimuli or shocks to which the inhabitants of modern urban environments were constantly subjected. Such stimuli demanded an increased level of consciousness and impaired the functioning of memory. In Wolf's reading too, excessive and overpowering novelty causes memory to malfunction—although not because consciousness rises like a shield, but because the assault on it is so great that it fails to do so. In short, in her reading, fascism overwhelmed and stupefied the mind, hypnotizing the subject. By implication, capitalism (the supermarket) has the same effect.[23]

In general, Wolf shares Brecht's suspicion of spontaneous emotive responses, such as those that performers, politicians and marketing strategists strive to elicit, and avoids provoking them in her writing. Her use of multiple temporal levels, which allows her to change gears abruptly when the reader might get carried away by a story, is an alienation effect that aims at encouraging her reader to reflect instead of reading for the plot or identifying with the heroine. Thus, for example, at the beginning of the story of the flight, she undercuts the potentially exciting story of "how the Germans experienced the end of the war" by abruptly cutting to an anecdote about present-day East Germans singing obnoxious ethnic songs abroad (417).

Parallel to the story of the family's trek, in the last five chapters of the book, a new drama in the present of writing unfurls: a story of illness (typical for Wolf), whose most prominent symptoms are anxiety attacks. Chapter 17 is devoted to the topic of fear. The narrator stresses the mysterious nature of her present fear (535, 545) and says that she does not understand the reason for it. Yet a closer look at the "Fear" chapter shows that Wolf attributes this emotion to two principal causes. First, fear is a by-product of the destabilization of identity. It is a fear of "Selbstverrat und Schuld", and it comes "von weit her [...] und von klein auf" (546).[24] Wolf shows how Nelly struggled with her identity as a schoolchild. Again and again, the child strained every nerve to live up to an ideal, to embrace an identity, to conform to a socially admired role that another part of her, a more instinctive part, rebelled against. It is indicative that when her teacher asks the class to name examples of emotions, Nelly suggests "pretending". The narrator concludes that throughout her childhood she denied her "true feelings", even to herself (236).

Wolf's adoption of Freudian theory stops short at childhood: her purpose, to show corruption, demands a different, Romantic child concept, one that implies natural innocence. Recovering Nelly's past attitudes and perceptions means discovering the sequence of selves and roles into which Nelly was split. It is a process that threatens to re-fissure her present identity. At the beginning of her project the narrator writes that she feels the child in her—her "inner child"—"move". Nelly, she recalls, left that child behind when she fled her home town after the war. Both "movements", the present movement of the inner child and the past movement of the flight, provoke fear: "Ein Gefühl, das jeden Lebenden ergreift, wenn die Erde unter seinen Füßen sich bewegt: Furcht" (43).[25] Twice she says that fear arises from internal conflict, from prying herself apart from a familiar role: "die Angst, sich selbst zu zerreißen, wenn man sich von der Rolle lösen muß, die mit einem verwachsen war" (557).[26]

The narrator recognizes that fear drives her writing—in the sense that she hopes writing will push back her fear. "Die besondere Natur des Leidens, das 'Angst' heißt, ist es, die jene Art von Produkten hervortreibt, in denen du dich erkennst [...]. Schreibend den Rückzug der Angst betreiben" (518).[27] Thus ostensibly she evaluates writing in the opposite way from acts of memory, which provoke fear. But in fact it becomes clear that both remembering and writing are undertaken out of a therapeutic intent, and both therapies could be seen as ones that initially make the problem worse by stirring up sleeping dogs. The narrator compares her writing to being in a cave ("tief in der Höhle der Erzählung" [507]), indicating that with writing she excavates her unconscious. Her cave dream sustains this idea. She dreams, "poisoned by fear", that she is lying in an abysmal, dripping cave; going "home" is denied to her, for when she reaches her apartment she finds that the racist historian Felix Dahn now lives there and refuses to relinquish it (535). The exploration of the unconscious by acts of remembering and writing is necessary in order to vanquish fear, yet in order to do so, they must themselves first arouse fear.

Wolf's second related point is that fear is released by reviving events that should have, but did not, trigger fear at the time. The narrator's main anxiety attacks, which lead to hospitalization at the time of writing, are intercalated with her account of the fear-provoking events of the flight, the sequence of traumas to which the teenager Nelly is subjected: her father vanishes and she believes him dead; low-flying bombers terrify the refugees; her family lives in perpetual fear of the Russians before being captured by the Americans, whereupon they fall into the hands of the Russians, after all; they are quartered on a remote farm that is regularly attacked by bandits. During this sequence of events Nelly is emotionally numb: she suffers from "Gefühlstaubheit" (432). Wolf's purpose here is to show that the repressed is pathogenic. The narrator implies that it deformed her personality never to have had a real youth, to have been obliged to cultivate "Strenge, Konsequenz, Verantwortungsbewußtsein, Fleiß" from the age of sixteen on (508).[28] Nelly got used to having to "pull on the emergency brake" (508). According to the narrator, this lack of feeling where there should have been feeling takes its toll. She insists, "Das Ungelebte ist das Wirksame" (507).[29] Now, in the present, she notices that her attempt to touch what has been off-limits, to say what she hitherto has not said, provokes fear (545).

At this point in the text, where Wolf describes the flight, the child Nelly once again stands for a larger collectivity. She represents a "survivor". This identification is not made without a certain awkwardness, since it lumps refugees and concentration camp survivors together under the umbrella of a single concept. Nelly suffers from the intricate problem of one who was herself victimized, in the sense of indoctrinated by the Nazis, but by the same measure implicated as a bystander in the atrocities, and then "punished" by the German defeat. The narrator nevertheless calls her teenage self a "survivor". She uses the word "Überlebende", "survivors", to characterize the group of refugees among whom Nelly finds herself in the village of Bardikow in Mecklenberg: "Das Dorf war mit Leuten vollgestopft, die ihre Katastrophe überlebt, und mit solchen, die keine Katastrophe bemerkt haben. [...] Zögernd nur mischte sie sich ein auf der Seite der Überlebenden, weil sie zu ihnen gehörte" (487).[30] She thereby appropriates for this group, and for herself, as an explanation for her own psychic condition, some of what is known about the psychic condition of concentration camp survivors: "Überlebenssyndrom: Psychisch-physisches Krankheitsbild bei Menschen, die extremen Belastungen ausgesetzt waren. Ausgearbeitet am Beispiel von Patienten, die Jahre ihres Lebens als KZ-Häftlinge oder als Verfolgte verbringen mußten. Hauptsymptome: Schwere anhaltende Depressionen mit zunehmenden Kontaktstörungen, Angst- und Beklemmungszustände, Alpträume, Überlebensschuld, Gedächtnis- und Erinnerungsstörungen, zunehmende Verfolgungsangst" (485).[31] The adult narrator's psychological and physical problems do not extend to this entire catalogue, but she does suffer from fear, guilt and nightmares. She contrasts the living ("die Lebenden") with the survivors ("Überlebenden"): whereas the living can freely range over past and present, survivors have no "Rück-sicht" and no "Vor-sicht" (517). She implies that they dare not approach the "hole in the ice", the traumatic past. It nevertheless dominates them, closing down the possibility of change and thereby the future.

In the present, too, the narrator represents herself as driving with the "emergency brake" on (506)—alluding to the conflict in her over writing the book.[32] Her conflict over excavating her past produces somatic symptoms: her heart races; she is hospitalized; in the hospital, she begins to experience attacks of fear. There is a parallel here to the symptom "joining in the conversation", as Freud says, when the analyst gets closer to the hidden cause of the neurosis (296). When the narrator experiences these symptoms she is, indeed, near the end of her book, where she will be cured to the point of finally managing to speak of herself in the first person, an indication of her (regained) self-identity.[33]

The trajectory of events followed here is curiously similar to that of Josef Breuer's famous patient Anna O., the first case given in *Studies on Hysteria*. Breuer observes that "the affect of anxiety dominated her psychical disorder" (28). During the so-called "incubation period" Anna O. was, like Nelly, under great stress. She spent long hours watching at her sick father's bedside. The pathogenic, hysterogenic material entered her when she was in a "hypnoid state" (equivalent to hypnosis). It split Anna O.'s self—just as Nelly believes that her self was split. Just as Nelly did not feel fear when she was emotionally numb, but only feels it later when she relives the events in memory, so Anna O. did not feel fear when the frightening material entered her in her "hypnoid state", but rather experienced it later, when her physician helped her gain access to the split-off part of her mind that contained the traumatic memories. While attempting to treat Anna O., Breuer famously invented the "talking cure", the germ of the psychoanalytic method. He and his colleague Freud claimed to cure hysteria by awakening the "dark" memories to consciousness and letting the patient expel them in words. In Anna O.'s case, Breuer states that her mind was completely relieved when, "shaking with fear and horror, she had reproduced these frightful images and given verbal utterance to them" (29–30).

Wolf's narrator likewise believes that her writing dispels fear and likewise suggests that her project is ultimately therapeutic. In fact, the "talking cure" idea informs the novel profoundly. As a child, Nelly was unable to voice her conflicted feelings. The Nazi regime usurped the sayable. No one dares speak his or her mind. Charlotte Jordan, Nelly's mother, puts herself at great risk on the few occasions when she rashly speaks out. Inability to speak surfaces in the narrator's dream of the torture victim who has no mouth (249). The solution in this dream, as Nelly thinks, would be for the victim to write. Granted, Nelly expresses her ambivalence about the efficacy of writing: implements for writing are produced, yet the victim continues to be tortured. In a previous dream, she casts doubt on the usefulness of her own writing by imagining that her writing hand is cut off (50). Yet writing proves, if not mighty like the sword, at least cathartic for the writer, for after Chapter 17, fear does not return. Throughout the book, Wolf engineers a play with pronouns to express her narrator's sense that she is not at one with herself. The narrator eschews the first person; she refers to Nelly (the child she does not identify with) as "she", and addresses her adult self as "you". A leitmotif in the text is the idea that the book would be finished if she could say "I". The book, in fact, ends ambivalently; the narrator does not declare the success of her venture, but poses questions about it, which she says she cannot answer. In spite of this, she *does* indeed say "ich" in the final four paragraphs of the book, thereby closing a fragile parenthesis to the first chapter, where the child Nelly first says "ich", a pronoun never to occur again until the end. This "ich" resonates with her earlier statement that "der Endpunkt wäre erreicht, wenn zweite und dritte Person wieder in der ersten zusammenträfen, mehr noch: zusammenfielen. Wo nicht mehr 'du' und 'sie'—wo unverhohlen 'ich' gesagt werden müßte" (507).[34]

A final peculiarity of Anna O's illness is that in the final period of the illness, the period during which Breuer used the cathartic method and gradually cured the patient, she spent part of each day living in the past, day for day. In the winter of 1881–82, she lived in the winter of 1880–81, that is, in the first phase of the illness. "This re-living of the previous year continued till the illness came to its final close" (33). Additionally, she relived the genesis of each hysterical symptom during the incubation period of the illness, which lay yet further back, describing, in reverse order, "all the occasions on which it had appeared" until she arrived at its "first appearance", whereupon the symptom was "permanently removed" (35). Without adopting the distinctive reverse chronological pattern of Breuer's cure, Wolf builds a similar reliving (as opposed to mere remembering) of the past into her narrator's story at the same stage of her illness, that is, after the narrator overcomes her fear. At the start of Chapter 18, the narrator starts to live in the past: "Es ist dahin gekommen, daß du dich konzentrieren mußt, um dich an den Fernsehfilm von gestern abend zu erinnern. Blaß, blaß. Dagegen: gestochen scharf Steguweits Küche" (558).[35]

Wolf became a writer in the era when the GDR writer had a social mission. The conviction that a work needed to have a broadly applicable moral message never left her and shapes her work generally. Perhaps this is why Wolf has inspired so much literary criticism: we critics like to identify these messages. Before writing *Kindheitsmuster*, she habitually used her fiction to make a point. She was an early feminist who, from 1969 on, wrote several stories that make a feminist point, notably "Unter den Linden", "Neue Lebensansichten eines Katers", and "Selbstversuch". A spate of feminist writing, of which her novel *Kassandra* (1983) is the outstanding example, followed *Kindheitsmuster*. What of *Kindheitsmuster* itself? Autobiography does not demand the transmission of a message, yet it can do so. Maxine Hong Kingston's contemporaneous autobiographical novel of childhood *The Woman Warrior* (1975), for instance, is a work that specifically addresses feminine issues and suggests a possible solution to the type of conflict experienced by a Chinese-American girl. In contrast, Wolf's work does not show the impact of National Socialism on girls or women in particular. *Kindheitsmuster* makes a point, but it is not a feminist one. The fact that the feminist agenda one might have expected is lacking reinforces the conclusion that Wolf had a different purpose in mind.

Writing about the "confession", which, she asserts, became a "distinctive subgenre of autobiography" in the 1970s and 1980s, Rita Felski notes that the women who write such "confessions" characteristically downplay the uniqueness of the protagonist/narrator in favor of emphasizing aspects that relate to a notion of communal female identity. They introduce fictional elements to the same end: to underscore communal identity. This trend, according to Felski, should be seen in the context of the contemporaneous emergence of what Keitel identifies as literary "counter-public spheres", which are concerned with affirming the oppositional values and experiences of a group, such as women or gays.[36] *Kindheitsmuster* shares some of the often-encountered characteristics of the women's "confessions" of the 1970s and 1980s: a fragmented, diary-like structure designed to awaken the impression of intimacy and authenticity; fictionalization; and a tendency toward self-castigation. The genealogy of these characteristics of women's writing, along with the notion of the "moral superiority of female expressiveness"[37] found in both Wolf and in the "confessions" certainly goes back at least as far as Bachmann. But the group that Wolf seeks to establish and speak for does not exclusively represent women but, rather, Germans of her generation.

As a woman's childhood autobiography, Christa Wolf's work is anomalous. Though written in the feminist 1970s by an author famous for championing women, it barely even touches on the issues that typically loom large in women's childhood autobiographies of any era, issues such as growing up female and the relationship with the mother.[38] To be sure, Wolf builds incredible landmarks in a girl's growing up, such as a young teen's crush on a woman teacher. Moreover, the mother, who remains unseduced by National Socialism, is an important figure. The narrator records an early fear of losing her mother's love (see 45) or losing her mother herself (e.g. the white ship memory [211f.]). She also puzzles over why, at the moment when it was imperative to flee L. at top speed, her mother opted to stay behind with the house instead of leaving with the children. But anxiety over possible maternal abandonment is kept small as a theme compared to the dimensions it assumes in other women's childhood autobiographies, such as, for example, Sarraute's *Enfance* or Jamaica Kincaid's *Annie John* (1983). Nelly has a credible relationship with her mother, but this relationship is not one of the book's pounding themes.[39] Most important: the woman who wrote *Nachdenken über Christa T.* does not say "I" herself. "I" means something different here than in *Nachdenken über Christa T.*, where it implied the assertion of one's individuality vis-à-vis the collective. Here its political punch has ceded to its psychological implications. It is a measure of mental health: "I" signals self-identity and psychic wholeness. Psychology dwarfs feminism in this childhood autobiography. Yet the subject position, as always in Wolf, is a feminine position. Her narrator embodies the positive qualities that Wolf typically imputes to femininity: sensitivity, insightfulness and moral superiority. Wolf gives fragility and suffering, in her work the indicators of an incorruptible conscience, considerable moral charge. The author may strategically (and, of course, also believingly) subject the narrator to the laws of psychoanalysis, but she does so without in the least adopting Freud's disempowering image of women.

By daring to quest for her Nazi childhood, the narrator shapes up as a wise and courageous figure. Correspondingly, if Wolf profiles herself through this book, it is inasmuch as she is the first major German writer who dares openly accuse herself of repressing a Nazi childhood.

Bibliography

Bartlett, Frederick C, Sir. *Remembering*. Cambridge: Cambridge University Press, 1932.
Bloom, Harold and Lionel Trilling, eds. *Romantic Poetry and Prose*. New York: Oxford University Press, 1973.
Brettschneider, Werner. *"Kindheitsmuster": Kindheit als Thema autobiographischer Dichtung*. Berlin: Erich Schmidt, 1982.
Breuer, Josef and Sigmund Freud. *Studies on Hysteria*. Translated by James Strachey. New York: Basic Books, n.d.
Burnett, Frances Hodgson. *The One I Knew the Best of All: A Memory of the Mind of a Child*. New York: Scribner's, 1893.
Coe, Richard N. *When the Grass Was Taller: Autobiography and the Experience of Childhood*. New Haven, CT: Yale University Press, 1984.
Felski, Rita. *Beyond Feminist Aesthetics*. Cambridge, MA: Harvard University Press, 1989.
Finck, Almut. "Subjektivität und Geschichte in der Postmoderne: Christa Wolfs *Kindheitsmuster*". In *Geschriebenes Leben: Autobiographik von Frauen*, edited by Michaela Holdenried, 311–23. Berlin: Erich Schmidt, 1995.
Freud, Sigmund. "Screen Memories". Translated by James Strachey, 299–322. Vol. 3 (*1893–1899: Early Psycho-Analytic Publications*) of *The Standard Edition of the Complete Psychological Works of Sigmund Freud*. London: Hogarth Press, 1953–74.
Greiner, Bernhard. "Die Schwierigkeit, 'ich' zu sagen: Christa Wolfs psychologische Orientierung des Erzählens". *DVjs* 55 (1981): 323–42.
Hörnigk, Therese. *Christa Wolf*. Göttingen: Steidl, 1989.
Kosta, Barbara. *Recasting Autobiography: Women's Counterfictions in Contemporary German Literature and Film*. Ithaca, NY: Cornell University Press, 1994.
Lange, Katrin. *Selbstfragmente: Autobiographien der Kindheit*. Würzburg: Königshausen & Neumann: 2008.
Leiris, Michel. *Biffures* [*La règle du jeu*, I]. 1948. Paris: Gallimard, 1991.
Lloyd, Rosemary. *The Land of Lost Content: Children and Childhood in Nineteenth-Century French Literature*. Oxford: Clarendon Press, 1992.
Martin, Elaine. "Autobiography, Gender, and the Third Reich: Eva Zeller, Carola Stern, and Christabel Bielenberg". In *Gender, Patriarchy, and Fascism in the Third Reich*, edited by Elaine Martin, 169–200. Detroit: Wayne State University Press, 1993.
Mitscherlich, Alexander and Margarete. *Die Unfähigkeit zu trauern: Grundlagen kollektiven Verhaltens*. Munich: Piper, 1967.
Rechtien, Renate. "Gelebtes, erinnertes, erzähltes und erschriebenes Selbst: Günter de Bruyns *Zwischenbilanz* und Christa Wolfs *Kindheitsmuster*". In *Günter de Bruyn in Perspective*, edited by Dennis Tate. 151–70. Amsterdam: Rodopi, 1999.
Reisinger, Roman. *Die Autobiographie der Kindheit in der französischen Literatur*. Tübingen: Stauffenburg, 2000.
Ryan, Judith. *The Uncompleted Past*. Detroit: Wayne State University Press, 1983.
Santner, Eric L. *Stranded Objects: Mourning, Memory, and Film in Postwar Germany*. Ithaca, NY: Cornell University Press, 1990.

Schaumann, Caroline. *Memory Matters: Generational Responses to Germany's Nazi Past in Recent Women's Literature*. Berlin: Walter de Gruyter, 2008.
Wilke, Sabine. "'Worüber man nicht sprechen kann, darüber muß man allmählich zu schweigen aufhören': Vergangenheitsbeziehungen in Christa Wolfs *Kindheitsmuster*". *Germanic Review* 66, no. 4 (1991): 169–76.
Wolf, Christa. *Auf dem Weg nach Tabou: Texte 1990–1994*. Cologne: Kiepenheuer & Witsch, 1994.
—*Die Dimension des Autors*. Frankfurt a.M.: Luchterhand, 1990.
—"Erfahrungsmuster: Diskussion zu *Kindheitsmuster*". In Christa Wolf, *Essays/ Gespräche/Reden/Briefe 1975–1986*, 31–72. Munich: Luchterhand, 2000.
—*Kindheitsmuster*. Munich: Luchterhand, 2003.
—*Patterns of Childhood*. Translated by Ursule Molinaro and Hedwig Rappolt. New York: Noonday Press, 1990.
Zahlmann, Christel. "*Kindheitsmuster*: Schreiben an der Grenze des Bewußtseins". In *Erinnerte Zukunft*, edited by Wolfram Mauser, 141–60. Würzburg: Königshausen & Neumann, 1985.

Notes

1. The most extensive study of childhood autobiography to date is Coe's study of the genre worldwide, *When the Grass Was Taller*. Werner Brettschneider's *Kindheitsmuster* and Katrin Lange's *Selbstfragmente* treat the German tradition specifically. The more extensive French tradition is addressed by Reisinger, *Autobiographie der Kindheit*; see also Lloyd, *Land of Lost Content*.
2. Leiris, *Biffures*, 24.
3. Burnett, *The One I Knew the Best of All*, vii.
4. See Martin, "Autobiography", 169.
5. Epigraph of Wordsworth's "Ode: Intimation of Immortality from Recollections of Early Childhood", *Romantic Poetry and Prose*, 176.
6. Greiner, "Schwierigkeit", 326. Greiner identifies, in an excellent analysis, the psychoanalytic tenor of the work and observes that "Erfaßt soll werden, was außerhalb des Bewußtseins zur Person gehört. Dies Erfassen verläuft auf dem von der Psychoanalyse gebahnten Weg."
7. Many critics have said the same. See, for example, Ryan, *Uncompleted Past*, 143. Kosta approaches the work from the standpoint of women's autobiography, as I do from the standpoint of childhood autobiography, and reaches several conclusions similar to mine. Thus she notes that Wolf "de-centers her position as author", noting that "the designation 'patterns' in the title emphasizes sameness, rather than the singularity of experience that Georges Gusdorf insists on in his delimitation of autobiographical representation as 'a conscious awareness of the singularity of each individual life'" (Kosta, *Recasting Autobiography*, 58–9). Rechtien rightly points out that "Die authentischen Erfahrungen des schreibenden Subjekts, auf denen das Erzählwerk deutlich beruht, sind [...] gleichzeitig kollektiver Natur" (Rechtien, "Gelebtes, erinnertes", 163).
8. Wolf, *Dimension*, 150. "I am writing a book about such a childhood at that time. [...] I try to be authentic by relying on my memory and then by checking this memory against any documents available to me" (my translation). Wolf has made a great many statements about *Kindheitsmuster*. All verifiable details correspond to the circumstances of her own life. Yet Hörnigk reports that

Wolf, while admitting that milieu and characters are authentic "in a literary sense", insists that they are not exactly as they were; she quotes Wolf as saying, "Ich habe vieles erfunden" (I invented a lot; Hörnigk, *Christa Wolf*, 7). In a 1975 discussion Wolf said, much in the same vein: "Ich kaschiere an keiner Stelle, daß es sich sozusagen um Autobiographisches handelt; das wird nicht verschwiegen. Wobei dieses 'sozusagen' wichtig ist, es ist nämlich keine Identität da" ("I nowhere conceal the fact that it's about so-called autobiographical material; that isn't kept secret. But this 'so-called' is important; there's no identity there"; Wolf, "Erfahrungsmuster", 40 [my translation]).

9   Hörnigk, *Christa Wolf*, 176–7. "Although in *Kindheitsmuster* a childhood and youth is narrated that is very closely connected to the author's early life and biography, the book can only be read in a limited fashion as an autobiography. The reworking of authentic experiences is intermixed with fictive elements" (my translation).

10 Wolf, *Kindheitsmuster*, 57, 75, 221. Further page references to *Kindheitsmuster* will be given in parentheses in the text.

11 "Memory, this system of treachery" (Wolf, *Patterns*, 152).

12 "The forgetting must have gratified a deeply insecure consciousness which, as we all know, can instruct our memory behind our own backs, such as: Stop thinking about it. [...] Because it is unbearable to think the little word 'I' in connection with the word 'Auschwitz'" (Ibid., 229–30 [translation modified]).

13 In a letter to Jürgen Habermas of 7 December 1991, Wolf writes: "Früh habe ich mich vor allem mit Psychologie beschäftigt, Freud, Mitscherlich, Reich waren wichtige Orientierungspunkte." "I occupied myself early on above all with psychology. Freud, Mitscherlich, Reich were important points of orientation" (Wolf, *Tabou*, 153, [my translation]).

14 Mitscherlich, *Die Unfähigkeit zu trauern*, for example, 24–7 (repression), 46 (neurosis), 65 (non-objective remembering).

15 Wolf, *Tabou*, 153.

16 Breuer and Freud, *Studies on Hysteria*, 268

17 "Well-sealed vaults of memory" (Wolf, *Patterns*, 69).

18 Breuer and Freud, *Studies on Hysteria*, 268.

19 "But twenty-nine years later you have to ask yourself how many encapsulated vaults a memory can accommodate before it must cease to function. How much energy and what kind of energy is it continually expending in order to seal and to reseal the capsules whose walls may in time rot and crumble" (Wolf, *Patterns*, 69).

20 "Especially at this particular point, when truthfulness would be most rewarding, which isn't always, perhaps only seldom the case, you come across a new type of amnesia. It doesn't compare to the gaps concerning your early childhood. [...] But now your consciousness itself seems to fall victim to a partial blackout, entangled as it is in the events it should rise above through remembering. It seems to be part of the cause of the darkening that you want to illuminate with its help" (Wolf, *Patterns*, 217 [translation modified and extended]).

21 Wolf, *Kindheitsmuster*, 318; *Patterns*, 217.

22 Breuer and Freud, *Studies on Hysteria*, 6–14.

23 This might be considered an instance of Wolf's pervasive strategy of

"Analogiebildung", as discussed by Wilke, "Worüber man nicht sprechen kann", 169–71.
24 "Self-betrayal and guilt" [that comes] "from far away [...] and from an early age" (my translation).
25 "The feeling that overcomes any living being when the earth starts moving underfoot is fear" (Wolf, *Patterns*, 24).
26 "The fear of tearing yourself apart when you have to detach yourself from the role that has become a part of you" (Ibid., 382 [translation modified]).
27 "It is the special nature of the suffering called 'fear' which brings forth that special type of product in which you recognize yourself" (Ibid., 357).
28 "Strictness, consistency, responsibility, diligence" (Ibid., 350).
29 "The unlived is the important influence" (Ibid., 349).
30 "The village was crammed with people who had survived their catastrophes, and with others who hadn't noticed any catastrophe. [...] Only hesitantly did she get involved on the side of the survivors, because she was one of them" (Ibid., 336).
31 "Survival syndrome: the psychosomatic pathology of persons who were exposed to extreme stress. As studied in patients who had to spend years of their lives in concentration camps or under other conditions of persecution. Main symptoms: severe, lasting depression, with increasing difficulty in relating to others, states of fear and anxiety, nightmares, survivor's guilt, disturbances of memory and recall, increasing fear of persecution" (Ibid., 334–5).
32 For an excellent analysis of narrator-protagonist relations at this stage, see Finck, "Subjektivität und Geschichte", 320.
33 Santner, then Schaumann, have paid close attention to the somatic ailments in *Kindheitsmuster* as "symptoms". Santner's psychoanalytically informed study reads these "symptoms" as I believe they must be read, as "traces of conflicts that have been repressed" (157). Schaumann reaches a similar conclusion—"illness is an alternative mode of expressing [unresolved conflicts]" (84)—without, however, reading psychoanalytically. Neither critic calls attention to the parallels to hysterical symptoms as Breuer and Freud discuss them.
34 "The final point would be reached when the second and the third person were to meet again in the first or, better still, were to meet with the first person. When it would no longer have to be 'you' and 'she' but a candid, unreserved 'I'" (Wolf, *Patterns*, 349).
35 "It's got so that you have to concentrate in order to remember last night's film on television. Pale, very pale. Whereas you remember the Steguweit kitchen with the utmost clarity" (Ibid., 383).
36 Felski, *Beyond Feminist Aesthetics*, 87, 93–5, 96–9, 105, 119. Felski refers to Evelyne Keitel, "Verständigungstexte—Form, Funktion, Wirkung", *German Quarterly*, 56 (1983). West German examples of this subgenre include Karin Struck, *Klassenliebe* (1973) and *Kindheits Ende* (1982); Verena Stefan, *Häutungen* (1975); Svende Merian's *Tod des Märchenprinzen* (1980).
37 Felski, *Beyond Feminist Aesthetics*, 119.
38 Critics disagree on this issue. Critics who share my point of view include Kosta in *Recasting Autobiography*—"Wolf largely elides questions of her gendered socialization" (59)—and Rechtien in "Gelebtes, erinnertes"—"Allerdings stehen bei diesem Prosawerk nicht geschlechtsspezifische Probleme an sich im

Vordergrund, sondern das Aufspüren der psychischen Strukturen, die sich im geschichtlichen Kontext des Faschismus herausbildeten" (163).
39 Zahlmann teases out a connection between the dominant theme of fear in the book and the narrator's anxiety over maternal loss, but I think she overemphasizes the narrator's "Gefühl des Verrats von Seiten der Mutter und die dadurch ausgelöste tiefe Unsicherheit" ("feeling of betrayal by her mother and resulting deep lack of confidence"; 154 [my translation]).

10. Provisional Existence

Walter H. Sokel

The University

I would first like to express my joy and gratitude for being present at this commemorative celebration and for being able to speak to you about a chapter in my life. We are commemorating two historical dates. One was progressive, pointing towards a glorious future: the founding of one of the most important universities in Europe. The other was exceedingly dismal, an event that robbed me of my home and robbed so many others, all too many, of their lives.

Since we are speaking of "historical" matters, I would like to admit that I have begun to find myself "historical" for some time now. For me "becoming historical" means that there are fewer and fewer people with whom to swap memories from a past that we lived through. In this sense three semesters in particular have also become historical: the three semesters from autumn 1936 to spring 1938, during which I attended the University of Vienna.

I would like to begin with a short background story about my emotional relationship to the university. Childhood memories bind me to that honorable building on the Doktor-Karl-Lueger-Ring Street. I was always a lad who was fond of reading. I valued academic study, knowledge, erudition, history, and especially stories. It was therefore almost a symbolic coincidence that the university was diagonally opposite the coffee house on the Mölker-Bastei Street, a so-called "artists café", where I was often brought along when my mother met up with her sisters and friends for their weekly teatime (*Jause*). While the women chatted, I would read whichever book I had with me. I recall reading *David Copperfield*, H. G. Wells' *The Time Machine*, and a Dostoyevsky novel there. The view of the university from the café laid the foundation for my life in and for literature.

At that time in my childhood there was not much talk of National Socialism. But only a few years later, in 1933, when I was in the fourth and fifth grade of *Gymnasium* and by then already suffering under Nazi persecution, we received terrible news from the university. We kept hearing more and more about Jewish students being brutally attacked. The son of my mother's cousin, whose last name was Abeles, was hurled down the steps of the university and suffered serious injuries. Before being thrown down the stairs he had been severely beaten.

When I arrived at the university three years later in the fall of 1936 these dreadful times were long over. Everyone seemed to have returned to the quotidian superficiality of civil comportment. The extensive measures taken by Chancellor Dollfus against the Nazis—made possible thanks to Mussolini's protective hand over Austria—resulted in a decisive turn of events in Hitler's Austria campaign. Most decisive was the containment of the Nazi putsch on 25 July 1934. Albeit forced by Mussolini's military mobility and readiness to support Austria, Hitler's temporary acceptance of Austrian independence brought with it a superficial sense of quiet and order to the university and beyond.

The tactic had changed but not the goal: the triumph of National Socialism in Austria and the incorporation of Austria into the anti-semitic Third Reich. A large number of students and the members of the educated middle class were more than just accepting of this goal. They drove it on. Even though there were no longer any beatings, rows or physical attacks on Jewish students, I still encountered early signs of what would later be called the Shoah at the university. I am referring here to the unofficial, silent exclusion of Jews from the community. As I would later come to understand it, this phenomenon corresponded precisely to Raul Hillberg's famous Shoah theory, in which segregation, the social exclusion of Jews, is the forerunner to their physical extermination.

We Jewish students (i.e., those who were considered non-Aryan) found ourselves isolated, left to our own devises, and with no camaraderie or social ties with our so-called Aryan classmates. I remember precisely my reflective sense of astonishment at the fact that I never had a single conversation of even the most limited significance with any of my non-Jewish university classmates. We "non-Aryans" were divided by what seemed to be invisible walls from our so-called "Aryan" peers. We were ghettoized.

The ghettoization did not take place at the university alone but also in the bourgeois echelons of older cohorts and adults. My mother was a close friend to the non-Jewish wife of a senior state official (*Hofrat*) for years. But around 1933/34 the first signs of distancing appeared and around 1935/36 the contact between the two friends had completely stopped. From then on my mother only mixed in social circles of Jewish women. The ghettoization conquered us long before the annexation (*Anschluss*). It was under these conditions that I entered the university.

At the start of the fall semester 1936/37, it should have been evident to all of us that our presence as Jewish citizens of Austria could not continue for long. Mussolini, who had been Austria's protector until now, withdrew his protective hand in the wake of the Second Italo-Abyssinian War and allowed Hitler to take possession of his country of birth. It is one of those ironies of history that Austria's fate was sealed in far-off Africa. Mussolini's war of conquest against the Ethiopians put him at odds with his western allies and gained him a new partner and soon-to-be ruler, namely the leader (*Führer*) of Nazi Germany. Thus the question was hardly *if* Germany would annex Austria but *when*.

Our fate was clear to us, or in any case it should have been. Nevertheless I decided, like so many others, to enroll at the university instead of emigrating. But why? It had certainly become very difficult to emigrate. The western European states that I would have considered had erected protective walls, implemented visa restrictions and put in place immigration blocks. But those were not the actual reasons or at least not the primary ones. For I would have been able to emigrate to America, where a sister of my father lived with her husband, a clockmaker. Indeed, two years later I would request an immigration visa for that country, which I received in Zurich in 1938. Still, at the time I could not imagine that I would have attempted to immigrate to a country without some pressing necessity forcing me to do so. Though certainly due to deep-set ignorance, to me the USA was a country whose supposed lack of humanistic culture and whose materialism directed by purely technological concerns caused me to tremble. I wanted to stay in my beloved Europe even though I knew it was hardly possible.

What was it, then, that I thought the future had in store for me, since I did stay in Austria and enrolled at the university despite the great likelihood that the Nazis would come to power? When I think back to it now, like so many others I behaved toward the annexation the way one behaves toward death. We all know that we will die at some point. But exactly when remains a mystery. And when that point in time remains undetermined (unlike in Elias Canetti's deeply meaningful play, *Die Befristeten* [*Their Days Are Numbered*]), it is impossible to believe completely in the certainty of anything. We know that it will come, but deep down we do not really believe it. As long as death has not come there is still the possibility, however absurd it might seem, that it actually will not come, at least not in this one particular instance. It seems at least feasible that a miracle of some kind will occur.

And this obviously absurd possibility of the impossible becomes even greater when we switch from our biological predisposition (to death) to historical events. For the extremely improbable is also possible in history. And it would not have seemed all that improbable if the Western Allies had made Austria the cornerstone of a new political strategy once they became tired of perpetually pacifying Hitler. Even an alliance between the West and the Soviet Union to protect Austria would have been feasible. But in fact a much more unlikely thing happened altogether: one-and-a-half years after the annexation, a pact between archrivals, the Nazis and the Bolsheviks, became a reality. Therefore preserving Austrian independence seemed thoroughly within the realm of possibilities if not the realm of probabilities.

I took courses in philosophy, art history, and romance languages and literature. Two professors dominate my memory: the one, Professor Robert Reininger, whose lectures on Nietzsche I attended, and the other, the Germanist Josef Nadler, known for being a Nazi and a favorite of Josef Goebbels.

Professor Reininger always started each lecture in the same infallible way that had a certain puppet-like effect. He would walk to his lectern with leisurely steps, then sit down, take his glasses out of their case, clean them carefully, look through one lens, then the other, lifting them each time carefully to the light. Then he would put on his glasses and begin his lecture. This mildly amusing routine embodied for me the pedantry of German (and obviously German-Austrian) professors that had become proverbial and which Heinrich Mann made the object of his satire in *Professor Unrat*. It seemed as if Professor Reininger had based his routine on watching the actor Emil Jannings.

But the content of Professor Reininger's Nietzsche lectures fascinated me and had a lasting formative influence on my approach to Nietzsche. Before I heard Professor Reininger's lectures, I only knew Nietzsche from *one* perspective, namely as the poet/thinker behind *Zarathustra*, who had continued to inspire me ever since I encountered him when I was eighteen years old. Professor Reininger taught me to recognize Nietzsche as a significantly multifaceted and paradoxical thinker. He presented us with an empirical and scientifically trained critic of idealism, a skeptic who left a mark on modernity that was in stark opposition to his other visionary and poetic facets. It was foremost the play of these two diametrically opposed sides of Nietzsche that granted him his momentous significance. Later, when I was continuing my studies in exile in America and getting to know the pragmatism of American thinking, I was astonished at the connections between certain American thinkers—William James and John Dewey—and Nietzsche. For a while I was planning on writing my dissertation on this connection as an exercise in a politics of reconciliation of sorts that would bring together Nietzsche, as the "typically German" thinker who was denounced for being the intellectual forefather of the

Nazis, and the most characteristic thinking in an America defined by democratic and positivistic principles. During that time I often thought back to Professor Reininger with the grateful realization of how much I owed to him. And he seemed to me to be the epitome of a good teacher, one who motivates his pupils to push the limits of their own thinking.

Even long before annexation, Josef Nadler was known as a national socialist. As I recall, the "moderate" Nadler was supported by Goebbels in his rivalry with Heinz Kindermann, who was known as being a much more radical Nazi. Nadler was a brilliant presenter. I did not officially enroll in his lectures but, like so many others, attended them occasionally as an auditor. One of my friends studied under Nadler. His name was Herbert Selkowitsch and years later he would become famous in Austria thanks to his novel *Gestörte Kreise* [Perturbed Circles].[1] Nadler's German literary history, based on the shared heredity of specific writers, definitely presented a Nazi world view in which parentage, blood and race were decisive. On the other hand, however, his approach pointed to the individuality of specific groups, thereby turning Germany into a colorful picture of cultural diversity. Years later I would be reminded of Nadler during my study of Herder's cosmopolitan or, as they say nowadays, multicultural nationalism. According to this type of nationalism, the individuality of each people [*Volk*] is a unique voice in the choir of humanity. The preservation and love of a people's distinctness brings with it at the same time the esteem of the Other's individuality and even a joy in that individuality. The richness and the diversity of non-interchangeable identities give existence its allure and worth.

This deeply humanistic nationalism is the exact opposite of intolerance, oppression, homogenization or the excision of the Other which characterized National Socialism. From this point of view, one might consider National Socialism as the extirpation of the cosmopolitan nationalism that Herder gave shape to. It was in this context that I would think back to Nadler. Was he not the opposite of the uninformed idiocy of Nazi homogenization with his emphasis on the individuality of each lineage? And as if to confirm this humanist core that I thought I espied in Nadler, I learned from Herbert Selkowitsch just what an exemplary humanitarian Nadler proved to be to his Jewish students. When Herbert emigrated to France and wanted to pursue his studies further at the Sorbonne, Nadler wrote a letter of recommendation for him to his French colleague in Germanics, Henri Lichtenberger, a letter that was crucial in helping Herbert continue his studies at the Sorbonne. I found Nadler's humanity endearing, the way the national socialist professor was prepared to recognize the ostracized racial Other and to help him. With his letter, my esteem for Nadler rose greatly, so much so that long after the war, when I heard that his permission to lecture (*venia legendi*) had been repeatedly revoked, I found the reprimand almost unjust—but only "almost", considering Nadler's overall impact. Still, I would have liked to mention his letter of recommendation in support of a Jewish student.

Ideology

I entitled the first part of my recollections here "The University". I had originally called the second part "Novels" because my actual inner life at that time did not belong to the university but to literary dreams in which I composed a novel about myself that allowed me to project myself into the future as a world-famous novelist. During the three semesters that I attended the University of Vienna, I was intensely engaged with novels. I was encouraged and spurred on by the writer Marcell Pellich, about whom I would primarily like to speak now.

Marcell Pellich, born 1908, gathered around him a circle of young, ambitious, hard-working literary talents. One member of this circle was Martin Esslin, whom we have to thank for the expression "theater of the absurd". At the time, Esslin's name was Julius Perszlenyi, and he was my best friend in seventh and eighth grade at the *Gymnasium*. We got to know Marcell Pellich in eighth grade, shortly before the *Matura* (high school graduation). He was a decade older than us, had published a volume of poetry, *Bilderbuch der Seele* [Picture Book of the Soul]—a second one was published in 1937, *Die Nachjagd* [The Night Raid]—and was working on a novel, *Das Vergrößerungsglas* [The Magnifying Glass], that was strongly influenced by Joyce and which he called "the story of a relationship". He was supported by a benefactor, a factory owner named Stern, who, as far as I know, also helped Robert Musil and Elias Canetti on occasion. Through Marcell I became familiar with Hermann Broch's *Schlafwandler* (*The Sleepwalkers*) and Canetti's *Blendung* (*Auto-da-Fé*). He also introduced me to Kafka's work. He gave me *Der Prozess* (*The Trial*) to read, but I have to admit that back then Kafka's novel bored me so much that I did not read it to the end. It was not until four years later that I picked up *Die Verwandlung* (*The Metamorphosis*) in the New York Public Library and began my second Kafka phase, which lead to an intimate long-term relationship.

Marcell's role-model and inspiration was Stefan George. But Marcell was part of a completely different time and world than the elite poet from the Catholic region of the Rhineland. Having grown up within the socialist, and later occasionally communist, youth movement, Marcell was strongly shaped by its concept of the world. I would like to put Marcell Pellich at the center of my discussion of the important role that radical-revolutionary ideologies played in our youth because he seems to me, from my present perspective, to be a key figure of contemporary history within that framework. I am referring here above all to the Nazis, who paid homage to an extreme ideology. Despite their close ties to conservative-reactionary traditions, they also exhibited tendencies that were radical-revolutionary, socially rebellious, and most notably anticlerical and all but socialist. This was especially the case during the period that came to an end with Hitler, the SS, and the murder of Ernst Röhm and his homosexual circle in the SA.

Marxism was the ideology that we, so-called non-Aryans, felt most attracted to, as long as we were not Zionists. When I was only in fifth grade at the *Bundesgymnasium VI Amerlinggasse*, I joined the Union of Socialist Middle-School Students (*Bund sozialistischer Mittelschüler*), which soon after became illegal. But I remained a member, and in seventh grade at the *Bundesgymnasium II Zirkusgasse* I was in charge of communications with the communists for a while. I was very proud of this assignment because "communist" sounded even more radical than "socialist", and anything that was radical had a lot of clout with my friends and me. Within our group, we actually worked together with a revolutionary Nazi, whom we found very amicable. He was in a Russian language course with my friend Julius Pereszlenyi (later known as Martin Esslin) because he planned to go to the Soviet Union later and start a rebellion with anti-Stalinist national revolutionaries. Before he could do so, however, he was arrested by the Austrian police for illegal activity and was severely beaten. I recall having a Nazi companion, which was certainly unusual; our work with him attests to my companions' and my image of ourselves as, first and foremost, radical revolutionaries. We thought of ourselves as a unifying alliance that could even include Nazis as long as they saw themselves first and foremost as social-revolutionary subversives. This alliance made all other differences relatively inconsequential.

But during the years that I am talking about, we leftist radicals experienced for the first time severe and depressing disillusionment. Stalinism continued to reveal itself as the horrible distorted image of all that we fervently believed to have been our spiritual homeland. And then Marcell Pellich stepped in to fill that void with his ideology that was born out of an extremely personal need and which initially appeared as a radical critique of ideology itself.

Whether on the left or on the right, Marcell would preach, radicalism was just a mask used to trick and seduce youth. And that is how it had always been throughout world history. Young people have been essential to every revolutionary movement. But they became mere tools. They were used to make it possible for aged men to claim the positions of power held by the former rulers. The seniors' will to power triumphed again and again. The actual force behind all revolutions, young people, was continually being betrayed and sacrificed. Nothing changed with regards to the grown men's authority. Nothing changed for the patriarchy. Whether on the left or on the right, whether under Marxism or National Socialism, it was the pseudo-revolutionaries who ruled. It was those frauds who promised liberation only in order to tighten the shackles of their apparatus that ensured the dominion of the patriarchs. As a result, youth became victims; they were reduced to cannon fodder. The status quo remained intact. It was only the words (called "ideas") that changed, and with these words their apparatus would conceal the truth. They would change according to whichever group of seniors was into bat. The basis of all ideology was the murderous, bellicose will to power of the fathers. Ideologies were nothing more than the colorful advertisements on hoardings meant to lure youth to self-sacrifice. What they presented as liberation would only turn into a new form of tyranny. The contents of ideology—race, class, nation etc.—were in fact related to real, partially oppressive measures. Germans under the Treaty of Versailles, the working class under capitalism, these groups were indeed oppressed and legitimately seen as victims. But the universal oppression of children by their fathers, which was much bigger and far-reaching, was not talked about.

According to Marcell, we were to expose all ideologies and the root of all oppression, namely the oppression of children by fathers. Only then could the real revolution begin: at last freedom from all domination. We were to demolish the patriarchy founded on the will to power and to replace it with the reign of those who had hitherto been powerless, the reign of youth. All men over thirty were impotent and obedient. If they resisted, they were to be shot. If they didn't, they were to put their experience and knowledge at the service of youth in order to bring about once and for all the emancipation of humanity from the will to power. Eros, in the form of *Knabenliebe* and the love of younger men, would help promote this strategy. Adults could only be auxiliary forces. Power belonged in the hands of those who had not yet fully developed their will to power—in the hands of youth, minors, no-one over the age of thirty.

Women barely counted for Marcell. They were only ever sidekicks to men. And it was only as supportive mothers that they could achieve the true fulfillment of their existence. It was not up to the women to destroy the patriarchy. That was up to the sons. Fatherlands were to become children's lands.

Today I see Marcell's critique of ideology as typical of ideology itself. For it proposed dethroning the will to power only to replace one group of powermongers with another. Sure authority would be in the hands of a group that had always been deprived of it before: young people. But just as in the Marxist system, where Marcell had come from, in his ideology there was no actual freedom from power inequality. Instead it was just a substitution: those who had up until then always had the power would be replaced by those who had up until then always been deprived of it. Marcell's idea that humanity would be liberated through the disempowerment of the fathers and the empowerment of youth was just as much a myth as Marxism was, in which all differences in power were to disappear once the workers ousted the capitalists. In both the realities of socialism and Marcell's ideal of the reign of the youth, power inequality persisted as it always had. Liberation meant disempowerment in both instances. And this is what turned Marcell's ideal into ideology. Back then I did not see it all this clearly; I only felt it. Marcell's idea of liberation did not feel liberating to me but foreboding. I had already celebrated my eighteenth birthday and soon enough I would have my nineteenth behind me. And then—oh God—the twentieth! And that would mark the beginning of the final decade, whose end was rapidly approaching, and then I would belong to them, to the pathetic old men, who were not granted any power, who were just accessory organs. Suddenly, I felt terribly old.

And yet, not long before that I was too young to be taken seriously. The girl whose love I longed for like crazy, my cousin Mary (she had begun to call herself Maria as an up-and-coming actress in the Max Reinhardt Seminar), explained to me explicitly that "A man under twenty-five does not even count in my book!" I was considered too young for real life, and now, according to Marcell's thoughts on our salvation, I would soon be a slave to the despised and lowly old men. At once too young and too old to partake in any part of true life. I would never be able to be in the right.

And then came annexation, the abrupt, long-awaited and yet hardly believable end of our world. Paradoxically, it came as a liberating response to my oppression. For it demanded action. Provisional existence changed overnight into a real existence, one that insisted on lifesaving measures. It was immediately necessary to risk everything in organizing our flight from impending extermination. I stopped writing my novel. In order to make sure that the story of my life would become a reality, I had to cast it and myself into the future.

Translated from the German by Japhet Johnstone

Notes

1 For works without published translations, the translator has provided English titles in brackets but not in italics. Titles in italics correspond to published translations.

Index

Adorno, Theodor W. ix, 12, 27, 34–5, 37, 39, 40n. 1, 43n. 42, 44nn. 54, 55, 116, 122n. 84
Allegorie 40n. 1
allegory vii, 4, 13, 27, 28–9, 70
Anderson, Mark 27, 39, 40, 41n. 8, 42n. 31
Anderson, Patrick 39
Andrian, Leopold von 53, 55, 58, 60, 61n. 8, 63n. 39, 64n. 62
Angst 56, 155–7
Anna O. (Bertha Pappenheim) 84, 157–8
anorexia 42, 44n. 56
anti-Heimat 97
anxiety 50, 87, 150–1, 155–7, 160, 164n. 30, 165n. 38
Aragon, Louis 74, 128–9, 136, 140n. 28
Aristotle 86
Arnds, Peter 115, 120n. 52
Aurnhammer, Achim 59, 63n. 41
Austerlitz (Sebald) 124, 126–8, 131–6, 138, 141nn. 50, 51, 62, 142n. 64
Austria x–xi, 5–6, 49, 50, 54, 58, 60, 84, 91, 93, 97–110, 112–13, 115–16, 117n. 8, 120n. 52, 123, 168–71
Austrian identity 5, 98, 108–10
Austrian Jews 103, 168

Austrian Social Partnership 98, 100–1, 107
Austria's Staatsvertrag 104
Autobiographie x, xi, 119n. 30, 149, 161–2n. 1
autobiography viii, 3, 6, 104, 108, 145–9, 151, 153, 155, 157, 159–61, 162nn. 1, 4, 7, 163n. 9
see also childhood autobiography
autonomous monologue 81, 87–90, 92

Bad Ischl 115
Bal, Mieke 87, 92
Bales, Richard 136, 141n. 50
Bartlett, Frederick C. 152, 161
Bauer, Felice 16, 25n. 23, 81
Bay, Hansjörg 22, 23n. 1, 40
Bebenburg, Edgar Karg von 55, 60, 62n. 37
Beck, Ulrich 101, 115, 117n. 13
Beckett, Samuel 16
Beicken, Peter 29, 39, 41n. 17
Beller, Steven 100, 115, 117n. 8
Benjamin, Walter vii, ix, x, 5, 65–76, 77n. 2, 133, 136, 139n. 19, 141n. 55, 145, 154
Bernhard, Thomas 97, 108
Beschreibung des Unglücks (Sebald) 123, 138, 141n. 60
Beyer, Marcel 74–6, 78n. 27

Beyond the Pleasure Principle
(Freud) 84–5, 93, 94nn. 15–17,
19, 154
Bhabha, Homi 118n. 17
Binder, Hartmut 18, 22, 25n. 30
biography 18, 25n. 23, 50–1, 57,
133, 163n. 9
see also autobiography,
childhood autobiography,
fictional biography
Bodenhausen, Eberhard von 59,
61n. 15
Booth, Wayne C. 1, 6–7n. 1, 69, 89,
92, 95n. 44
Bray, Joe 136, 141n. 59
Brazil 103, 107
Brettschneider, Werner 147, 161,
162n. 1
Breuer, Josef 83, 84, 94n. 13, 151–2,
154, 157–9, 161, 163n. 17, 164n.
32
Brief an den Vater (Kafka) 15, 17,
19, 22
Briefe an Felice (Kafka) 16, 22, 25n.
20
Briefe an Milena (Kafka) 16, 22,
25nn. 25, 26
Broch, Hermann 87, 122
Brockmann, Stephen 115, 120n. 42
Buck-Morss, Susan 76, 77n. 2
Bülow, Ulrich von 137–8, 140nn.
30, 31
Burckhardt, Carl J. 49, 54, 59–60,
64n. 58
Bürger, Jan 76
Bürger, Peter 102, 115, 118nn. 18, 22
Burgtheater 58, 60
Burnett, Frances Hodgson 147–8,
161, 162n. 3
Burnett, Jacob 20, 22, 26n. 41
Butler, Judith 98, 101–2, 115, 117n.
3, 118n. 17
Butor, Michel 5, 124–5, 127–8,
136–8, 139nn. 7–9, 16–18

Calasso, Robert K. 20, 22, 26n. 41
Campo Santo (Sebald) 130, 138,
140n. 30
capitalism 5, 32, 38, 67, 72, 117,
154, 174
Caruth, Cathy 2, 6, 7n. 6, 83–4, 90,
92, 94, 95n. 46
Caspian Sea 132, 141
The Castle (Kafka) 11–13, 18–24, 26
Catling, Jo 137, 138n. 5
Chatman, Seymour 86, 92, 94n. 26
childhood autobiography viii,
6, 145–9, 151, 153, 155, 157,
159–61, 162nn. 1, 7
China x, 114, 122
Coe, Richard N. 147, 161, 162n. 1
Cohn, Dorrit 1, 6, 7n. 1, 87–9, 92,
94nn. 34–6, 95n. 41, 134, 137,
141n. 57
Corngold, Stanley vii, ix, 4, 11,
22–3, 26n. 42, 27, 39, 41n. 6
Corsica 129, 130–1, 140
counterfactuals 21
Coyne, James C. 91, 93, 95n. 49

Dakyns, Janine 129, 137, 140n. 29
Das kleine Welttheater
(Hofmannsthal) 55
Das Schloß (Kafka) vii, 4, 11–22,
23nn. 3, 4
"Das Urteil" (Kafka) 3, 12, 16, 19
Decker, Hannah S. 92, 95n. 48
deconstruction 72, 102, 113
Degenfeld, Ottonie Gräfin 57–8, 60,
63n. 51, 64n. 59
Deleuze, Jacques 42n. 31
Der Abenteurer und die Sängerin
(Schnitzler) 58
"Der Erzähler" (Benjamin) 141n. 55
"Der Hungerkünstler" (Kafka)
39–40, 41nn. 10–13, 16–17, 23,
42nn. 30–1, 43n. 37–9
Der Mann ohne Eigenschaften
(Musil) 97, 116

Index

Der Mythos der Zerstörung im Werk Döblins (Sebald) 138
Der Prozeß (Kafka) 12, 15–16, 22–3, 172
Der Turm (Hofmannsthal) 59
Der Verschollene (Kafka) 71, 76
Derrida, Jacques 22, 25nn. 27–8
Descombes, Vincent 137, 141n. 56
dialectical 5, 99, 101–6, 109–10, 113–14, 117n. 6, 118n. 16
The Diaries of Franz Kafka 22
Die Ausgewanderten (Sebald) 138, 139n. 11
Die Eurokokke (Goll) vii, 5, 65–6, 74–6, 77n. 4
Die Logik der Dichtung (K. Hamburger) 6, 7n. 2, 87, 94n. 29
Die Ringe des Saturn (Sebald) 4, 7, 124, 126–7, 129–31, 134–6, 138, 139n. 10, 140n. 29, 142n. 63
direct discourse 82, 91, 134–5, 141n. 49
displacement 3–4, 123, 136, 141n. 50, 152
Don Quixote 103, 109
Doppelgänger, Freud and Schnitzler as 82
Dora (Ida Bauer) vii, 5, 81–2, 90
Dora (Freud) 82, 89–90, 93, 94n. 6, 95nn. 47, 48
drag 98, 102, 113
Drucke zu Lebzeiten (Kafka) 22, 24nn. 16–17, 40n. 2
Dujardin, Edouard 141n. 60

Einstein, Albert 11
Eisenach, Herbert 107, 116, 120n. 44
entrapment xii, 110
exile vii, 3–5, 7, 50, 65, 170

fashion 113
fear 23n. 7, 52–3, 55, 57, 61n. 17, 63n. 46, 70, 74, 77, 106, 112, 125, 132, 155–60, 164nn. 24–6, 30, 165n. 38
Feijoo, Jaime 112–13, 116, 121n. 75
Felski, Rita 159, 161, 164nn. 35–6
feminine (characteristics) 110, 112–13, 159–60
femininity 102, 160
feminism ix, 92–3, 115, 160
fiction ix, 1–4, 6, 7, 40, 50–1, 54, 58, 61n. 3, 67–8, 75, 81, 86–9, 92, 95n. 44, 124, 128, 134–7, 145–7, 149, 159–61
see also narrative fiction
fictional biography 50–1
fictionality 2, 61n. 3
Finck, Almut 161, 164n. 31
Finney, Gail vii, ix, 5, 81, 92, 94n. 8
flânerie x, 73, 75, 78n. 20
flâneur 66–8, 70, 73–4, 129
Flaubert, Gustave 5, 21, 124, 129–30, 134–7, 140nn. 29, 31–2, 37–40
Fludernik, Monika 87, 89, 92, 94n. 30, 95n. 43
fragment xii, 5, 12, 18, 22, 39, 55, 59, 63n. 41, 64n. 67, 66, 75, 81, 86, 88, 93
Fragment of an Analysis of a Case of Hysteria (Freud) 5, 81, 93
fragmentation 75, 86, 115, 118n. 13, 120n. 52
fragmented bodies xi, 116, 117n. 5, 160
Fräulein Else (character) vii, 5, 7, 25, 34, 81–3, 85–95
Fräulein Else (Schnitzler) 5, 81, 86–8, 93nn. 1, 2, 94n. 37–8, 95nn. 39–40, 45, 141n. 60
Freud, Sigmund ix–x, 2, 5, 58, 81–6, 89–93, 94nn. 7–8, 13, 15–17, 19, 21–2, 95nn. 42, 47, 109, 145–6, 150–5, 157–8, 160–1, 163nn. 1, 17, 164n. 32

and Breuer, *Studies of Hysteria* 84, 151–3, 157, 161, 163n. 17
see also *Beyond the Pleasure Principle*, *Fragment of an Analysis of a Case of Hysteria*, *Moses and Monotheism*, "On Narcisissm: An Introduction", "On the Psychical Mechanism of Hysterical Phenomena"
Fritsch, Gerhard 98, 101, 113, 116, 118n. 15
Furst, Lilian R. 93

Gemert, Guillaume van 101, 107, 116
gender viii–x, xii, 3, 5, 6, 98–9, 101–2, 109, 112–15, 117n. 3, 118n. 17, 145, 161, 164n. 37
Genette, Gérard 87, 93, 94nn. 31, 33
genius 102–3, 105
Geschichte 44n. 55, 50, 116, 117nn. 2, 11, 118nn. 21, 24, 26, 119nn. 31–2, 120nn. 41, 45, 121n. 75, 161, 164n. 31
Geschlecht xii, 164n. 37
Gilman, Sander 116, 121n. 73
Glauert-Hesse, Barbara 74, 76, 77n. 1, 78n. 26
globalization x, 115, 117n. 13, 118n. 13
Goebel, Rolf J. vii, x, 4–5, 7, 65, 76
Goll, Yvan vii, 2, 5, 65–77
see also *Die Eurokokke*
Gomperz, Marie von 55, 60–1, 63n. 38
Gray, Richard T. 3–4, 7, 11, 38–40, 45n. 48
Greiner, Bernhard 161, 162n. 6
Guarda, Sylvain, 39, 42n. 31

Haas, Willy 54, 60, 62n. 25
Habsburg 49, 52–3, 61n. 16, 107, 115
empire 49, 52–3, 61n. 16, 107

Hamburger, Käte 1, 6, 7n. 2, 87, 93, 94n. 29
see also *Die Logik der Dichtung*
Hamburger, Michael 59, 63n. 41, 64n. 67
Hanssen, Beatrice 76, 77n. 2
Hardt, Michael 116, 117n. 10
Harman, Mark 22
Heath, Stephen 130, 137, 140n. 38
Hegel, Georg W. F. 32, 103, 116, 118n. 24, 120n. 52
Heidegger, Martin 17, 22, 25n. 29
Heimat 49, 60n. 1, 123, 128, 138, 140n. 27
Hellmann, Irene and Paul 57, 59, 64n. 55
Hirsch, Rudolf 59, 60, 64n. 56
history x–xii, 1, 5–6, 7n. 5, 12, 16–18, 32, 38, 40, 41n. 2, 42n. 31, 69, 72, 78, 83, 85, 91–3, 94nn. 5, 11, 22, 98–9, 102, 104, 106–7, 109–15, 117n. 8, 120n. 41, 132, 146, 151, 154, 167, 169, 170–3
Hofmannsthal, Hugo von vii, xi, 2–3, 5, 40, 49–59, 60nn. 1–2, 61nn. 3–7, 8–9, 15, 17, 62nn. 18–21, 25–7, 31–3, 36–7
see also *Das kleine Welttheater*, *Der Turm*, "Reitergeschichte", *Timon der Redner*
Holocaust 2, 4, 85, 112, 121n. 70, 151
memoirs 85
Horkheimer, Max 34–5, 37, 39, 43n. 42, 44nn. 54–5, 116, 122n. 84
Hörnigk, Therese 149, 161, 162n. 8, 163nn. 8–9
"Housewife's psychosis" 90
"The Hunger Artist" (Kafka) vii, 4, 27–39, 40n. 2, 41nn. 10–13, 15–17, 23, 25, 42nn. 30–1, 37, 43n. 37–9
hypnosis 82, 154, 157

hysteria 5, 81, 84, 92–3, 151–4, 157–8, 161, 163n. 17

identity ii, 3, 5, 17, 54, 74, 97–9, 102, 108–13, 115, 119n. 36, 139n. 23, 155, 157, 159–60, 163n. 8
"In der Strafkolonie" (Kafka) 13, 16
"In the Penal Colony" (Kafka) 40
interior monologue 66, 87, 89, 141n. 60
internal focalization 87
interwar (Europe) 5, 97

Jameson, Fredrick 116, 118n. 16
Jelinek, Elfriede 97
Jesenská, Milena 13, 16, 22, 25n. 25
Jesus 31, 42n. 31
Joyce, James 74, 87, 172
"The Judgment" (Kafka) 38

Kafka, Franz iii, vii, ix–xii, 1–5, 7, 9, 11–13, 15–22, 23nn. 1, 3–6, 24nn. 15–17, 25nn. 19–20, 23–6, 26n. 42, 27–9, 31–3, 35–40, 41nn. 2–3, 8, 10–11, 15–17, 42nn. 31–3, 71, 76, 87, 172
   see also *Brief an den Vater*, *Briefe an Felice*, *Briefe an Milena*, *The Castle*, *Das Schloß*, "Das Urteil", "Der Prozeß", *The Diaries of Franz Kafka*, *Drucke zu Lebzeiten*, "The Hunger Artist", "In der Strafkolonie", "In the Penal Colony", "The Judgment", *Nachgelassene Schriften*, *Tagebücher*, *The Trial*
Kafka-memes 11–13, 16, 18, 21, 25n. 23
Kapitalismus 44n. 55
Kaplan, Ann E. 83, 85, 93, 94nn. 12, 20
Kappacher, Walter 50–1, 53, 55–8, 60, 61nn. 3, 6–7, 10

Kessler, Harry Graf 52, 56, 59–60, 61n. 16, 63n. 46, 64n. 66
Kindheitsmuster (Wolf) viii, 6, 145–9, 151–2, 159–61, 162n. 1, 163nn. 9–10, 164n. 32
Kleinwort, Malte 23
Kohl, Helmut 106, 115
Kosta, Barbara 161, 162n. 7, 164n. 37
Kracauer, Siegfried 76, 77n. 13
Krieg 52, 54
Kritische Theorie 115, 118nn. 18, 22
Kubinyi, Laura R. 126, 137, 139n. 13
Kuzniar, Alice A. 27, 40, 41nn. 4–5

La Varende, Jean de 129, 137–9, 140n. 32
LaCapra, Dominick 2, 7, 82–3, 86, 91, 93, 94nn. 5, 11
Lakoff, Robin Tolmach 91, 93, 95n. 49
Lange, Katrin 161, 162n. 1
Lange-Kirchheim, Astrid 40, 42n. 31, 43n. 38
Leiris, Michel 145–6, 161, 162n. 2
leisure 23, 70, 72–3, 170
Lenau, Nicolaus 53, 60, 62n. 23
Leys, Ruth 86, 93, 94nn. 9, 14, 23
Lloyd, Rosemary 161, 162n. 1
Logis in einem Landhaus (Sebald) 123, 138
Lüders, Detlev 60

Maier, Thomas 40, 44n. 56
Mann, Thomas ii, xi, 11
Männlichkeit x, 60, 62
Marcus, Steven 93, 94n. 6
Martens, Lorna viii, x, 6, 126, 137, 139nn. 14–15, 145
Martin, Elaine 161, 162n. 4
masculinity vii, xi, 5, 97–103, 106–14, 116

masochism xii, 40–1, 42n. 31, 43n. 40
Mauriac, Claude 137, 140n. 43
memory x, 3, 4, 6, 15, 62n. 28, 84, 92, 128, 135–6, 139nn. 23–4, 145–6, 149–56, 158, 160–2, 163nn. 11–12, 16, 18, 164n. 30, 170
Menasse, Robert vii, 2, 5, 97–116, 117nn. 1–2, 4, 6–7, 11–12, 118nn. 14–15, 19–20, 23, 119nn. 27–30, 35, 37–8, 120n. 41, 45–7, 50, 52–3, 121nn. 54, 74, 76–7, 122nn. 82, 83
  see also *Trilogie der Entgeisterung*
metropolitan 66, 69, 74–5
Meyer, Imke i, vii, ix–x, 4–6, 27, 60, 62n. 19
Mieszkowski, Jan 31, 40, 42nn. 31, 33
Miller, J. Hillis 17, 22, 25nn. 27, 28
Mitchell, Breon 22, 40, 42n. 31
Mitscherlich, Alexander and Margarete 151, 161, 163nn. 13, 14
Moderne x–xi, 39–40, 44n. 54, 59
modernism iii, vii, x, 1–3, 5, 7, 40, 41n. 3, 75, 10
modernity ii, 5, 39, 44n. 54, 65–6, 68–73, 75, 83, 106, 170
Momus 19
Moses 31, 85, 93, 94nn. 21–2
Moses and Monotheism (Freud) 85, 93, 94nn. 21–2
Mosse, George 106, 116, 120n. 43, 121n. 73
Müller, Michael 22, 28, 40, 41n. 13, 59
Münchberg, Katharina 137, 139n. 23
Musil, Robert ix, 62, 97, 116, 172
  see also *Der Mann ohne Eigenschaften*

Nachgelassene Schriften (Kafka) 22, 25n. 19
Nachträglichkeit 84
narcissism 88–9, 95n. 42, 151
narrative iii, vii, x, 1–7, 11–13, 15–16, 18, 20–1, 27, 33, 40, 66–7, 75, 79, 81–3, 85–9, 91–3, 94nn. 31, 33, 99–100, 103–6, 108, 110, 114, 118n. 24, 119n. 36, 123–7, 129–31, 133–7, 139, 141nn. 51, 59–60, 145, 149–50
theory vii, 1, 3–7, 11, 97, 81, 86, 89, 93, 124
narratology vii, 3, 5, 50, 81, 83, 86–7, 92, 94nn. 31, 32, 95n. 43
narrator 1, 4–6, 28–30, 32–4, 36, 39, 68, 70, 74, 89, 92, 99, 104–6, 108, 112, 114–15, 119nn. 34, 36, 125–9, 131–6, 138, 141n. 59, 142n. 62, 150, 153–61, 164n. 31, 165n. 38
National Socialism 98, 159–60, 168, 171, 174
nationalism 171
Nationalsozialismus 117n. 2
Negri, Antonio 116, 117n. 10
Nehring, Wolfgang 93, 94n. 8
Neumann, Gerhard 22, 40, 41nn. 11–12, 16, 42n. 31
neurosis 84–5, 87, 151, 157, 163n. 14
Norris, Margot 29, 40, 41n. 18, 42n. 31, 43n. 40
novel of consciousness 87

O'Neill, Patrick 86, 93, 94nn. 24–5
"On Narcisissm: An Introduction" (Freud) 89, 93, 95
"On the Psychical Mechanism of Hysterical Phenomena" (Freud) 84, 92, 94n. 13
Oppenheimer, Felix 64
Orr, Mary 137, 140n. 39
Österreich xi, 50, 60, 116, 117nn.

Index 183

1–2, 4, 11–12, 118nn. 14, 15, 120nn. 44–5, 48, 121n. 76

Paris 5, 65–9, 73–6, 77nn. 4, 6–7, 129, 133, 136, 141n. 52, 148
performance 2, 30, 39–40, 42n. 31, 66, 98, 102, 112–13, 118n. 17
phantasmagoria 68, 77n. 19
postcolonialism xii
postmoderne 118, 120, 161
postmodernism xi, 102
post-dialectical 5, 99, 102–4, 109, 114, 117n. 6
post-traumatic stress disorder (PTSD) 85
Proust, Marcel, 5, 87, 124, 128, 131–8, 139n. 23, 140nn. 25–6, 141nn. 45–7, 49, 51–2, 56, 58, 150
psychoanalyse 162n. 6
psychoanalysis viii, 6, 84, 109, 145, 148–9, 151–3

ragpicker 70, 77n. 13
Rangaran, Sudarsan 138, 139n. 12
Rechtien, Renate 161, 162n. 7, 164n. 37
recovered memories 85
Redlich, Josef 50, 55, 60
Reisinger, Roman 161, 162n. 1
"Reitergeschichte" (Hofmannsthal) 3, 62n. 19
repetition compulsion 85
return of the repressed 85
rhetoric 1, 6, 7n. 1, 89, 92, 95n. 44, 126
The Rhetoric of Fiction (Booth) 89, 92, 95n. 44
Richter Horst-Eberhard 98–9, 116, 117n. 5
Rieckmann, Jens i, vii, xi, 5, 49, 60, 62n. 20, 63n. 53, 64n. 61
Rilke, Rainer Maria xi, 50, 59, 61n. 4, 67–8, 76, 145

Robertson, Eric 76, 77n. 3
Rolleston, James 27, 28, 40, 41nn. 3, 14
romanticism 145
Roth, Philip 110, 109, 116
Russian and Czech formalism 86, 116
Ryan, Judith vii, xi, 5, 123, 161, 162n. 7

Santner, Eric L. 161, 164n. 32
Sartorius, Joachim 74, 76, 78n. 25
Schaumann, Caroline 162, 164n. 32
Schlipphacke, Heidi vii, ix, 5, 97, 116
Schmid, Martin E. 60, 62nn. 26–7, 32
Schnitzler, Arthur x, 2, 5, 52, 55–6, 58, 60, 62n. 33, 63n. 44, 64n. 63, 81–2, 86–7, 89, 92–3, 94nn. 7–8, 37, 138, 141n. 60
see also *Der Abenteurer und die Sängerin, Fräulein Else*
Scholes, Robert 1, 7n. 1
Sebald, W. G. iii, vii, xi, 1–5, 7, 123–37, 138nn. 1, 3–6, 139nn. 6–7, 17–21, 23, 140nn. 26–31, 35, 7, 39–43, 141nn. 45, 49–51, 60–2, 142n. 63
see also *Austerlitz, Beschreibung des Unglücks, Campo Santo, Der Mythos der Zerstörung im Werk Döblins, Die Ausgewanderten, Die Ringe des Saturn, Logis in einem Landhaus, Unheimliche Heimat*
sexuality 85, 109, 146
shell shock 84
Sheppard, Richard W. 28, 40, 41n. 10
Spengler, Oswald 54, 62n. 28
Stanzel, Franz Karl 1, 7n. 2
Stern, Sheila 131, 133–4, 138

Stifter, Adalbert 21, 138, 141n. 62, 142n. 62
structuralism 86, 116
subjectivity 35–7, 39, 41n. 16, 44n. 52, 102, 109, 117, 128
Subjektivität 45, 161, 164n. 31
Succi, Giovanni 42n. 31, 86
survival syndrome 164n. 30
survivors 85, 156–7, 164n. 30

Tagebücher (Kafka) 22, 23n. 6, 25n. 31, 40, 76
talking cure 84, 158
Tasso, Torquato 85
technology 68
Timon der Redner (Hofmannsthal) 54–5, 59, 61n. 6
Todorov, Tzvetan 85
totality 115, 120
translation ii, ix, 6, 22, 35, 74, 123–4, 128, 131–2,
translator 123, 175n. 1
Transvestismus 117nn. 2, 4, 121n. 76
trauma vii, ix, 2–7, 81–6, 88–92, 93n. 3, 94nn. 9, 12, 14, 20, 23, 148, 151, 156–8
theory 3, 5, 81, 86
traumatic neurosis 84–5
Traumnovelle (Schnitzler) 138, 141n. 60
The Trial (Kafka) 22–3, 172
Trilogie der Entgeisterung (Menasse) 102–3, 113, 115–16

Unheimliche Heimat (Sebald) 123, 128, 138, 140n. 27
unreliable narrator 89, 92
urban x, 2, 66, 68–9, 74–5, 125, 129, 139n. 16, 154

ventriloquization, literary 82
Verdrängung 60, 62n. 20
Vienna ii, x, 6, 20, 51–2, 54, 59–60, 62nn. 18, 21, 82–3, 86, 92, 95n. 48, 101, 104, 107–8, 110, 119n. 41, 167, 172
Vilain, Robert 76, 77n. 3

Wagner, Benno ix, 21–3, 26n. 42
Walser, Robert, 21, 23, 26n. 43
Walsh, Richard 138, 141n. 61
Waugh, Patricia 2, 7n. 4
Weber, Max 32–3, 39, 40, 42n. 34, 60, 61n. 17
Weinzierl, Ulrich 60, 62n. 20
Weiss, Robert O. 86, 93, 94nn. 27–8
Wertheimstein, Josephine von 61n. 9
White, Hayden 1, 7n. 1
Wien x–xi, 52–3, 120n. 46
Wilke, Sabine vii, 1, 162, 163n. 22
Wolf, Christa vii, ix, xi, 2, 6, 145–56, 158–61, 162nn. 7–8, 163nn. 8–11, 13, 15–16, 18–20, 22, 164nn. 24, 33, 37
see also *Kindheitsmuster*
Wood, James 130, 138nn. 35, 37–8
Woolf, Virginia 87
World War I 84
World War II 97
writing x, 44n. 52, 50, 85–6, 89, 124–9, 131, 134–5, 147, 150, 155–60
writing trauma 82, 85–6, 89, 93

Zahlmann, Christel 162, 165n. 38
Zweig, Stefan 49

www.ingramcontent.com/pod-product-compliance
Lightning Source LLC
Chambersburg PA
CBHW052045300426
44117CB00012B/1982